MURDER AT LORDSHIP

Also by Pat Marry

The Making of a Detective: A Garda's Story of Investigating Some of Ireland's Most Notorious Crimes

*

After being turned away by An Garda Síochána at 17 for being too young, **Pat Marry** joined the force eight years later. He went on to investigate some of Ireland's most high profile cases, including the killings of Rachel O'Reilly and Garda Adrian Donohue. He retired in 2018 at the rank of Detective Inspector. In 2019 he published a memoir, *The Making of a Detective*.

Robin Schiller is a journalist for Mediahuis Ireland covering Independent.ie, the *Irish Independent* and the *Sunday Independent*.

PAT MARRY AND ROBIN SCHILLER

MURDER AT LORDSHIP

INSIDE THE HUNT FOR A DETECTIVE'S KILLER

ALLEN&UNWIN

First published in Great Britain in 2024 by Allen & Unwin

A CIP catalogue record for this book is available from the British Library.

Trade paperback ISBN 978 1 80546 122 7
E-Book ISBN 978 1 80546 123 4

Allen & Unwin
An imprint of Atlantic Books Ltd
Ormond House
26–27 Boswell Street
London WC1N 3JZ

www.atlantic-books.co.uk

Printed in Great Britain by CPI Group (UK) Ltd, Croydon CR0 4YY

10 9 8 7 6 5 4 3 2 1

MIX
Paper | Supporting
responsible forestry
FSC
www.fsc.org   FSC® C171272

To all the members of An Garda Síochána who
have lost their lives in the line of duty

CONTENTS

PROLOGUE

25 JANUARY 2013:
MURDER OF A DETECTIVE

The four masked shadowy figures were crouched behind the wall of Lordship Credit Union car park, waiting patiently and out of sight for their moment to strike. One figure, wearing a dirty and soaked tracksuit as he stood out in the pouring rain, tightly held the long-barrelled shotgun in his hands as the convoy was about to leave. The credit union workers were transporting several thousand euro in cash and would make for an easy target. The gang's only obstacle was the armed garda escort shadowing the employees, but they had planned for this; the shotgun was loaded and ready to use, while another raider was armed with a handgun. They were motivated by greed and were callously determined that nothing would stop them.

Suddenly, a dark-coloured Volkswagen Passat appeared from the main road and drove at speed towards the exit, its tyres screeching as it came to a sudden stop, blocking the convoy from leaving. It was the sign for the four robbers to move. Two of them vaulted over the four-foot wall and made their way directly and with purpose to the unmarked garda-escort car. Detective Garda Adrian Donohoe had stepped out of the passenger seat to establish what was happening, with his line of sight directed at the car blocking the exit. He didn't even see the two masked men approaching out of the darkness from his right side.

The only visible detail on the first gunman's face was his intense stare through the slits in his balaclava as he held the shotgun against his right shoulder, trained the firearm over the roof of the garda car and aimed the muzzle directly at the head of Adrian Donohoe. The masked man was intent on savagery and never said a word as his right index finger hovered over the trigger. No demands were made of the detective, and no warning was given. As the rain swept down on the dark credit union car park, he squeezed the trigger, applying the five pounds of pressure necessary to discharge the 12-gauge pump-action shotgun. A loud, thunderous bang erupted as he fired, discharging a cartridge containing some 250 lead pellets that left the muzzle of the shotgun at high speed.

Standing just seven feet away, Adrian Donohoe never stood a chance. He was struck on the right side of the face and dropped onto the wet tarmac beside his patrol car. Such was the speed and organisation of the attack that he didn't even have a chance to reach for his weapon. It was still safely clipped into the holster on his hip. The recoil of the shotgun caught the masked gunman off guard and he stumbled back several feet, almost falling to the ground. He regained his balance and stood up before pointing the shotgun forward once again. The job wasn't finished yet. They continued their violent mission, targeting the other armed detective and the volunteer staff in the car park. The raider with the shotgun this time focused his attention on Detective Garda Joe Ryan, who was sitting in the driver's seat of the patrol car. Opening the door and training the firearm at the terrified detective's head, the gunman shouted: 'I'm going to fucking kill you, I'm going to shoot you. Give us the money.' One of his accomplices had turned his attention to the car of Bernadette McShane, a credit union volunteer of 25 years, who was sitting in her Nissan Micra. He smashed the driver's side window in on top of the traumatised worker, screaming at her: 'Give me the money. Give me the fucking money.' Another gang member focused on the Mazda being driven by Pat Bellew and secured a bag containing just under €7,000 in cash from the employee's vehicle. Almost simultaneously, the four young, athletic men sprinted to their getaway car, which was still blocking the exit. They jumped in and its engine roared as it sped away from Lordship Credit Union and into the night. In just under a minute, the five-man gang had carried out a daring robbery that would shock the nation. In their murderous wake they had left Detective Garda Adrian Donohoe mortally wounded on the car-park ground. In those 58 seconds, they had also left his children fatherless, his wife a widow, and his local parish without a pillar of their community.

Over the next decade his colleagues at Dundalk Garda Station would lead an international manhunt for the killers that spanned three continents. The full resources of the Irish state were afforded to the murder inquiry with support from the Northern Irish security services, counter-terrorism officers in Australia, and federal agents in the United States. The suspects had fled to the far corners of the globe, boasting about their crimes in the bars of New York and living off their reputations as men to be feared, all while believing they were out of the reach of gardaí. But the investigation team were resolute, determined, and driven: they would never rest until they got justice for their murdered colleague.

1

POLICING BANDIT COUNTRY

With over 300 open crossings leading into a different jurisdiction, and an ambivalent attitude towards law enforcement passed down through generations, the border area has been one of the most difficult and dangerous areas of Ireland to police over the last 50 years. This wasn't always the case, and for the first two-thirds of the 20th century towns like Dundalk in County Louth were policed like any other large provincial town in the country. The border, established in 1921 and dividing Ireland into two separate states, meant that there were higher rates of smuggling of illegal contraband, but the region was no more violent than any other garda district.

That all changed in the 1960s with the outbreak of the Troubles, the violent Northern Ireland conflict that spread south of the border and raged for 30 years. What started as a civil rights campaign over the treatment of Catholics in the North escalated into warfare, with the deployment of British troops to the region and the emergence of the Provisional Irish Republican Army (IRA). Known as the Provos, the terror group was formed in late 1969 following a split with the original IRA movement, and it adopted an approach of physical force

republicanism, initially focused on defending Catholic communities but escalating to a guerrilla warfare campaign against
the security forces by the 1970s.

A unique unit within the movement was the South Armagh
Brigade, which became known for its militancy and independ-
ence, retaining a battalion structure throughout the conflict,
and was the most active Provisional IRA unit during the
Troubles. A senior figure within the brigade was Thomas 'Slab'
Murphy, who resided on a farm straddling both sides of the
border in Armagh and Louth. During the conflict, he would
also allegedly be elected a member of the IRA's Army Council,
linked to a bombing campaign in Britain and accused of stock-
piling weapons imported from Libya.

The main base for the South Armagh Brigade was
Crossmaglen, a small village with a predominantly nationalist
community located three kilometres from the southern border.
Despite a population of just 1,257 at the time, its proximity to
the border, the rough terrain of the surrounding landscape, and
a sense of rebellion stretching back centuries made the lawless
enclave a stronghold for the Provisional IRA. The village
became synonymous with much of the violence during the
Troubles, and in August 1970 two Royal Ulster Constabulary
(RUC) officers were killed by a booby-trapped bomb planted
under a car near Crossmaglen. They were the first RUC officers
killed by republicans during the conflict, and the incident set
the tone for the area's links to the ensuing bloodshed over the
next decades. The Provos' campaign in Crossmaglen escalated
in 1971 after Harry Thornton, a 28-year-old sewage worker,
was shot and killed by the British Army. The fatal incident led
to heightened tensions in the village, with locals outraged at the
killing of a civilian, providing new recruits to the republican

movement and creating an even more hostile environment for security forces in the area.

From then until 1997, the South Armagh Brigade is estimated to have been responsible for the deaths of over 120 British soldiers and more than 40 members of the RUC, with many of the killings happening in Crossmaglen. In the same period, the RUC recorded more than 1,200 bombings and 1,550 shootings in a ten-mile radius of South Armagh. The region was branded 'bandit country' in 1974 by then Northern Ireland Secretary Mervyn Rees and became the most dangerous posting for members of the British Army. At one stage, soldiers stationed in and around the village outnumbered the local population, while elite paratroopers from the Special Air Service (SAS) were also deployed to try and combat the violence in the region. To add to the bloodshed, another dangerous dissident organisation was formed in 1974, the Irish National Liberation Army (INLA), which began targeting security forces in the North while also carrying out attacks on gardaí.

With the conflict escalating, the Irish government re-established the Special Criminal Court, first introduced under the Offences Against the State Act 1939 to prevent the IRA from subverting Irish neutrality during the Second World War. The court, composed of three judges and sitting without a jury, was reintroduced to prevent jurors being intimidated or swayed by the dissident campaign during the Troubles, and it remains in place to this day.

Just 18 kilometres south of Crossmaglen across the border is Dundalk, a large town that also became a hotbed of dissident activity. Gardaí in the division, which at the time also policed areas including Omeath, Carlingford, Drogheda and Ardee, became all too familiar with the violence of the Troubles in

1972. On the night of 21 September, the garda barracks was attacked by a mob of around 200 people armed with firebombs and other missiles. The group also tried to force entry into the station and only retreated after a detective discharged several shots from a machine gun over their heads. Patrol cars and the private vehicles of gardaí were firebombed, and the army was called in to disperse the mob. It was one of the first major incidents linked to the Troubles involving Dundalk gardaí, but it wouldn't be the last.

The area was also vulnerable to attacks from loyalist paramilitaries, highlighted by a no-warning bomb blast in 1975. Six days before Christmas, a car bomb was detonated at Kay's Tavern on Crowe Street, resulting in the deaths of two civilians. In a coordinated attack hours later, a bar in the village of Silverbridge, close to Crossmaglen, was targeted and three men, including a 14-year-old boy, were shot dead. The atrocity was carried out by members of the Ulster Volunteer Force (UVF), a loyalist terror organisation operating during the Troubles.

Two years later Dundalk gardaí were involved in investigating the abduction and murder of a British Army intelligence officer, Captain Robert Nairac, who was forcefully removed from a pub in South Armagh by the Provisional IRA during an undercover operation. He was brought from the bar in Dromintee across the border to Ravensdale and subjected to a violent interrogation during which he was beaten with weapons before being shot dead. Although several people have been convicted in relation to the incident, his body has never been recovered.

Gardaí in Dundalk were also involved in the investigation into the 1979 Narrow Water Ambush, across the waters of Carlingford Lough in the County Down village of Warrenpoint.

The guerrilla attack by the Provos killed 18 British soldiers and injured 6 others. During the atrocity the soldiers, believing they were under attack from the southern side, opened fire. A civilian, William Hudson, had gone to the Omeath shoreline to see what was happening when he was hit by a bullet and died. Three days later there was large-scale sectarian violence in the town during a European Cup game between Belfast team Linfield and Dundalk at Oriel Park, during which the away fans rioted, resulting in some 100 civilians and gardaí being injured.

Members of the public and gardaí were at constant risk of serious injury or death as the sectarian conflict raged on both sides of the border. Several members of An Garda Síochána would be killed in bombings and shot dead in bank robberies, the latter being carried out under the veil of fundraising for the republican movement. In 1985, Sergeant Patrick Morrissey became the first garda member to be murdered in the Dundalk district during the conflict in a killing carried out by dissident republicans. On the afternoon of 27 June, 49-year-old Sergeant Morrissey was on duty when he was notified of an armed robbery at the local employment exchange in Ardee. He and two colleagues set up a checkpoint in the village of Tallanstown to intercept the raiders. They came across two men on a motorbike and gave chase, with the bike crashing into a car at Rathbrist Cross. The raiders, Michael McHugh from Crossmaglen and Noel Callan from Castleblayney in County Monaghan, were both connected to the INLA. They fled the scene on foot and were pursued by Sergeant Morrissey. As the officer caught up with the men, he was initially shot and wounded by McHugh, who then stood over Sergeant Morrissey, a married father of four, and shot him in the head.

The raiders were later arrested during a major search operation involving the army and tried before the Special Criminal
Court in Dublin. They were charged with capital murder, a
special provision relating to the murder of a garda or prison
officer acting in the course of their duty, for which the punishment on conviction was death. Both men were found guilty and
McHugh, then aged 23, shouted at the judges after the verdict:
'Victory to the INLA. You are pro-British.' He was initially
sentenced to death for the murder, but this was commuted to
40 years' penal servitude by then President Patrick Hillery,
seven days before the execution was due to take place. For his
courage and heroism, Sergeant Morrissey was posthumously
awarded the Scott Gold Medal, the highest honour in An
Garda Síochána. The death penalty was abolished under the
Criminal Justice Act 1990 and replaced with a life sentence,
with a minimum period of 40 years' imprisonment. The
legislation, which also has special provisions for politically
motivated murders of the head of a foreign state or member of
government, remains the most serious offence on the statute
books. McHugh and Callan would be the last people convicted
of capital murder in the 20th century.

The Provisional IRA announced its ceasefire in 1994, and
its political wing, Sinn Féin, became involved in the Northern
Ireland peace process, eventually leading to the signing of the
Good Friday Agreement in 1998. The accord also provided
for the early release of prisoners jailed for crimes related to
paramilitary groups as long as they agreed to an unequivo-
cal ceasefire. The agreement ended most of the violence of
the Troubles, although splinter groups such as the Real IRA
rejected peace and were intent on continuing a violent campaign. On 15 August 1998, the group was responsible for the

deadliest single incident of the conflict when it detonated a car bomb outside the courthouse in Omagh, County Tyrone. The bombing killed 29 people and injured over 200 others, leading to condemnation both nationally and internationally.

The Real IRA didn't relent in its campaign, and the following year 10 suspected members of the group were arrested at a firearms training camp in Stamullen, County Meath. One of those detained was Dubliner Alan Ryan, who was later jailed by the Special Criminal Court for receiving training from other persons in the use of weapons. He subsequently moved up the ranks to become the leader of the Real IRA in Dublin, before he was shot dead in September 2012.

Dundalk became a central area of operations for the dissident group, who were carrying out attacks on security services in Northern Ireland. Gardaí in the district, supported by counter-terror units, were pivotal in curbing the threats posed by the terror group at the beginning of the 21st century. In one operation in 2010, a dissident arms dump was discovered in Dunleer, County Louth, which included a homemade mortar, three kilos of TNT, bomb-making equipment, a pipe bomb, and ammunition. It highlighted the constant threat posed by dissidents operating in the border area long after the conflict had ended.

One investigator with vast experience of policing the border region in the post-Troubles era was Pat Marry. Graduating from the Garda Training College in 1986, he was first stationed in Dublin before being transferred to Clones in County Monaghan. Upon being promoted to detective sergeant, he moved to Balbriggan Garda Station in north Dublin and led the investigation into the high-profile murder of Rachel Callaly, a mother of two who was killed at her home in Naul. Her husband, Joe O'Reilly, would later be convicted of her murder and is currently serving a life sentence. Upon further promotion, Marry served two years as detective inspector in Drogheda before moving to Dundalk Garda Station in 2010, overseeing the gardaí's response to serious crime in the area. While the violence of the Troubles had dissipated, splinter groups such as the Real IRA remained active in the region. Speaking about policing the region, Detective Inspector Marry says:

In my two years in Clones I got a fair taste of border life with people from the town and surrounding areas. At the time there were only two pubs in Clones that gardaí were comfortable drinking in. There was a blanket of suspicion and pure silence with people having to encounter the gardaí. Dundalk was no different, and in fact worse. This was because of the political factors at play in the area, while 34 border crossings in the district of Dundalk alone made it impossible to police. Did the criminal dissident fraternity know this? Policing was difficult and the gardaí would regularly chase a car to the border but weren't allowed to follow and the criminal would get away.

Dundalk was where I first heard the term 'IED' [improvised explosive device]. These were explosive devices which dissident republicans engaged in making. These people were highly skilled fabricators, and it was clear some of them were trained in chemistry, as evidence was present of mercury fulminate in detonators. These people took an innovative approach to the technical issues; they used airbags as gas generators to propel the devices. They used plastic pipes as the bomb body, easily shattered. They had a good command of multifunctional digital rail timers. The dissidents were very active between 2008 and 2012, placing roadside IEDs to murder mostly PSNI (Police Service of Northern Ireland) officers. I got to know what a mark 21 IED monitor rocket was as, when I was not long in Dundalk, in November 2010, one was discovered in a roadside near the border. It was with the brave work of both past and present detectives from Dundalk, and support from colleagues in the Special Detective Unit and intelligence from the Garda Crime and Security branch, that individuals were identified and associated with this new group, the Real IRA.

By 2005 the British government had announced a full demilitarisation plan, and it closed all army bases in South Armagh two years later. The full responsibility of policing the area was handed over to the PSNI, which had replaced the RUC in 2001. While many of the landmarks from the Troubles were removed from Crossmaglen, the heavily fortified police station surrounded by high fences made of corrugated iron remains in the centre of the village and is a reminder of the violence that raged for decades. Located directly behind the barracks are the grounds of Crossmaglen Rangers, whose pitches were used to land army helicopters during the conflict. The club would become one of the most successful Gaelic football clubs in the country at the turn of the century.

Despite efforts by many to move on from the area's past, the historical prominence of the IRA on both sides of the border would have an impact on the generations to come, with a deep distrust of authority remaining to this day. 'The Fighting Men of Crossmaglen', a rebel song lamenting the area's fight against the British forces, remains popular among younger generations in the village. There also continues to be an especially malevolent attitude towards informers, colloquially referred to as 'touts', with the code of silence of omertà deeply engrained in the community. One investigator who spent most of his career policing the border region said of this: 'People in the area would be subjected to severe threats, or threats to life, if found to be speaking with the authorities about criminal activity of any nature. There are a lot of decent people there, but there are sections that would have an extreme ambivalence towards gardaí, sympathies towards certain groups, and vested interests in areas such as smuggling.' Another investigator, when explaining the attitude specifically towards those who cooperate with law enforcement in the South Armagh village, said: 'There is a saying among certain groups in Crossmaglen: the only thing worse than a paedophile is a tout.' Cross-border smuggling and diesel laundering – the process by which dye is removed from discounted agricultural diesel and sold as regular fuel at an inflated price – became the most lucrative forms of criminality in the area, with Crossmaglen a key location for both. Crime groups involved in robberies and burglaries would also take advantage of the border to cross between jurisdictions without fear of being pursued. Gardaí in Dundalk had to deal with not just their own local criminals, but also those from the North who would cross south for their criminal exploits, with uniformed gardaí and detectives attached to the crime unit at the forefront of efforts to stop them.

2

A PILLAR OF THE COMMUNITY

One of the members of the crime unit in Dundalk tasked with investigating violent gangs and dissident republican groups was Detective Garda Adrian Donohoe. Born on 14 January 1972, to Hugh and Peggy, he grew up on the family farm in Kilnaleck, a small village in County Cavan. Adrian was the eldest and had five siblings: Mary, Alan, Colm, Anne, and Martin. He attended St Patrick's College in the village, where he was a model student. He was also an accomplished Gaelic footballer, playing in midfield and at forward for the school's team while also lining out for local club Crosserlough GFC. In 1989 he scored four points from midfield as the club won that year's minor championship, and a month later he fisted the winning goal in injury time as Crosserlough won the U-21 title. The following year he played on the school team that made it to the semi-final of the MacRory Cup and sat his Leaving Certificate exams that summer. His footballing ability was also recognised at inter-county level, where he represented both the Cavan minor and U-21 teams.

In 1994 he applied to join An Garda Síochána and departed for the training college in Templemore, County Tipperary, becoming a sworn member of the force on 28 September 1995. His siblings looked up to him, both literally and metaphorically. Standing at 6 feet 4 inches, he was a large presence and described by those who knew him as a gentle giant, and Colm and Martin later followed his career path by also joining the guards. Upon graduating from Templemore, with the reg number 26222F, he was allocated to Dundalk Garda Station and moved to the north-east coast. Despite the three-hour round journey back home, Adrian never missed family occasions and made a point of returning for the many gatherings back in Kilnaleck. The following March another trainee, Darren Kirwan, was placed on Adrian's unit. The two young recruits became close friends and later joined St Patrick's GAA club, known as 'the Pats'. While in the Garda College Adrian had also met Caroline Deloughery, a trainee from the coastal village of Kilkee in County Clare, who was also later transferred to Dundalk and worked in the immigration unit. The pair began dating, later marrying and having two children, Amy and Niall. The family lived in Lordship, a small village on the Cooley Peninsula overlooked by the Slievenaglogh Mountains and looking out onto the shore of Dundalk Bay.

Around 500 people live in the village of Lordship, which sits on the outskirts of Dundalk on the R173, known as the Carlingford Road, that loops around the Cooley Peninsula. The village has several cafés and shops dotted around it, while St Patrick's GAA club is located at the heart of the parish and close to where the Donohoes lived. Adrian became a central part of the community, playing for the senior team while also helping to coach the under-age footballers. In 2003 he won a county medal with the Pats, and that same year he was appointed as a detective to the crime unit. His and Caroline's children were enrolled in Bellurgan national school, a short drive along the R173 towards Dundalk, where Adrian would give talks to the children about the role of gardaí and the importance of road safety. The school sits directly across from Lordship Credit Union, an old single-storey building facing out onto the Carlingford Road. Its large car park is surrounded by four stone walls, around four feet in height, with the rear wall facing onto fields with rough terrain leading to the shoreline of the bay. While one of the smaller credit unions in the area, it provides an important financial service for the local communities in Bellurgan, Lordship, and Jenkinstown. After being moved to the crime unit, Detective Garda Donohoe worked under Detective Inspector Marry, who had command of serious crime in the Dundalk district. Recalling the man with whom he worked on a daily basis, Detective Inspector Marry says:

Adrian was an exceptional detective, but he was much more than a garda. He lived his life giving to others and was embedded in the local area, a real pillar of the community. GAA was his love, apart from his family, whom he adored, and he was an exceptional husband and father loved by all and highly respected. The Donohoe family, both in Cavan and Louth, were well known and well respected.

As far as work went, I always found Adrian to be very aware of his job and his interactions with dissidents and the criminal fraternity. He knew them all and he pursued criminals without fear, favour or malice towards them. He was someone who, when tasked with a job by myself, would always do it within the timeframe necessary. His attention to detail was exceptional and his report writing was excellent. I didn't regularly socialise with the detectives, and I mainly knew Adrian from a work perspective. In December 2012, we all went on a night out to the dogs in Dundalk where we placed bets, had some food and pints. I was sitting beside Adrian and we engaged in chit-chat, and I could see how much of a decent guy he was. That night at the same dog meeting were a cohort of border criminals who had gathered not far from our table, and we had no doubt they were trying to intimidate us. Adrian and some of the detectives paid them a visit and asked them to leave, which they did. They would later become of particular interest to gardaí in the area. Adrian was a decent human being with an appetite for all things good: family, community, and the job of being a detective.

Outside the metropolitan area of Dublin, the Dundalk garda district was one of the busiest in the country, as it dealt with dissident crime, drug-related shootings, smuggling, and robbery gangs that exploited the border. At that time there were several high-profile crimes in the area, including the murder of Irene White in April 2005. The 43-year-old mother of three was stabbed 34 times in a frenzied attack after answering the door to her home on the Demesne Road in Dundalk. A year later drug dealer Paul Rea was shot dead at Marley's Lane in Drogheda, a murder inquiry which was also overseen by Detective Inspector Marry and his team. There was also a criminal inquiry into historic allegations of sexual assault against Michael Shine at Our Lady of Lourdes Hospital in Drogheda, while detectives were investigating the cold-case murder of Ciara Breen, who was aged 17 when she disappeared from her home in Dundalk in 1997.

Gangland criminality in Dublin would also spill out of the capital and up to the border region. In March 2012, Dubliners Joseph Redmond and Anthony Burnett were found shot dead in a burnt-out car in Ravensdale Park, a forested area within a kilometre of the Northern Ireland border. The two men had been lured to the secluded area in a double-cross after falling foul of Dublin criminals. The Real IRA and other dissident groups also continued to hold a presence in the region and were the targets of many investigations by Dundalk gardaí. Detective Inspector Marry said that the work of his colleagues helped solve many of the crimes while they dealt with the ever-present threats of dissident criminals:

It was the tireless work from the detectives in Dundalk, Adrian Donohoe being one of them, that kept these dangerous dissidents at bay by constant coalitions, intelligence, and active policing, including regularly stopping and searching these individuals. I relied on a handful of detectives to keep me informed of what was new or concerning with the dissidents. The Irish public don't know how the detectives from Dundalk, with their dedication and knowledge, saved lives and recovered bombs, firearms, and the proceeds of crime while bringing very dangerous characters before the courts. Detective Garda Donohoe was a very skilled investigator and he knew each and every dissident. He was an invaluable detective and servant of the state. The border was then a very difficult region to police; diesel laundering was rife and cigarette smuggling also. These activities were very profitable and generated huge sums of money for dissident activity.

As the financial crisis gripped the country and led to increased crime rates, police agencies on both sides of the border had to deal with a spate of armed robberies. In a two-year period, between 2011 and 2013, gardaí and the PSNI investigated 12 armed robberies that all had a similar modus operandi. In many of the crimes, gangs used the border to escape from police in one jurisdiction, knowing they couldn't be pursued. One of these raids happened on 5 August 2011, when Lordship Credit Union was targeted. John Kenwright was working in the branch that night and in charge of transporting the cash takings to the local bank in Dundalk. Credit unions in the area had been seen as a soft touch, with mostly volunteer employees tasked with transporting thousands of euros. A decision had been made that they would be shadowed by armed detectives to offer protection and ensure that the staff could safely deposit the large sums they were carrying.

That night, after the other staff had left, Mr Kenwright sat in his Toyota Corolla as he waited for the armed escort to arrive. The armed garda on the cash escort that night was Detective Garda Donohoe, but the credit union was hit before the gardaí got there. Shortly after the employee sat into his car, a black Audi A3 drove at speed from the Dundalk direction through the credit union gates and reversed towards the entrance door where he was parked. Two masked men got out and one, holding a shotgun, shouted at him: 'Give us the money.' The terrified credit union worker feared for his life as the firearm was pointed in his face. The gunman then ran to the passenger-side door, smashing the window and reaching in to grab the money bag before jumping back into the Audi, which sped out of the car park. The raid was well-planned and meticulously executed, netting the gang over €22,500 in cash in just 27 seconds.

After the gang fled, John Kenwright called the emergency services and relayed what had happened. 'I've just been robbed outside the credit union in Lordship,' he told the garda operator before confirming that money was taken from the car. In a statement later given to gardaí, he described the raiders as youngish, aged in their early 20s, having 'fairly local accents', being of average height and of stocky build. He also said that the weapon produced was a sawn-off shotgun and that the getaway car had a Northern Irish registration plate. Detective Gardaí Stacey Linnane and Andy Barron made their way to the scene that night and took the initial information from the injured party. The Audi A3 was later recovered burnt out in the Flagstaff area, a remote location across the border in County Down, and investigations established that the car had been stolen in a creeper burglary earlier that month.

While inquiries were being carried out into that crime, a similar robbery took place nearby several weeks later. The racecourse in Dundalk was and remains a popular Friday-night venue for local punters and once again drew a sizeable crowd for the racing on 28 October 2011. Fionnan McCoy was a bookmaker working at the track who had a relatively successful night. The racing finished shortly after 9 p.m. and around 25 minutes later he was walking through the car park with £1,725 and €6,825 in cash. As he made his way towards the main entrance of the stadium, two masked men, who had been crouching behind a vehicle, emerged in front of him. One was armed with an iron bar and the other was holding a double-barrelled shotgun. Mr McCoy was threatened before being forced to hand over his profits from the night's racing. The raiders then fled to a waiting grey Audi car, with two men getting into the front and another lying across the back seat, before it drove off. As the bookmaker attempted to give chase, he noticed that the raiders had dropped the shotgun while fleeing the scene. Gardaí were alerted and Mr McCoy later told them that both suspects were of average height and wore balaclavas. Detective Garda Donohoe was tasked with investigating both robberies, and his inquiries would lead him to a cross-border crime group.

In a five-month period the following year, 10 armed robberies were carried out on a number of financial institutions and shops in Louth and Armagh. On 9 September 2012, a cash-in-transit van was robbed at the Ballymascanlon Hotel, just a four-minute drive from Lordship Credit Union. Workers from a private security firm were collecting cash from the premises when they were approached by a lone man armed with a hammer, who threatened them before fleeing the scene with a cash box. On 6 October, the Esso garage in Omeath was targeted by a four-man gang armed with a hammer and a pole, during which a worker was struck in the face. On 10 October, McKevitt's Filling Station in Newry, County Armagh, was hit and would be targeted again less than two months later. On 5 November, an establishment at Morgan Fuels in Ravensdale was robbed. The gang fled with less than €1,000 while an employee was also shot in the knee by one raider brandishing a firearm. On 23 November, the credit union in Forkhill, County Armagh, was raided when three men, one armed with a black handgun, hit the premises and forced workers to hand over cash. The same branch was once again robbed on 7 December by two men, one armed with an orange-handled hammer. A week later the Spar store in Newry was the scene of a robbery while the Riverstown Post Office in Louth was another premises to be targeted twice in a short space of time, once on 14 November and again on 11 January 2013. In the second raid a stolen car was used by the gang, who were armed with a hammer and a gun. While not all the crimes were carried out by the same gang, gardaí believed that several, including the robberies at Lordship, the Dundalk racecourse, Morgan Fuels, and Forkhill, were all the work of the same criminal network. While in most of the raids security staff and employees escaped physical harm, the crime at Morgan Fuels showed that the criminal gangs had no qualms about inflicting violence and using their firearms.

Up until that year, district detectives had been equipped with the Israeli-designed Uzi, a powerful submachine gun capable of penetrating body armour with an effective range of 100 metres. But in 2012 garda management decided to withdraw the weapon from use, stating that it no longer fulfilled requirements, and detectives were instead issued the Swiss SIG Sauer 9mm semi-automatic pistol. The decision was heavily criticised by gardaí, not least those in the border areas, with Detective Inspector Marry sending an internal submission to his superiors on how the withdrawal of the Uzi would impact frontline services. At the time he had planned to initiate armed checkpoints to enhance anti-terrorist operations along the border, but he submitted that this would now be greatly restricted. In his report he stated: 'The border area around Dundalk is unique both in terrain and dissident activity. Authorising detectives in Dundalk to use the Uzi machine gun in limited circumstances, in particular on checkpoint duty and in doing searches, is something that has to be seriously considered.' Speaking about the withdrawal of the submachine gun, he says:

It was all over the newspapers that the Uzi was withdrawn from detectives along the border. Representative bodies highlighted this, and how right they were that their members were being put in a vulnerable position. The authorities replied by stating that there was now adequate armed cover with the newly formed regional support units. At that time there were two regional support unit hubs, one in Letterkenny in County Donegal and the other in Dundalk. When the unit in Louth were resting, the Letterkenny unit would be working, so the unit in Donegal would have to respond to an armed incident in Louth and vice versa. Figure it out: there was no armed cover in the Louth divisions for vast periods of time.

I remember one incident where the gardaí in Drogheda stopped a car at 5 a.m. and discovered the lone driver had a shotgun between the consul in the car. When questioned, he drove off at speed. The gardaí found the car parked up in the quay area of Drogheda and on approach the occupant of the car discharged a shot. The uniform car pulled back and requested armed assistance. There was no armed assistance available, no regional support unit. I was contacted and I requested that command control in Dublin be contacted, and they sent an armed unit to Drogheda from Naas. Eventually the regional support unit gathered, having been contacted. They conducted the approach to the car and on doing so discovered the body of the lone occupant. He had taken his own life with the shotgun. It's all very well saying there are regional support units to deal with armed incidents, when in reality that degree of cover was not there and detectives on the border were vulnerable. The training and the refresher courses for the Uzi users, which happened three times a year, were costly and this move to revoke the gun was purely to save money on the garda budget.

Just two weeks after the second Riverstown Post Office robbery, a criminal gang would once again show their predisposition to violence, but this time on a cold, calculated, and appalling scale.

3

58 SECONDS

The evening of 25 January 2013 started like any other normal work night for Adrian Donohoe. He left the family home in Lordship, saying goodbye to his wife and children, before making the short car journey across to Dundalk Garda Station. He hadn't been due to work that night but, true to his selfless nature, filled in for a colleague at the last moment to ensure there were enough armed members to police the vast region the station covered, including the busy town centre and rural hinterlands. His detective duties required him to wear plain clothes, as opposed to the operational uniform worn by many frontline members. Dressed in a white checked shirt, black trousers supported by a black leather belt, dark laced boots, and a black zipped jacket, he set off from home into the rainy evening.

His first task that night would be to shadow the credit union officials transporting cash takings from the four branches across the Cooley Peninsula and safely escort them to the bank in Dundalk town centre. There was good reason for the armed escort following the previous robbery at the credit union in 2011. The branches were seen as a lucrative target, with workers transporting tens of thousands of euros in cash on any given Friday night. That night Adrian would take part in the escort with Detective Garda Joe Ryan, an experienced member of the local crime unit. At the time Joe Ryan had more than two decades' service in the guards, having joined in 1991. He was first stationed in the sub-district of Dromad before moving to the district headquarters in Dundalk three years later. In 1995 he was transferred to the crime unit before being appointed a detective in 1998.

That evening Joe Ryan took up duty at 6 p.m. and was catching up on some paperwork when his colleague arrived in the office to begin their first job of the night. Adrian clipped his garda issued SIG Sauer P226 semi-automatic pistol into the black leather holster on his right-hand side, and at 8.05 p.m. they left the station in their unmarked patrol car, a grey 06-registered Toyota Avensis. Their call sign for the night, to make them identifiable to other garda units, was Papa Bravo One-Six. The weather conditions that night were miserable as heavy rain and wind swept across the Cooley Peninsula. The detectives set out into the dark January night and would first head to Omeath Credit Union, then travel to the branches in Carlingford, Cooley, and Lordship, before escorting the convoy to Dundalk. Detective Garda Ryan was driving the patrol car with his colleague acting as observer in the passenger seat. They stopped off at Ballymascanlon service station on the way to get petrol, while Detective Garda Donohoe went in to get a packet of chocolate peanuts and a bottle of water. As they pulled out of the service station they were contacted by Garda Kevin Cleary, stationed in Omeath, enquiring if they were on their way. Detective Garda Ryan apologised to his colleague for the delay and said they would be there shortly, making their way over the Cooley Mountains towards Omeath.

It was a busy night in the garda district, and as they drove through the mountains in the torrential rain they received a callout over their radio from the garda control room about an incident in the town centre. The cash escort was mandatory, and the detectives informed control that they would be unable to attend the other scene. The adverse conditions were also causing issues on the roads around the peninsula. As the gardaí reached the post office at Jenkinstown, they came across heavy flooding and barely managed to pass through the roadway. Detective Garda Ryan checked his rear-view mirror to ensure they weren't being followed by any motorists who could come into difficulty with the deluge, but nobody else was in sight.

In Omeath, Gardaí Alan Lynch and Tony Golden, who later lost his life in an unrelated tragic incident, decided to begin the escort and meet their colleagues along the way so as not to delay matters. Deirdre Campbell was working in Omeath Credit Union that night and was in charge of transporting the cash to her colleagues in Cooley. She placed roughly €3,500 in cash as well as cheques into a laptop case and got into her car to begin the 7 kilometre journey to Carlingford. She was shadowed by the marked garda patrol vehicle and would later recall that she didn't notice anything unusual as they drove along the windy coastal road running alongside Carlingford Lough.

While the cars were in transit, a group of men were getting themselves into position several kilometres away near the Lordship branch. At 8.49 p.m. a car travelling along the R173 slowly drove past the building and turned right on to New Road, a small lane leading towards the shoreline and on to lands directly behind the credit union. A minute after entering the laneway the car returned and drove back along the R173. Out of sight from the main road and credit union CCTV cameras, four young men wearing dark clothing and balaclavas had emerged from the car. They were also heavily armed, with two carrying loaded weapons. The gang forced their way into a barn on land nearby to keep themselves out of the tumultuous weather conditions as they waited. As the minutes passed, they moved themselves into position at the credit union's rear wall, making sure to conceal their presence from the view of the car park. Another car integral to their plan was being put into position near the credit union, watching it from a distance. Everything was now in place, and all the gang had to do was wait for their target.

Detective Gardaí Ryan and Donohoe would have been unaware of the sinister developments taking place as they caught up with the escort at Cooley at 8.45 p.m. The grey Avensis pulled into the credit union car park, where the armed detectives exchanged pleasantries with their uniformed colleagues, discussing the torrential weather conditions. Garda Lynch also informed them that the licence plate on the front of their Avensis had partially come off. Detective Garda Donohoe got out of the car to inspect the damage and adjusted the plate before Gardaí Lynch and Golden left to let the armed officers take up the escort. Mary Hanlon was working in the Cooley branch that night and was responsible for transporting the cash and cheques to Dundalk from the three credit unions. In total four bags, containing €27,375 in cash made up of notes and just under €90,000 in cheques, were put into her black Nissan Qashqai. While the workers would on occasion chat with the gardaí ensuring they could travel safely, it wasn't a night to stand outside on ceremony. She signalled to the detectives that she was ready to go, and the two cars set off at 9.12 p.m. towards their penultimate stop.

Working in Lordship Credit Union that evening was Pat Bellew, a retired engineer, along with Bernadette McShane, who had volunteered there for 25 years. The branch had closed its doors at 8.30 p.m. and the employees spent the next hour balancing reports and sorting out cash. Ms McShane was looking after the takings that night and placed just under €7,000 in cash as well as cheques into a zip-locked AIB bag. The cash float had initially been reduced following the previous raid and had only been increased again in recent weeks. Security measures put in place after that raid also meant that the two employees had to wait inside the building until the garda escort arrived.

At 9.26 p.m. Pat Bellew looked up at the monitors in the back-office, which displayed a real-time feed from the cameras overlooking the credit union car park. Two cars had just pulled in, and at the same time he received a phone call from Mary Hanlon telling them that they were outside. 'We'll be out now shortly,' he told her as he keyed in the alarm code and secured the building while turning off the car-park lights. The Nissan Qashqai and Toyota Avensis were stationary outside as both workers exited the building, gesturing to the convoy while making their way towards their own cars. Bernadette McShane had parked her red Nissan Micra facing the wall that looked out onto the main road, and she waited a moment to start the ignition so that the convoy knew it would be Pat Bellew joining them that night. He had made his way to his gold Mazda parked on the opposite side of the car park, facing the wall that looked out on to land and fields. Mr Bellew opened the rear door of the car and placed a laptop bag with documents in the back, before getting into the driver's seat and putting the cash bag down beside him. He got into the driver's seat and turned the key in the ignition to join the convoy. The three cars began slowly making their way out of the car park towards their final destination that night. They never made that journey.

As the cars were about to drive out, a dark-coloured Volkswagen Passat, which had been watching from a distance, sped towards the credit union from the Carlingford direction and parked across the exit, blocking it with perfect timing. Mary Hanlon would later tell gardaí that the driver, who she initially believed was a woman with blonde hair wearing a black beanie hat, had their eyes fixed straight ahead and their hands tightly gripped on the steering wheel. Simultaneously, the four masked men that had taken up their positions in the field vaulted over the credit union wall beside Pat Bellew's car. It was obvious to him that a robbery was now taking place and they were being hit.

The first two raiders ignored his car and made their way with purpose directly towards the garda vehicle. Both men were wearing balaclavas and were armed – one carrying a long-barrelled shotgun and the other holding a handgun. It was an indication of the planning involved, given that the only robbers carrying firearms targeted the garda vehicle. Detective Garda Donohoe had, by this point, stepped out of the Avensis on the passenger side to establish what was blocking the exit. His line of sight was directed at the Volkswagen Passat, and he would not have seen the masked gunmen running directly towards him from his right side. The robber wielding the shotgun had made his way to the driver's side of the garda car and stood within seven feet of the detective. He lifted the shotgun up to his right shoulder, training the muzzle directly

at the detective's head. Without saying a word or giving any
warning, he pulled the trigger, leading to a thundering bang
echoing around the car park. Detective Garda Donohoe wasn't
even looking at the raider as he was blasted in the right side of
the face, dropping to the ground. He never even had a chance
to draw his weapon, which was still safely clipped into the
holster. The robber, who had now also become a murderer,
stumbled back several feet from the recoil of the shot. He
staggered, almost losing his footing and falling to the ground,
before regaining his balance and running back towards the
garda car. His accomplice holding the handgun also briefly
retreated after the shotgun was discharged before running
back to the Avensis.

The two gunmen then trained their weapons on Detective
Garda Ryan and opened the driver's door. The killer rested his
shotgun against the shoulder of his dirty tracksuit and pointed
the weapon into the car, aiming it along the detective's body
and up at his head. The other raider fixed his handgun on
Detective Garda Ryan as he was hemmed into his seat, fearing
for his life. All that was visible through the black masks were
their stares as one shouted at him: 'I'm going to fucking kill
you. I'm going to fucking kill you. I'm going to shoot you. Give
us the money.' One of the gunmen then reached down and
removed the key from the ignition to neutralise the garda car.
'Don't shoot. I've no money,' Detective Garda Ryan shouted
back as he pleaded for his life. The daunting thought came into
his mind that, if he were to be shot, he would have a better
chance of survival if it was with the 9mm handgun.

While the two gunmen were focused on suppressing any
potential threat from the detectives, their two accomplices
targeted the credit union staff. They had made their way,

separately, to the cars of Pat Bellew and Bernadette McShane. The masked raider who focused on Mr Bellew's Mazda had a hammer in his right hand and swung it against the driver's window, smashing the glass inwards on top of the shocked employee. Without saying a word, he opened the driver's door and reached over Mr Bellew to the passenger seat. Struggling to grab the cash bag, he made his way around the car to the passenger side and grabbed the bag containing the cash takings from the Lordship branch. The red-handled hammer used to break the car window was left at the scene.

The other robber focused on Ms McShane's Nissan as he smashed the driver's window in. Shouting at the terrified volunteer, he told her: 'Step out, step out, hand it out, hand it out.' She screamed in panic as the masked man continued to shout at her: 'Give me the money. Give me the money. Give me the fucking money.' She eventually managed to let out a response to his terrorising demands, pleading with him: 'I don't have the bag. I don't have it.' Further threats were made for her to open the glove compartment, which was empty. Fearing for her life, Bernadette McShane grabbed her handbag from the passenger seat and threw it out of her window towards the robber. The gang were using walkie-talkies to communicate, and a signal came over their devices that it was time to go. 'Are you right there, lads?' a voice said through the transceiver. The four raiders almost simultaneously sprinted from the car park towards the Volkswagen Passat. The raider at Bernadette McShane's car seamlessly bolted over the credit union wall as he made his way to the getaway vehicle. The only car they hadn't focused their attention on was Mary Hanlon's Nissan Qashqai, containing more than €27,000 in cash from the other credit unions. Having been on the phone as the raid was happening, she believed that the guards had fired a warning shot and that the gang cleared off.

The raiders jumped into the Passat and its tyres screeched along the tarmac as it sped away from the scene. The entirety of the heist, from the point at which the getaway car arrived until its departure, had lasted just 58 seconds. It had netted the gang around €7,000, with nearly four times that figure left behind. Their greed and callousness had also cost Detective Garda Donohoe his life.

As the gang were fleeing, Detective Garda Ryan managed to free himself from the driver's seat and jumped out of the car, drawing his handgun from its holster. He pointed the weapon at the car as it sped away but, believing there was no further immediate threat to life, decided not to discharge the weapon at the fleeing car. He then ran around to the passenger side of the car to check on his colleague. He initially thought that the gang had simply fired a warning shot but became aware of the seriousness of the situation when he saw the garda lying on the wet tarmac with blood forming around his head. It was clear to him that Detective Garda Donohoe had been fatally wounded. Detective Garda Ryan then went to check on Mary Hanlon to see if she was hurt before rushing back to the garda car to inform his colleagues of what had just happened. It would have been evident to the gardaí who heard Detective Garda Ryan's distressed call for urgent assistance that something terrible had happened.

D/Gda Ryan: 'Bravo to Papa Bravo One.'

Control: 'One-Six to Bravo. Go ahead.'

D/Gda Ryan: 'Ambulance. Over.'

Control: 'Roger. One-Six you need assistance?'

D/Gda Ryan: 'Roger urgent assistance. Over. Urgent assistance.'

Control: 'What's your location?'

D/Gda Ryan: 'Can we get somebody?'

Control: 'What's your location?'

D/Gda Ryan: 'Lordship Credit Union. Over.'

The dispatcher then requested members of the armed regional support unit to the scene.

Control: 'Any detail Joe?'

D/Gda Ryan: 'I think he's been fatally shot. Over. Dark-coloured car is all I got … shotgun to my face.'

After the alert was placed over the garda radio, a separate call was also made to 999 by a person at the scene, informing emergency services of what had just occurred, with the detective being handed the phone.

D/Gda Ryan: 'Hello. Who's this?'

Dispatch: 'This is Drogheda Garda Station.'

D/Gda Ryan: 'Joe Ryan, Dundalk. Just had a member shot, member shot.'

Dispatch: 'Joe? Are you a member?'

D/Gda Ryan: 'Yeah. I'm on an escort.'

Dispatch: 'What's the story, Joe?'

D/Gda Ryan: 'We had a robbery there on escort. One man shot.'

Dispatch: 'Dead?'

D/Gda Ryan: 'Yeah.'

Dispatch: 'On way out. What did you see there?'

D/Gda Ryan: 'Shotgun in me face, all I saw was two men.'

Dispatch: 'Shotgun in your face?'

D/Gda Ryan: 'Shotgun and handgun as well.'

The callouts triggered a significant emergency response from across the division, with personnel racing to Lordship Credit Union to come to the aid of their colleagues. Gardaí Lynch and Golden were in Drumullagh near Omeath when they heard Joe Ryan's call for urgent assistance. They activated their lights and sirens and sped towards Bellurgan, where they were one of the first units on the scene. Sergeant John O'Flaherty had also arrived and was issuing instructions over the garda radio, directing members where to go and to cordon off the area. A helicopter from the Garda Air Support Unit was also deployed and circled over Dundalk in search of any sign of the robbery gang, while the PSNI were also put on alert. However, the speed at which the getaway car fled, and the scene's proximity to the border, meant they had long passed into Northern Ireland before they could be intercepted.

After leaving the scene the dark-coloured Passat drove at speed along the R173 towards Ballymascanlon Roundabout. Stephen Toal was driving on the road that night with his wife and in-laws and would later describe how his own car vibrated with the speed at which the Passat overtook them. His brother-in-law, Felix Smith, turned to Stephen and remarked: 'Look at that eejit the way he's driving that car. He won't have it long.' As the car approached the roundabout, they watched on, expecting it to skid into the island. But the person behind the wheel was clearly experienced in driving at high speed, even with the treacherous conditions, and jammed on the brakes before seamlessly switching lanes as the car made its way around the roundabout and off into the night. Two days later it was found by a forest worker burnt out on Cumsons Road, a remote site off Chalybeate Road near Newtownhamilton in County Armagh. Enquiries would establish that it had been stolen in a creeper burglary three nights before the credit union raid from a residential property in Clogherhead, County Louth.

Back at Lordship more emergency personnel from across the region were making their way to the scene. Barry Redmond, a paramedic based in North Leinster, was on duty that night when he received a call to attend the credit union. He arrived there at 9.51 p.m., grabbing his equipment from his car and going over to where Detective Garda Donohoe lay. The paramedic turned on his automated external defibrillator, a device that provides visual monitoring of the heart circulation system, but there were no signs of life. The paramedics began assessing the other people at the scene, including Mr Bellew, who had bleeding to the right side of his face from the glass fragments of the smashed driver's window. The little pieces of very fine glass looked like glitter across his face, and he was treated for minor injuries. Detective Garda Ryan was also assessed and found to have a considerably elevated blood pressure of 178 over 139, due to the shock of what he had just witnessed. Dr Alina Coroliu arrived at the scene a short time later and formally pronounced Adrian Donohoe dead at 10.36 p.m. Dr Khalid Jaber, the deputy state pathologist, was called to the scene to carry out preliminary examinations on the deceased detective.

Detective Garda Donohoe's best friend, Detective Sergeant Darren Kirwan, was off duty that night when he received a phone call shortly after the shooting informing him of what had happened. Upon hearing the devastating news, he brought his children home and made his way to the Donohoe house. There Adrian's wife told him that she wanted to visit her husband at the crime scene where his body lay. Their children were still asleep in bed, unaware of what had happened, minded by friends and family who had come to the house, as she made her way to Lordship Credit Union, arriving there shortly after 11 p.m. It was a sight that Caroline Donohoe would never fully recover from.

Recalling that night, Detective Inspector Marry says:

The 'station of the quivering lip' is an image that has stayed with me since 25 January 2013. It is a night neither I nor any of my colleagues and friends will ever forget. A horrible night. A violent night. A desperately sad night. At around 9.35 p.m., as the rain battered the ground, I got a call from Superintendent Gerry Curley: had I heard about Adrian Donohoe? I had not. I listened as he told me that my detective, our colleague and friend, was dead. He said that Adrian had been shot by armed raiders at Lordship Credit Union whilst on a cash escort. The words were clear, but my brain couldn't process them. The shock and disbelief were immense. A young man out doing his job had been killed. Shot dead in cold blood. A garda, killed on duty. The impact of those words was phenomenal. It was inconceivable to me that Adrian had been taken from us. Only the day before he had stuck his head into my office to see how things were going and what needed to be done. That was typical of Adrian, always enthusiastic and interested, a dedicated and dependable detective, a kind and gentle human being.

I arrived at Dundalk Garda Station just after 10 p.m. Everywhere I looked, uniformed and plain-clothes gardaí were either crying openly or fighting back the tears with their fists clenched and the tell-tale quivering lip, indicating pure emotion, pure anger, and sadness. It is an almost uncontrollable reaction, but it is unmistakable. My colleagues were transformed that night by raw grief and anger. The emotion coated the station; it was on the walls, the floor, the roof. It was in the air. Adrian's murder had changed the atmosphere. It was almost hard to breathe.

The first person who approached me was one of my detective sergeants who, barely able to contain his anger, said: 'If Adrian had the Uzi, this would not have happened.' He was referring to the application I'd made to senior management to have the Uzi machine gun restored to the detectives working on the border and, in particular, to Dundalk detectives. We felt strongly that this was important because border policing is unique and we knew the Uzi commanded respect, and therefore afforded our officers more protection. On that night at Lordship Credit Union, Adrian was armed only with a standard issue handgun. He didn't stand a chance against the full-barrel shotgun that the raiders were carrying. It was like bringing a sword to a gunfight. Useless.

We were all distraught, but we had to get to work. Our friend was murdered, and we were the only people who could solve this case and get justice for him. We had to pour ourselves into the work and be professional in our response. It gave some respite from the white-hot anger that the grief was wrapped up in. We knew that we had to work quickly if we were going to find out who had committed this horrific crime. On my car journey to Dundalk I'd phoned certain people to get the ball rolling. I needed a good team of detectives in a well-set-up incident room. We focused on that, the job at hand. There was going to be a huge amount of work to get through. But like all investigations, you have to get the basics right at the start. Make sure everything is done perfectly. No shortcuts. As hard as it was, we had to channel our grief and fury and turn it into something productive.

I distinctly remember that no one was sitting around the conference table. Everyone was standing and waiting for someone to take charge. That someone was me. I remember scanning the room as I sat at the top of the table, and there were familiar faces of colleagues I knew, but there were also unfamiliar faces. This always stuck with me, the number of gardaí who had heard about the shooting on the news and just got up and came to Dundalk, giving their own time to help out. There were gardaí from all over the region, from Dublin, from the Midlands. I was hugely impressed with the members who just had the sense that one of us was killed, murdered, and were here to help in any way they could. I had a job to do even though my lip did quiver at times. I knew the decisions I made that night would pave the way for the investigation to follow.

I remember it was 3 a.m. that morning before I got to visit the scene, I was so busy putting things in place for the 10 a.m. conference. I had to read the statements from the witnesses in case there was something they had to offer that could be worked on straight away. The scene was preserved by Sergeant Vincent Connell and he had everything in place and properly cordoned off. I spoke with the crime scene manager from the Technical Bureau, Sergeant Tom Carey, and I was satisfied all was in order as I would expect.

In the incident room that night, as Detective Inspector Marry looked around, he saw Detective Garda Ryan who, just hours earlier, had come face to face with the two armed men involved. He brought him and Detective Sergeant Kieran Reidy into his office and they sat around his desk, asking Detective Garda Ryan to recollect what information he could about the men involved.

Joe was focused. I specifically asked Joe what accents had the culprits. Joe was very sure, he said, they were not Traveller accents, they were not Dublin accents, and they were not northern accents. He stated that they were local border accents. Joe had spent over 20 years on the border, he was an experienced detective, and he would know his accents. This was the key piece of information for me to get up and running. On returning to the incident room, I picked two of my experienced detective sergeants to go and make a list of known border criminals who could do such a thing or be part of it. In the meantime, I divided the personnel I had into teams of two. I tasked a number of them to seek out witnesses and to take detailed statements from them. I needed to know what they saw and heard.

The detective sergeants set off to compile a list of potential suspects and returned a short time later. They handed the piece of paper to their detective inspector with 12 names scribbled on it. It contained persons known to gardaí for involvement in criminality in or around the border region, among them armed robbers, violent burglars, dissident criminals, and fuel smugglers. The fifth name, jotted down in black ink on the piece of paper, was a young criminal from Crossmaglen named Aaron Brady.

4

A CROSS-BORDER
CRIMINAL GANG

By the time of the Lordship murder and robbery, Aaron Brady was frequently appearing on garda radar and was well-known to detectives in Dundalk. In his mid-teens he was suspected of involvement in an assault within the district, before his involvement in criminality progressed to diesel laundering, car thefts, and burglaries. He was also on bail at the time of the raid and under a curfew over a dangerous garda pursuit in Dundalk during which he rammed a patrol van and three taxis. Because of his progressively worse offending, along with his ties to violent criminals in the border area, gardaí believed he was more than capable of being involved in the credit union robbery.

Aaron Brady was born on 16 February 1991 to Tony and Caroline, and the family lived in the Monaghan village of Iniskeen before relocating to Nottingham in England. There Tony Brady worked as a milkman while also studying physiotherapy, which was financed by an aunt living in Dublin. They had two daughters, Sonya who was born in 1994 and Laurene who was born in 1999, and after a number of years in England, the family moved to Crossmaglen. Aaron Brady was enrolled at Abbey Grammar School, where his father's cousins had attended and won All-Ireland medals with County Armagh, but after one year he moved to St Joseph's High School in Crossmaglen. There he met James 'Jimmy' Flynn and the pair would become close friends.

He left school aged 16 with unremarkable GCSE results, going on to work as a manual labourer and apprentice electrician between Crossmaglen and County Cavan. He also enrolled in a training and employment course in County Sligo, but in his late teens the electrical work dried up and Brady moved to the Gold Coast in Australia. After four months he returned home, following the death of his grandmother, and later in the summer of 2010 he met up with James Flynn, who was working in Massachusetts. The Flynn family all had American citizenship and at the time operated a tarmacking business in Quincy, a coastal city south of Boston. After living there for three months, Brady returned home and worked in his father's business selling advertisements for an internet company in the border area. The business declined as the economic recession took hold, and Tony Brady began working as a physiotherapist with Crossmaglen Rangers, and would later become chairman of the successful football club. Aaron Brady had played for the junior teams and later occasionally lined out as a forward for their second team.

Away from the football pitch and attempts at legitimate employment, Brady would regularly find himself on the wrong side of the law. As early as December 2007, when he was aged just 16, Brady was suspected of involvement in a minor assault in Carrickcarnan, Dundalk. He kept relatively quiet over the next three years, although he was linked to public-order incidents on Park Street in the town in 2009 and 2011. His criminal convictions in his teenage years were mainly for road-traffic offences, including a £450 fine and 18-month driving ban at Newry Magistrates' Court for driving without insurance and taking a motor vehicle without authority. While Brady was gradually making a name for himself, he couldn't blame the offending on his background, coming from a family with no links to criminality or dissident groups. Brady's mother, Caroline, had previously worked for a company contracted to Vodafone at their call centre in the Ramparts, Dundalk, from 2005 until the centre was closed during the financial crisis in 2011 and the jobs outsourced.

His involvement in crime continued, and in 2011 he was investigated for nine burglaries in County Monaghan over a six-month period. Some of the break-ins were creeper burglaries, in which a gang gain access to a home in the middle of the night by popping the barrel of the door lock to take valuables or car keys, before driving off with the stolen vehicle. These types of crimes would become the main modus operandi of Aaron Brady and his criminal associates, and his offending was only escalating.

In the early hours of 2 October 2011, gardaí were investigating the theft of a stolen Volkswagen Golf when they came across the car in Dundalk. The car had been stolen in a creeper burglary in Cootehill, County Cavan, a month earlier and was fitted with false number plates from a car stolen in a separate burglary in Stockport, England. Shortly before 4 a.m. gardaí saw Brady behind the wheel of the car with two other men, including his friend Liam Crozier, an electrician from Lismore Park in Crossmaglen. Brady pressed his foot down on the accelerator while keeping the handbrake up, making

the wheels of the vehicle spin and releasing a cloud of smoke
from the rubber skidding off the tarmac. Gardaí pulled up
alongside the Golf in their patrol van on Park Street, but
Brady gave them the finger and drove off at speed towards the
Demesne. Garda Sergeant John Moroney was in the patrol van
and immediately became concerned for the safety of pedestri-
ans and other motorists in the area. At Crowe Street, Brady
rammed a taxi before continuing to drive through the town
centre at high speed. At one junction he hit another taxi which
was parked up, causing the Golf to become partially airborne
and drive on two side wheels.

Gardaí believed the stolen car would overturn but Brady
continued driving and made his way back to Park Street,
where he deliberately reversed into a third taxi. When the
officers attempted to pull in front of the Golf to prevent any
further carnage, Brady rammed into the side of the garda van.
From there, Brady drove towards McSwiney Street and Legion
Avenue, where again he rammed the patrol van as it tried to
pull out in front of him. A car was coming in the opposite
direction and Brady swerved towards it, but the other driver
managed to avoid a collision by taking evasive action. At this
point gardaí feared that Brady would make it to the busy
Castletown Road, accessible by a blind junction, and pulled
back from the chase. The stolen car eventually came to a stop,
having driven a considerable distance with a damaged left front
tyre. The three men fled from the Golf, but Aaron Brady and
Liam Crozier were arrested a short distance away. The pursuit
had caused more than €10,000 worth of damage.

Brady was brought to Dundalk Garda Station for questioning but wasn't cooperative and, sticking to the Crossmaglen
code of omertà, invoked his right to silence and refused to

answer questions during interview. While nothing probative was gained from this process, the eye-witness accounts from gardaí and bystanders, along with the CCTV footage of the incident, meant there was enough evidence to prosecute him. He was brought before Dundalk District Court and charged with a number of offences, including unauthorised taking of a car, dangerous driving, criminal damage, and driving without insurance. On 11 December 2011, he was successful in applying for bail but certain conditions were attached in order for him to be released from custody. This included a 9 p.m. curfew to an address in Whitestown in Carlingford, County Louth. The property was owned by his grandfather and used by the Brady family as a holiday home.

Despite the bail conditions, he would normally stay outside of the gardaí's jurisdiction in the family's new home at New Road in Silverbridge, County Armagh. In 2012 he also began renting a property on Lough Road, a three-bedroom Portakabin sitting on more than three acres of land near Crossmaglen, with his friend Colin Hoey. The property was used as a party house at the weekends, with Brady and his friends returning there after socialising in nearby nightclubs to continue their sessions into the early hours of the morning. That September he also began dating Jessica King, a 17-year-old who lived with her parents on the Concession Road in Cullaville, South Armagh.

Despite serving a driving ban, Brady had access to several vans and cars, while he would also use James Flynn as his personal driver to ferry him around. Born 24 November 1990, Flynn was the youngest son of Eugene Snr and Philomena Flynn, who later separated. James, along with his mother and older brother, Eugene Jnr, lived in a large detached property called Dunroamin House, located just off the Carlingford Road

near Lordship Credit Union. Eugene Flynn Snr was known
to authorities in the UK for involvement in fuel laundering
and in 2000 was convicted for evasion of excise duty. He was
sentenced to three years and nine months' imprisonment and
ordered to pay £650,000 (€776,100) to the British Exchequer
after police raided an industrial unit at Ossett, West Yorkshire.
He later absconded from prison and returned to Ireland, where
he was living unlawfully at large. He had also some years earlier
been the victim of a shooting when a gang of men stormed his
home and wounded him. The son of a senior IRA figure was
suspected of carrying out the shooting, but no one was ever
prosecuted over the incident. James Flynn would spend half of
the year, from March to October, in the United States, where he
worked with a half-brother from his mother's previous relationship, and would return to Ireland for the other six months of
the year. Unlike Aaron Brady, Flynn had not come to prominent
garda attention in his younger years, but did have some minor
infractions. In January 2011 he was convicted of threatening and
abusive behaviour as well as being intoxicated in a public place
for which he was fined €200 at Dundalk District Court. By the
time of the robbery at Lordship Credit Union he was going out
with Colleen McCann, a hairdresser from Crossmaglen who
was living in the County Monaghan town of Castleblayney.
The young woman had also had past brushes with gardaí. On
20 July 2012, she had been involved in a serious road crash
in which teenager Ciaran McKenna died. The 17-year-old,
her then boyfriend, was discovered fatally injured behind the
wheel of the car. However, following an investigation, gardaí
established that another person had been driving the car at the
time of the collision and that Ciaran McKenna's body had been
moved into the driver's seat after it crashed.

Flynn's tarmacking business was going well, and in late 2012 he purchased a BMW 5 Series with the registration plate W608 BDY for around £15,000. The grey sports car had a 3-litre turbo engine and stuck out when being driven around the area because of a metallic wrapping on the car that he had had applied after buying it. The Flynn family also owned a yard on Concession Road that was locally known as the firework house. The premises was used for fuel-laundering activity, and the sludge from diesel waste would be brought there in cubes and loaded onto trailers before being dumped in ditches and lands around the region.

The site was being rented from Philomena Flynn by a young man from Crossmaglen who was aged just 19 at the time of the credit union robbery. Hailing from a family of suspected smugglers in Armagh, he also became involved in the trade, and intelligence linked him to operating a significant diesel-laundering operation. For legal reasons, he is referred to as Mr C. Gardaí had information that several criminals including this man and Aaron Brady operated 'freelance' in the dumping of diesel waste cubes for which they would be paid between €100 and €200. Mr C had come to the attention of the PSNI previously, after he drove through a police checkpoint and led officers to a shed in which he was storing 24 cubes of diesel sludge. He later received a punishment beating from his uncle, a well-known cross-border smuggler, who owned the fuel-laundering facility. Police on both sides of the border also believed Mr C was involved in the theft of motor vehicles that were broken down for parts and sold. Just over a week before the credit union robbery he had a disagreement with Eugene Flynn Snr, who wanted the operation at 155 Concession Road closed down, as he was still being sought by authorities in England.

In his late teens Aaron Brady also began associating with a dangerous local criminal, Brendan 'Benny' Treanor. Gardaí believe that they formed an organised crime gang with Flynn, Mr C and others, which up to January 2013 was involved in a spate of creeper burglaries, diesel laundering, and armed robberies of petrol stations and credit unions around the border region. The gang were also suspected of stealing cars that were dismantled and sold for parts. Born 3 June 1988, Treanor was already earning a reputation in the border region in his teens as a violent offender linked to burglaries and armed robberies. While his mother lived in Dundalk, Treanor mainly resided in the North and lived at Slieve View in Silverbridge. The youngest of four siblings, Treanor was kicked out of the family home when he was 17 because of his wild behaviour and involvement in criminality. In between carrying out audacious raids he would work as a lorry driver, while he was also involved in rally driving as a hobby. Brady and Treanor got to know each other through Treanor's partner, Charlene O'Callaghan, a hairdresser from Crossmaglen. Her younger brother Danny was a successful footballer with Crossmaglen Rangers but was also connected to criminality. Despite Brendan Treanor's links to a litany of offending, he had few serious criminal convictions, having mainly received various fines before Newry Magistrates' Court for driving with no insurance or licence.

On 17 September 2010, he was arrested, along with another man, for the unauthorised taking of a Teleporter from a shop in Carlingford. Detective Garda Donohoe had arrested him and interviewed Treanor, who was later charged, although the case was struck out due to insufficient evidence. Gardaí also arrested Treanor over a serious assault that highlighted his propensity for violence. In September 2011, he allegedly stuck a broken glass bottle into another man's neck, which caused serious injuries and required 37 stitches. Despite his being quizzed over the attack and later charged, the case was subsequently dismissed. His most serious criminal convictions were for handling stolen property, for which he was jailed for six months, and for perverting the course of justice in relation to a rape, but Treanor himself was not involved in the serious sexual assault.

Socially, he would regularly hang out with Aaron Brady at Ma Brady's restaurant (no relation) and Ridley's nightclub in Dundalk, as well as the Cartwheel pub in Crossmaglen. Treanor was also known to use cocaine and would spend many Saturday nights gambling in the casino in Dundalk. His name was also scribbled down on the list, given to Detective Inspector Marry hours after Adrian Donohoe's murder, of local criminals capable of involvement in the Lordship Credit Union raid. One of the main reasons for this was that he was a suspect for a previous armed robbery at the branch, which had a similar modus operandi. Shortly after the 2011 raid, gardaí received confidential information that he was one of the men involved and that he was showing off the proceeds of crime at a pub in Dundalk days later. One garda said of this: 'There was information that he was essentially flashing the cash and buying everyone drinks in the bar, and bragging about how easy it was to rob a credit union.' Treanor was also being named by confidential informants as the person who carried out the robbery of the bookmaker at Dundalk racecourse two months later.

The garda tasked with investigating both robberies at that time was Detective Garda Donohoe, and while gardaí wanted to question their chief suspect, this was hampered by the fact that he lived across the border outside of their jurisdiction. Gardaí got a break a year after the robberies when they were notified that Treanor was due to appear before the district court in Monaghan over a separate matter on 24 September 2012. Gardaí decided they would arrest and question him about both armed robberies, with Detective Gardaí Donohoe and Barron dispatched to detain him. The two detectives walked into the courtroom that morning and sat down at the back, awaiting Treanor's arrival. After a few minutes they spotted their suspect walking into the courthouse with a group including Aaron Brady and Charlene O'Callaghan. Treanor's case was adjourned, and as he went to leave, he was approached by the detectives. At 11.30 a.m. Detective Garda Donohoe arrested Brendan Treanor under Section 30 of the Offences Against the State Act, 1939, on suspicion of the unlawful possession of a firearm and the robbery of the bookmaker. He remained calm during the arrest and didn't appear in any way surprised or irate at the developments. The suspect, who had just been put in handcuffs, even turned to the detectives and said: 'Sure I knew you must have been here for me.'

They escorted him to their patrol car, with Detective Garda Donohoe driving and Detective Garda Barron sitting in the back with the prisoner. During the car journey to Dundalk Garda Station the mood was mostly civilised, with no angry words exchanged as they engaged in general conversation. However, at one point Brendan Treanor turned to Detective Garda Donohoe and asked: 'How's all in Railway Village?' Revealing that he knew the home address of the detective who was leading investigations into his gang was a clear attempt at intimidation. Unfazed by the comment, Detective Garda Donohoe simply replied 'Grand' as he continued driving.

They arrived at Dundalk Garda Station at 12.25 p.m. and shortly afterwards began interviewing Brendan Treanor about the racecourse robbery. His attitude during the interviews bordered on carefree, invoking his right to silence while also goading his interrogators. At one point during the interview Treanor sat forward and told them: 'I'd like you to start showing the evidence against me.' After the first interview, Detective Garda Donohoe decided that a second interrogation in relation to the racecourse raid would prove pointless and reap no reward, as Treanor knew the evidence against him was minimal. At 7.25 p.m. the interview process began for the Lordship robbery, for which he was also detained, with Detective Sergeant Darren Kirwan taking over. However, no new information was gleaned during the process and Brendan Treanor was released from custody after 10 p.m., pending the emergence of new evidence. A file was sent to the Director of Public Prosecutions, but Treanor was never charged with either armed robbery.

A few weeks after Treanor had been arrested, Brady was back before Dundalk Circuit Court on 12 October 2012 over the dangerous-driving incident. He was arraigned on three counts of dangerous driving, using a stolen car, and criminal damage, pleading guilty to all three charges. The judge adjourned the matter for sentencing to 14 January, but on that day it was again adjourned to a later date.

As gardaí gathered in Dundalk Garda Station late on 25 January 2013, Sergeant John Moroney was tasked with locating Aaron Brady and establishing his whereabouts for that night. At 1.45 the following morning he was accompanied by

Detective Garda David Gantley and Garda Eamon Kissane as they called to the address in Carlingford where Brady was meant to be residing as part of his bail conditions. There was no answer at the property and no sign of life.

In the early hours of 26 January, checkpoints had been placed on the roads around Lordship Credit Union to cordon off the scene. The checkpoints were dotted along the Carlingford Road all the way up to Ballymascanlon Roundabout to preserve the scene, with only residents permitted within that zone to go to their homes. A further roadblock had been positioned just off the R173 near Dunroamin House. Dr Jaber had finished his preliminary examinations at the scene at 3 a.m. and was being driven back to Dundalk by Garda Finbarr Gurhy when they came across a car travelling towards them. The vehicle was signalled to pull over so Garda Gurhy could establish what it was doing inside the cordon. The grey BMW was being driven by James Flynn, who was known to the garda. Flynn said that he had been in and out of the cordon on a number of occasions that night and was heading home. Garda Gurhy saw a passenger in the front seat but didn't take any notice and, following the brief exchange, the garda car and the BMW continued on their separate journeys.

The following afternoon a team of around 30 gardaí began combing the route the getaway car had taken from Lordship Credit Union. Sergeant Moroney was leading the search team at Ballymascanlon Roundabout when at 12.25 p.m. he noticed Flynn's BMW heading towards them. The familiar face of Aaron Brady, whom he had unsuccessfully attempted to locate in Carlingford hours earlier, stared back at him from the passenger seat. Flynn was instructed to pull over while Gardaí Joanne Moore and Anthony Quinn carried out a search of the vehicle. The sergeant brought Aaron Brady away from his friend and they sat down on the barrier at the side of the road. Brady appeared calm and composed as he confirmed his details to Sergeant Moroney and called out his phone number, swapping the last two digits. He then went on to give an account of his movements the previous night.

Brady claimed that he was with Flynn between 4 p.m. and 5 p.m. before going to the Superbites fast-food restaurant in Crossmaglen. He said he was then dropped to Jessica King's home in Cullaville at 7 p.m. and that he stayed there until he was collected by James Flynn, who drove them back to Flynn's house where they played video games and stayed the night. After taking down the details of Brady's account, the sergeant asked him a more direct question: did he know anything about the murder and robbery at Lordship Credit Union? Aaron Brady denied having any knowledge of the crime and claimed that he first heard about it after waking up that morning. This appeared strange to Sergeant Moroney, as the two men had been staying at a house within the cordon put in place in response to the murder. It was reasonable to believe that he must have known about the events the previous night. As they conversed, the information Brady was giving was relayed back to him to make sure an accurate account was being recorded. He was then again asked if he had heard anything about the murder, to which Brady replied: 'It might help me with my circuit court case.' Gardaí took this to mean that, if Brady were to pass on any information about the crime, it might help him in getting a lesser sentence for the dangerous-driving incident he was charged with.

The sergeant then returned to the BMW and, out of earshot of Brady, asked his friend to account for his movements the previous night. Flynn appeared nervous and gave an account that contradicted the version given by Aaron Brady moments earlier. He said that he was in Crossmaglen from about 6 p.m. to 10 p.m. with Brady and that he went to his friend Ryan Conlon's house in Lismore Park to get a ticket for a poker event, arriving there at around 10.30 p.m. He continued that he then collected Brady from his house, failing to mention where Brady had been in the meantime or where he had dropped him off, and that he then took him to Cullaville. Flynn stated that he went to his own house to charge his phone, arriving there between 11 p.m. and 11.30 p.m., before travelling to his girlfriend's home at 12.30 a.m. Sergeant Moroney then sought to clarify certain matters with Flynn, who said he'd dropped Brady off at his home sometime between approximately 8 p.m. and 9 p.m. – he wasn't sure of the time. He said he then went to Ryan Conlon's house and was there for up to an hour, and that Aaron Mostyn was also present, and that he then col-lected Aaron Brady from Cullaville.

Having given their accounts, the two men were allowed continue their journey. As Sergeant Moroney read back over his notes it became obvious that one of the men, if not both, were lying about their movements the previous night. Because of the inconsistencies in their accounts, along with Brady's claim that he only heard about the shooting that morning and Flynn's nervous demeanour, Sergeant Moroney decided to compile a note of the encounter and send it up to his superiors when he returned to Dundalk Garda Station. In his report he stated: 'On analysis there is a conflict on the times being presented by both men. There also appears to be a conflict that James Flynn stated that he spoke to the gardaí on the barrier yet Aaron Brady claimed not to have known about the incident until the next morning. It appears that a more formal interview of these two individuals will be necessary.' Gardaí decided to begin looking more closely at the pair. Phone examinations later established that Aaron Brady made a flurry of calls directly after the encounter with Sergeant Moroney. He rang his girlfriend and his father, while also failing to get through to Brendan Treanor, and then called Mr C and another friend involved in diesel laundering.

Immediately after the encounter, gardaí notified the PSNI and asked them to send officers to Jessica King's home to corroborate the accounts given by Brady and Flynn. Within an hour two police constables knocked on the door of the King family home and spoke to her. She confirmed that she was in a relationship with Aaron Brady and that he had been at the house between 7.30 p.m. and 9.30 p.m. that previous night. After the constables left, Jessica King and Aaron Brady made several more phone calls to one another. Having consulted with their colleagues in the south, the PSNI returned to the house later that day and requested that she attend Crossmaglen Police Station to give a formal statement. Jessica King and her sister Amy were driven to the barracks and were asked to wait in the lobby area. By this stage the schoolgirl realised that matters were more serious than she initially thought and took out her phone, hastily deleting several text messages between her and her boyfriend.

She was then brought into an interview room where she gave a statement to Detective Constable Robert McAllan about the events of the previous day. Having spoken to her boyfriend in between her interactions with the PSNI, Jessica King told Detective Constable McAllan that Brady had arrived at her home at 8 p.m. the previous night before leaving at around 2.30

the following morning. This account was similar to the one given by Aaron Brady to Sergeant Moroney hours earlier but would again prove to be false. Detective McAllan then asked Jessica to hand over her mobile phone so it could be examined and analysed by gardaí.

Her friend Jade Fitzpatrick had also been with her in the house on the night of the murder and was asked to make a statement. She told investigators that she'd arrived there at 7 p.m. and that Aaron Brady arrived between 7.30 p.m. and 8 p.m. She recalled him being dropped off by James Flynn in his BMW and joining the two teenagers in the bedroom. He was wearing a red hooded sweatshirt, she told the PSNI, adding that he left at around 9.30 p.m. However, the following day Jade Fitzpatrick made a further statement indicating that she wanted to change aspects of her initial account. She clarified that she hadn't arrived at Jessica King's home until 9.30 p.m. on the night of the murder and that Aaron Brady only showed up between 10.30 p.m. and 11 p.m. It was clear that Brady was using his girlfriend and her friend to create a false alibi for himself. This, along with the inconsistencies in his statement and his claim that he hadn't heard about the shooting until the following morning, made him a person of interest to the investigation within 24 hours of the murder. Gardaí made applications to review Brady's phone records, and the records of those associated with him, through the Crime and Security section, with Detective Inspector Marry explaining:

> He was a person we wanted to look into more. I was looking for Aaron Brady's call data because he was on the list drawn up relating to people who may be involved in that type of robbery, he could not be traced that night,

and the next day Sergeant Moroney stopped him with James Flynn and their stories did not match up. I was thinking: 'Why was someone telling lies?' It was important to tell the truth because it was such a serious incident. We needed to look into it more.

5

KEY PERSONNEL

The shock and revulsion at the murder of a detective carrying out his duties was palpable not just in Dundalk but across the entire country. Adrian Donohoe had become the 87th member of An Garda Síochána to lose his life in the line of duty and the first to be murdered since Detective Garda Jerry McCabe was shot dead by the Provisional IRA in Adare, County Limerick, on 7 June 1996. The shooting of Detective Garda Donohoe also came at a time of unprecedented cuts across the organisation and there was widespread anger that, at a time when the government was slashing resources and closing down garda stations, a detective had lost his life serving his community. On the week of the murder a total of 95 garda stations were shut all over Ireland, while the training college had been closed for new recruits since 2010. The moratorium on recruitment meant that the garda was the only national police force in Europe that was not hiring new personnel to its ranks.

Garda management and government officials were quick to defend these unprecedented measures. At a media briefing the day after the murder, Garda Commissioner Martin Callinan told reporters: 'Resources will not be an issue and will never be an issue when it comes to this type of an investigation.' The justice minister of the day, Fine Gael politician Alan Shatter, also gave a statement to toe the party line, saying that the organisation had sufficient capabilities. In an interview published in the *Sunday Independent* on 27 January, he was quoted as saying: 'The gardaí have very, very substantial resources. They are engaged in smart policing. We are ensuring that as many members of the force as possible are engaged in these areas of crime prevention and crime detection and gardaí are not unnecessarily engaged in desk jobs that can be done by civilians.' He also said that Adrian Donohoe was 'given no chance' and that those involved had 'no respect for human life'. The leader of the opposition, Fianna Fail TD and future Taoiseach Micheál Martin, said that his party would support the government in what he described as a 'key moment where politics faces a major test', adding that the killing was a 'tipping point', similar to the murders of Jerry McCabe and crime journalist Veronica Guerin in 1996. 'The situation could not be graver. Democracy and the rule of law need the foundation of a strong, well-resourced garda force. Instead, morale within the force is at an all-time low. The thin blue line is becoming ever thinner,' Mr Martin said.

Detective Inspector Marry was formally appointed senior investigation officer (SIO) of the murder investigation by Chief Superintendent Pat McGee, overseeing the mammoth inquiry that in the early stages involved hundreds of gardaí, and set about putting his key personnel in place for the investigation. The 14 sections established for the murder and robbery probe included teams for inquiries, phone analysis, interview strategy, exhibits, house-to-house interviews, searches, analysis, working with the PSNI, and liaising with the family, as

well as CCTV viewing and collection. A team had also been
appointed to review associated crimes for similar patterns and
modus operandi. The main lines of inquiry in the initial stages
included stolen shotguns, cars taken in creeper burglaries, robberies, and the evaluating of intelligence, which was handled
by senior detectives.

Local gardaí were backed up by divisional units in Louth
and across the wider northern region while also being given
support by national garda units based in Dublin. This included
detectives who specialised in major crimes from the National
Bureau of Criminal Investigation (NBCI) and anti-terror gardaí
attached to the Special Detective Unit (SDU). The garda's highly
trained tactical unit, the Emergency Response Unit (ERU), were
also sent to Dundalk to help gardaí with the investigation and
assist in searches and checkpoints. The National Surveillance
Unit (NSU) were utilised to help with the discreet monitoring
of targets. The Stolen Motor Vehicle Unit were later called in
to assist the investigation and provide expertise relating to car
thefts, given that the car used was stolen in a creeper burglary.

At Dundalk Garda Station case conferences were held
regularly to give updates on the progress of the inquiry. On the
responsibility of overseeing the major investigation, Detective
Inspector Marry says:

> Being a senior investigating officer and to be put in charge
> of the biggest murder inquiry the state has seen is not for
> the faint hearted. I knew I was experienced, and I had a
> good sense of how to motivate my teams, and I knew I
> was good at planning strategies and moving an investiga-
> tion. However, this case was something different. I knew
> I had to plan for a protracted investigation and what

that entailed. I drew up a chart of what sections or areas evidence may come from and put a sergeant in charge of each one, while also planning for what backup would be required. I needed key people in positions to take on not just running an incident room but also the responsibility of detective tasks. Firstly an incident-room coordinator had to be picked, and I assigned Detective Garda James Doherty for this task. He was my right-hand man during the Niall Dorr murder inquiry, and I was very happy with our relationship and understanding.

James is one of the best incident-room coordinators in the country, if not the best, and a marvellous good character. We understood each other and he had my back as I did his. I also needed an incident-room manager, someone who takes notes, makes sure administrative work is done and in order, and someone who is an all-rounder when it comes to a major case. I assigned Detective Sergeant Ciaran Clancy to this task. What a skilled detective – there was many a hard day I could not have got through without Ciaran's dedication and professionalism. He is one in a million and the best incident-room manager in the country by far.

I needed an exhibits officer, someone with an eye for the importance of maintaining a comprehensive responsibility for all exhibits from the time they come into their possession to the day they are needed in court. A huge task with equal responsibility, I assigned Detective Garda Karen Coughlan to this. She excelled at the job, and I could not talk highly enough about her. I needed someone to coordinate statements. This is where someone I assigned would read each and every statement with a view to seeing if anything of evidential value could be gathered from the witnesses. This person had to have experience of major investigation and be someone who was sharp and that I could trust. I assigned Detective Garda John Kissane of the NBCI to this task. His skill and awareness would later lead to the first real break in the case.

These were the first key persons I needed to get the show on the road and were people I could trust. They also trusted and respected my position as senior investigating officer, and that I would make the decisions to progress matters. I was happy with my people, who were excellent investigators with skills to match the task at hand.

Although suspicion fell on Aaron Brady and his associates within hours of the murder, other potential suspects had to be investigated, and the person-of-interest list would grow to 207 names. The focus of any criminal inquiry is to investigate the offence, rather than any individual person or persons, meaning that all other possibilities have to be ruled out. Because of the region where the crime occurred, and the cross-border element, gardaí could not dismiss dissident republican involvement. In the days and weeks after the robbery, the Garda's SDU was tasked with tracking down approximately 50 known republicans and violent criminals to establish their whereabouts on the night of the murder.

One of the first persons the anti-terror unit approached was Gerard Mackin, a ruthless criminal from Belfast who was a leading member of the INLA. In 2008 he was convicted by the non-jury Special Criminal Court in Dublin of the murder of taxi driver Edward Burns (36) on the Falls Road in Belfast on 12 March 2007. It was the first time a person had been convicted in a Dublin court for a murder in the North under the Criminal Law Jurisdiction Act of 1976. However, Mackin's conviction was overturned, and a chief prosecution witness later refused to give evidence at the retrial, telling a High Court judge he had been threatened and told he would be shot dead if he testified. Prosecutors entered a 'nolle prosequi', meaning the matter would not be prosecuted, and Mackin walked free from court as his supporters applauded and cheered. In the years after his acquittal, Gerard Mackin remained involved in criminality and has since been convicted for his role in an attack, during which a man was tortured and had his foot nailed to the floor, and of money laundering in the Special Criminal Court. Within hours of Adrian Donohoe's murder, detectives sought to establish Mackin's whereabouts on the night. When members of the SDU finally caught up with Mackin, he stated that he was in a bed and breakfast in Castlebellingham, around 25 kilometres from Lordship Credit Union, on the evening of the crime. His account was corroborated by the bed-and-breakfast owner, and gardaí quickly ruled out Gerard Mackin as a person of interest.

Many of the criminals tracked down refused to give formal statements but were happy to provide alibis ruling them out of involvement in the crime. Others, however, were less than helpful in interacting with the gardaí to rule themselves out, even if there was little reason to believe they were even involved. One such person was a double murder suspect originally from the North who was living in Dundalk at the time of the armed raid. The man, now aged in his 40s, cannot be named for legal reasons as he is currently facing serious charges before the courts. When gardaí attempted to speak to him at Dundalk Garda Station in the days after the robbery, he refused to account for his whereabouts that night and declined to give gardaí a statement. Members of the SDU decided to conduct a follow-up interview with the criminal and ascertain where he was on the night of the murder. The inquiry once again hit a brick wall, with the man becoming 'very aggressive' and 'uncooperative' when approached by detectives, according to one report. It wasn't until weeks later that he stated that he was home on the night of the murder and robbery and was not involved in it. Gardaí found there was no evidence to link him to the crime and ruled him out of their inquiries.

Other people visited by the anti-terror unit were Real IRA member and bomb-maker Philip McKevitt; Oliver Traynor, who was named in the House of Commons as being linked to the Omagh bombing; and Derek Murphy, who at the time was on bail for, and would later be convicted of, firing shots at gardaí during a post office robbery in Portmarnock, Dublin, the previous November. They were all subsequently ruled out of having any involvement in the credit union raid.

Other potential suspects came to the attention of gardaí through tip-offs from observant members of the public. One report came in from a woman in the days after the murder, who raised concerns about an individual who was on her flight from Belfast Airport to London on 26 January. She had become concerned about the man sitting near her on the plane, recounting that he was acting suspiciously. The man, she said, was on the phone and spoke in a 'thick Southern accent'. One comment she overheard him make to the person on the other end of the line was: 'No I'm on a plane. No, I am. I am telling you the truth, I'm on a plane to London. Did you hear about the Garda, that was some job.' A few seconds later he referred to 'going to London to lie low for a while', that he 'may be heading to Magaluf', and he enquired with the other caller about staying with certain people. She became concerned and raised the issue with a member of the cabin crew, before later reporting the matter to investigating gardaí at Dundalk. Garda inquiries established that the individual was a Traveller living in the Newry area.

The matter was of interest to Detective Inspector Marry and the investigation team. This interest was further piqued after inquiries were made into the man in Northern Ireland. It emerged that on 26 January at 1.31 a.m., just hours after the credit union raid, the PSNI were called to a house in Newry following reports of several individuals acting suspiciously in a garden. When the police arrived, they discovered six males at the property, including the man on the plane, and noticed a distinct smell of petrol. This was of potential significance as the house was located just 20 minutes from where the getaway car used in the Lordship raid was burnt out. PSNI intelligence also indicated that a Traveller gang from Newry were involved in a previous robbery at Newry Credit Union in November 2012 during which £2,000 in cash was stolen. Detectives began focusing on the man on the plane and set about establishing his whereabouts at the time of the murder. Investigators even considered obtaining a warrant to intercept his telephone calls due to his suspicious behaviour on the plane and the encounter with the PSNI hours after the robbery. Ultimately, though, he was able to establish that he was not near Lordship Credit Union during the murder and was eliminated from inquiries as part of that investigation.

The murder had also led to a wave of information flowing into the investigation team from a multitude of informants, formally referred to as covert human intelligence sources (CHIS). The CHIS system had been established following the Morris

Tribunal in 2004, which investigated allegations of abuse and corruption by certain gardaí in County Donegal. In its first report the tribunal said that the garda's Crime and Security section had at the time 'not come to grips' with the informant system and called for a robust review of the process. The new CHIS system introduced several changes, including a code of practice to govern the relationship between a source and their handler and a rigid structure of registration and assessment for informants, while mandating that a minimum of two people should be involved in handling a CHIS. The system remains in place to this day.

In the days and weeks after the robbery, the names of Aaron Brady, Brendan Treanor, and James Flynn were at the forefront of intelligence relating to the crime, while detailed information about their links to previous criminality was also coming to light. One informant stated that Aaron Brady was involved in the murder of Detective Garda Donohoe and that he was also responsible for separate armed robberies at Morgan Fuels and at the Dundalk racecourse. Another source told gardaí that Brady 'was on the racecourse job' and that the gang had laughed about Aaron Brady dropping the shotgun used in the raid. It was also stated that he received the nickname 'Butterfingers Brady' among criminals after the incident.

A further piece of intelligence stated that Brady was involved in the theft of a four-by-four jeep months earlier that contained a shotgun. Gardaí would later establish that this vehicle was stolen by Brady during a creeper burglary in Kingscourt, County Cavan. Inquiries determined that the jeep was later returned to the owner without the firearm and that Aaron Brady had this shotgun in the attic of his house at Lough Road for a number of weeks. It was stated that this was the weapon used by Brady to murder Detective Garda Adrian Donohoe. Investigators were also told that the car used in the shooting was parked in close proximity to Aaron Brady's house for a number of days prior to the murder. This was again in reference to the Portakabin on Lough Road where Brady had been living offside at the time of the murder. Gardaí were also told that Brady was the person who'd carried out the actual shooting, that he was linked to a criminal gang who specialise in stealing expensive cars, and that his gang carried out the first major robbery at Lordship in 2011. While the information from confidential sources is often hearsay and can't be used as evidence in a court of law, it did show the level of suspicion around Brady and his associates in the border community and criminal fraternity. Detective Inspector Marry said that he 'couldn't ignore' the level of information coming into the incident room about the gang.

In late January gardaí became aware that, while on a trip to Belfast with their girlfriends and two others on 27 January, James Flynn told Brady that an unspecified event should not be discussed. That evening Flynn was also heard talking to another man about media reports that stated that gardaí were focusing on a border gang and that a burnt-out car had been recovered, with these news reports appearing to worry Flynn. Gardaí also received a tip-off that two days after the robbery Flynn and another man engaged in 'cleaning the house' at Lough Road and that the men discussed moving a 'small package' that weekend. There was also further information that Aaron Brady had been associated with what was found, which related to the getaway car that was discovered in Cumsons Road. The investigation team were also made aware that Aaron Brady was considering advancing the argument that he was involved in other criminality on the night of the murder to account for the discrepancies in his alibi given to Sergeant John Moroney.

Further intelligence available to gardaí indicated that Flynn and Brady were continuing to concern themselves with confirming alibis on the night of the murder and were fearful they would be arrested soon. Both men also believed that speculation in the media about who was involved in the murder stemmed from their association with Brendan Treanor and Aaron Brady's general involvement in criminality. Gardaí received information that on 2 February 2013, James Flynn instructed Mr C to go and collect a 'parcel' immediately from Aaron Brady as he couldn't hold on to the unspecified item for long.

Plenty of details were also being shared about the alleged involvement of other people in the shooting. Sources were telling gardaí that a woman connected to the gang was 'on the job in Bellurgan', with informants describing her as 'ruthless', 'a good driver', and 'mad'. Brendan Treanor's name featured heavily among the pieces of information gardaí were receiving too. One source stated that Treanor was involved in three previous robberies: Forkhill Credit Union, Morgan Fuels, and the Dundalk racecourse raid. Other informants were claiming that Treanor was concerned over newspaper articles about the murder, but he was confident that investigators couldn't put him at the scene on the night or disposing of anything, and he was cautious of using his mobile phone. There was also information that Treanor had 'a grudge against the Garda who was shot'. Another source said they didn't believe there was any personal animus against Detective Garda Donohoe or other gardaí investigating serious criminality in the area.

The murder of a garda also led to a major focus and crackdown on cross-border criminality. As part of the murder inquiry a checkpoint strategy was deployed involving the ERU and SDU to gather intelligence and identify suspect vehicles on both sides of the border. The dissident groups running lucrative fuel-laundering and smuggling enterprises in both jurisdictions were enraged, not that a garda had been shot dead in cold blood, but because the increased police activity was affecting their illicit businesses. Thomas 'Slab' Murphy had moved on from his armed campaign and by this stage had become heavily involved in cross-border smuggling operations. In 2006, he was the subject of a major investigation by authorities in Britain and Ireland that resulted in illicit contraband and around €800,000 in cash being seized. At one point the BBC's 'Underworld Rich List' estimated that he had amassed £40 million from his illegal activities. The attention being given to the area by authorities was bad for business, and in February gardaí received intelligence that Murphy and other unknown IRA associates were conducting their own investigation into the murder and robbery at Lordship Credit Union.

According to the intelligence, the IRA believed that Aaron Brady and Brendan Treanor were both involved, and within days of the credit union robbery the PSNI gave Treanor a verbal warning that he was under threat from dissident republicans. Further intelligence available to gardaí stated: 'Because of the high-level of garda attention in the Cooley Peninsula and the disruption of illegal activities, members of the dissident groups are to take direct action against Benny Treanor, and it is assessed there is an imminent threat to the life of Treanor.' Gardaí were also informed separately that another republican branch, the Continuity IRA, were aware through their own enquiries that Treanor carried out the 2011 robbery at Lordship Credit Union after a republican unit was sent to investigate the crime at the time. Treanor was summoned to meet them but refused and moved into a safe house near Chalybeate Road. This, gardaí noted, was very close to the remote location where the Volkswagen Passat was burnt out after the credit union raid.

The detailed planning and execution of the robbery showed that the gang were forensically conscious. Despite extensive searches, no traces of DNA evidence linked to any of the suspects was recovered at the crime scene or Cumsons Road. They were also technologically aware, having used walkie-talkies to communicate during the raid so that no mobile phone activity could be traced to the scene. Within days of the murder Detective Inspector Marry had requested call-data records from Aaron Brady and people close to him including his family, James Flynn, and Brendan Treanor. Upon closer inspection it showed a large amount of phone contact between the three men. Detective Inspector Marry says of this:

> The phone data for these men was telling and something that couldn't be ignored. Both Jimmy Flynn and Aaron Brady had been in contact with Benny Treanor on the day of the robbery. This was significant as the last time the credit union was the subject of an armed robbery, Treanor was the main suspect. More significantly the modus operandi was the same: a stolen car taken in a creeper burglary was used in the crime and the car was found burnt out across the border. Firearms were used and the window of the injured parties' car was smashed during the robbery. It was too much of a coincidence to ignore.

The net was later cast wider to include phone records of other known associates of Brady, including Mr C and one of Brady's closest friends. The call data showed a flurry of activity between the gang in the hours before and after the robbery. Crucially, it also identified a two-hour silent period of the suspect's phone at the time of the robbery. James Flynn's phone was last used before the raid at 7.58 p.m. Aaron Brady was using two phones at that time, neither of which was used after 8.01 p.m., when he had received a phone call from Mr C, the last time Mr C's phone was also used before the gang targeted the cash escort. Brendan Treanor had made eight unsuccessful calls to Brady between 8.17 p.m. and 8.29 p.m., before Treanor's phone went dead. The silent period for all four phones lasted more than two hours, during which the credit union had been robbed and Detective Garda Donohoe shot dead. Over an hour after the raid their phones were active again within 12 minutes of one another: Flynn's at 10.37 p.m., Mr C's at 10.42 p.m., Treanor's at 10.45 p.m., and Brady's at 10.49 p.m. That night was also the last time Treanor's phone would be used. The phone traffic was significant, as Detective Inspector Marry explains:

Their phones were inactive an hour before and after the murder and robbery at Lordship. A witness from the credit union during the robbery observed one of the raiders with a walkie-talkie, so they were communicating via these devices and not mobile phones. They were phone savvy, but we turned the fact that their phones were not operational into evidence. I made the point that why on this night, between 8.30 p.m. and 10.30 p.m. approximately, were these suspects' phones non-operational when the robbery was taking place? I could see from records of the previous two Fridays that in that same time period their phones were operating as normal.

Further evidence recovered from Jessica King's phone would cast more suspicion over Aaron Brady. While the texts didn't contain any admissions, it was evident that Brady was planning to come into a substantial amount of money on the weekend of the robbery, and far more than the €100 he would get for moving laundered diesel waste cubes. Three days before the raid, during a text conversation about lending her money to buy a car, Brady told his girlfriend: 'I dont mind babes I was promised money this week and im selling the van and have money to pay the whole car off this weekend with all going well.' Further texts from the day of the robbery showed he was letting his girlfriend know that he would be unavailable that night. At 4.25 p.m. he sent Jessica King a message saying: 'I was away there for a while had to meet a man there now ... I have work at 8 till about half ten then thats it.' At 6.58 p.m. he told her that he was waiting for Mr C and another man, and that he then had 'a bit of work at about 8 finished in an hour or 2 then am doing nothing'. At 7.54 p.m. he sent her another text which read: 'Just have to load the lorry but will only take an hour or 2. This phone is gonne go dead. ill text ya soon as am home and get it charged love you x.' This was one of the messages deleted by Jessica King while waiting in the PSNI station but later recovered by garda phone experts.

In his first message to her after the robbery, Brady texted his girlfriend at 10.51 p.m. saying: 'You awake babes. Sorry me phone went dead I couldn text ya.' Another deleted message, sent from Brady's phone at 2.40 p.m. the day after the robbery, showed that he was concerned about what was happening. He texted his girlfriend saying: 'Please Jess I just want to get away till this blows over ill prob just go into them tomorrow everythin will be ok. Tell them its fine I just wanna go and get something to eat away from here and go to the cinema am just pissed off please.'

The text messages added further weight to the belief that Aaron Brady had lied to Sergeant Moroney about his movements on the night of the robbery and this, along with the phone records, ensured that Brady and his associates were cemented as the main suspects for the murder of Detective Garda Donohoe. They were now the main focus of the garda investigation under a special operation codenamed Operation Sinuous.

6

RUMOURS AND DENIALS

Five days after he was mercilessly shot dead in the car park of Lordship Credit Union, a state funeral was held for Detective Garda Adrian Donohoe. It was an extremely poignant sight as thousands of gardaí lined the streets of Dundalk to make the final journey with their fallen colleague. The sea of blue walked solemnly behind the hearse, carrying his tricolour-draped coffin to St Joseph's Redemptorist Church, in a powerful and eloquent show of strength against his killers. His family and closest friends led the cortège through the rain before his colleagues carried his coffin into the church for the funeral mass. His garda hat and gloves sat on top of the coffin as a reminder of the career for which he had given his life.

The service was attended by state officials including President Michael D. Higgins, Taoiseach Enda Kenny, and most of the government cabinet, while Sinn Féin leader Gerry Adams and Detective Garda Jerry McCabe's widow Ann were also present. There was also police and political representation from Northern Ireland with PSNI Chief Constable Matt Baggot, Secretary of State Theresa Villiers, and Justice

Minister David Ford attending to show condemnation of the murder across the border. Hundreds of mourners packed into the church while thousands more stood outside and listened through speakers as Colm Donohoe gave an emotional tribute to his older brother. 'We are devastated with the senseless and tragic loss of Adrian and the occasions he will miss as the kids grow up,' he told the congregation. 'We take some comfort from the fact that he packed so much into a short life. He lived life to the fullest, always with a smile on his face. Rest in peace, Adrian.'

Chief celebrant Fr Michael Cusack also spoke out strongly against the murder, telling mourners that sometimes 'evil becomes personified, almost Satanic'. He also said in his homily: 'The idea that there can be people in our society who can destroy the lives of so many young people through the trading of drugs. The idea that sin itself can be imprisoned and still manage to run drug baron circles and markets right around our country. It is like Satan laughing at us.' The priest made an impassioned plea from the altar to the people harbouring the killers to help bring them to justice. 'If there is anyone who knows anything about that, if you have any semblance of goodness in you, for God's sake, turn these people in. If not, you're allowing Satan to ruin the lives of more and more people. He was a man of honour, who could do this?' After the emotional ceremony Adrian Donohoe's remains were taken to his final resting place at Lordship cemetery.

The following day, the investigation room at Dundalk Garda Station was back fully operational with all available resources of the state being afforded to the inquiry. Senior officers from across the country would also attend the briefings, much to the annoyance of Detective Inspector Marry:

The degree of brass that attended each conference in the first two weeks was top heavy. At one conference the minister himself was flanked by the commissioner and deputy commissioner. I had to give them an update, but during this other brass kept interrupting me so they could have their say with the minister. Talk about bullshit. I knew the breaking of the case would come from hard work by members on the ground of the investigation. The hanging around of brass was people waiting for the golden nugget, the arrest, the solving, but it was not coming, and they did what they do best, disappear. We knew if a break came and a charge was to be preferred, they would descend on Dundalk like vultures to have their names associated with a solve.

A €100,000 reward for information leading to the prosecution of those involved had also been put forward by Crimestoppers, and augmented by The National League of Credit Unions, The Dundalk Chamber of Commerce, and a private donor from Cork, in an effort to entice people with knowledge of the crime to come forward. The robbery suspects were beginning to feel the strain of the garda attention and the rumours around Crossmaglen about their involvement in the murder. Aaron Brady's name was widely circulating in the community as being involved, with his girlfriend's name also bandied about. In one statement to gardaí Jessica King outlined how she was being linked to the crime despite having absolutely no involvement. 'There's loads of rumours that me and Aaron had something to do with this, there's even a rumour that I was the getaway driver, that I was involved. My sister Amy got an email from a friend in America saying that me and Aaron were arrested for the murder of the guard,' she told gardaí. Her parents told Brady that he should go in to gardaí and give an account of his movements that night to stop the rumours spreading about him and Ms King.

On the evening of 5 February, Aaron Brady arrived at Dundalk Garda Station with Danny McNamee, a solicitor who was well known in South Armagh. He had previously been convicted of the IRA bombings in Hyde Park, London, in 1982 that claimed 11 lives. In 1999, the Court of Appeal overturned the conviction after finding that material had been withheld from the defence in the original trial. Danny McNamee had already been freed under the terms of the Good Friday Agreement and the court declined to order a retrial. Fourteen years after that acquittal, the solicitor was accompanying Aaron Brady to profess his own innocence. The lawyer had earlier received a phone call from Tony Brady, who said that his son was being connected to the murder and they were concerned about this. Mr McNamee strongly advised his client that, if he had any involvement in the events at Lordship Credit Union, he should not give a voluntary statement to gardaí. They presented at the station that evening and informed gardaí that Brady, who had left his phone at home, wanted to speak to them about the murder investigation.

Two detectives from the garda's major crimes unit, Detective Sergeant Mark Phillips and Detective Garda Jim McGovern, were tasked with taking the statement. Two experienced investigators attached to NBCI in Harcourt Square, Dublin, they had already been involved in several high-profile inquiries and were among the highest trained garda interviewers in the force. Detective Sergeant Phillips had previously been involved in the successful prosecution of Barry Doyle, a gangland hitman who carried out the 2008 murder of rugby player Shane Geoghegan in Limerick. During garda interviews Doyle had admitted to Detective Sergeant Phillips that he was the man who carried out the shooting and he is now serving a life sentence. Phillips's colleague, Detective Garda McGovern, had also been involved in the successful prosecution of Joe O'Reilly for the murder of his wife Rachel Callaly. The detectives brought Aaron Brady and his solicitor into an interview room in the garda station to take his statement. As it was a voluntary act, they couldn't interrogate him on any matters and only took details of what Brady told them. He was informed that he was not under arrest and that he could leave the station at any time. Detective Garda McGovern began taking down his statement as Brady outlined his life growing up and his circumstances leading up to the robbery.

He told them that he had been working with his father 'trying to get money together' to pay off compensation for the damage during the garda pursuit in 2011. Brady also said that the previous year, while playing as a forward for Crossmaglen Rangers' second team, he'd broken his hand. He had previously chipped a bone in the same hand two or three years earlier while out socialising with James Flynn and said that 'it never really healed'. He told them that on 7 December 2012, at the Royal Hospital in Belfast, he had a plate and two screws inserted in the hand in an operation. 'I was just doing physio with my father trying to get a bit of strength into it, power into it. It's my right hand the hand I use, my dominant hand. I've struggled to lift more than 20kg, 30kg with my right hand long term. I've seven or eight dissolvable stitches, still freshly scarred. I had a splint on it up until I went to work last Tuesday,' he told them. Brady also said that he had received £4,000 in compensation the previous year from a car accident in Newry.

He told the detectives that he spent 24 January with James Flynn and that night they collected their girlfriends from Ridley's nightclub in Dundalk. '[Jessica] meant to stay in mine, but we had an argument. Jessica was wearing some fella's American style hat when she came out of the nightclub. The argument continued between me and Jessica until the next morning by text on the phone, she was basically saying she was all for breaking up and I was sorry for over-reacting and all that.' He told the gardaí that he stayed in Dunroamin House with James Flynn that night and that, on the day of the robbery, he woke up at around midday. 'We had nothing to do that day,' he told them. He said they collected Treanor from his house at around 1 p.m. and went to get food at McCaughey's filling station in Castleblayney and later returned to Dunroamin House where, according to Brady, the three men played video games up until 6 p.m. before having dinner. 'I remember Benny saying we had to leave as he had to sign on as part of his bail conditions at Crossmaglen Police Station,' Brady said, and described the route they took to the PSNI barracks across the border. At the time of the robbery Treanor was on bail for aiding and abetting a rape. CCTV footage would later show Flynn's BMW arriving at the police station at Crossmaglen at 7.20 p.m. with Treanor briefly entering the barracks to sign on. From there, Brady claimed, they dropped Treanor home before driving to Concession Road, where they stayed for 15 minutes.

At this point Danny McNamee asked for the process to be halted in order to consult with his client in private. The detectives left the room and a short time later the solicitor emerged and said that his client was reluctant to account for his movements on the record out of fear of being prosecuted. Detective

Sergeant Phillips informed the lawyer that all they wanted was a true account of his movements. Off the record Aaron Brady then claimed that he went to the diesel-laundering site on 155 Concession Road at around 8 p.m. where he tried to get a forklift started. He said he stayed there for around 15 minutes before leaving again. While this was left out of his voluntary statement, the detectives took notes of the account being given. He then continued: 'We stayed in Jimmy's car, his BMW, then I got Jimmy to leave me down to Colin Hoey's house because Jimmy was on about going home to his house and I couldn't be arsed sitting in his house. Colin's house is in Annaghmare about three miles outside Crossmaglen. He dropped me off around 9 p.m.'

Brady then told the gardaí, who were documenting every word, that they watched *Fast & Furious 5*, describing a specific scene in the movie to give an indication of the length of time he was in the house. He added that James Flynn then collected him at around 10 p.m. 'I asked Jimmy what he was doing for the rest of the night, he said waiting for Colleen to wake up and then going down to her house,' adding he was dropped to Jessica King's home on Concession Road.

I walked into Jessica's house and shouted 'hello', the door was open, and I just walked in. Jessica was upstairs with her friend Jade Fitzpatrick. I walked upstairs then. I was sitting on the bed for around 10 or 15 minutes then her mother rang my phone or her phone telling us to come downstairs. She showed me the news, I'm not sure what time but the RTÉ news of what was after happening the guard in Bellurgan that was shot. She goes 'Where were you all night?' joking. I sat and watched the remainder of the news and went back upstairs to Jessica. Then we tried to watch a DVD on her laptop from the internet.'

He also outlined how he had known Brendan Treanor for about two years but, since the previous year, hadn't hung around much with him. Brady had been in Dundalk Garda Station for several hours at this point and decided to leave and return the following morning without his solicitor. His statement from 7 February began: 'I understand I'm here at Dundalk voluntarily and know I am free to leave here at any time I wish. I know I am not under arrest.'

Taking up from where he had left off, Brady said it wasn't until 3.30 a.m. on 26 January that James Flynn arrived to collect him and that, on their way to Dunroamin House, they passed through the garda cordon. He said he woke up at midday and went downstairs, where they spoke with Jimmy's mother, Philomena. 'We talked about what happened the night before up the road from his house, the guard had been shot. Jimmy's mother said it was terrible, we agreed, and the three of us just chatted generally. She asked us did we see or hear anything about it, we said no we hadn't,' he told gardaí. Aaron Brady also said he wanted to clarify a matter with the detectives, telling them:

I just want to say about the first time I heard about the guard being shot it was in Jessica's on the Friday night 25th January 2013. It would have been around quarter to 11 by the time I arrived at the house. Jade had seen it on Facebook that a guard had been shot, she just said it was somewhere near Bellurgan. The three of us, me, Jessica and Jade, were in Jessica's bedroom at this time. I was on Jessica's laptop watching Django trying to get it going when [her mam] Allison called me downstairs. I went downstairs and she goes 'Did you hear what happened?', then she says 'Look at this'. The RTÉ news was on and showed the guard had been shot at Bellurgan. That's when I knew exactly where it happened, it said a guard had been shot dead in a failed attempt of a raid ... when Allison asked me where I was, I told her I was down at Colin Hoey's house before I came over.

Brady said that on the day after the murder he visited BoyleSports bookmakers in Castleblayney with James Flynn, where they stayed for several hours betting on horses and football matches, while also meeting Liam Crozier there. Referring to the impact the garda clampdown was having on the border region, he said: 'Everyone is angry cause the police are everywhere and no diesel can be moved.' As he concluded his voluntary statement, Aaron Brady told the detectives: 'I came in to give a statement to hopefully clear my name of all the rumours going around Crossmaglen. Just that people are pointing the finger at me over the murder of the guard Adrian. That's it.' Detective Garda McGovern then read over the statement to Aaron Brady, who said he was happy with the account and signed it before he was collected by his father. After Brady had left the station Detective Sergeant Phillips typed up a report of the meeting, including Brady's account of where he had claimed to be at key times on the day of the murder.

The following day James Flynn presented himself at a PSNI station to give his own voluntary statement and account for his movements. He outlined a similar version of events on the day of the murder to that given by Brady, including collecting

Brendan Treanor from his home to go for food. In Flynn's statement he said that Brady 'had been told to stay away from [Treanor] by a Garda because of something previous they had been involved in. The Garda had told him Benny was bad news. This was when I was in America so I'm not exactly sure what it was.' Flynn said that after getting food in Castleblayney they drove to a store near Lordship Credit Union before returning to Dunroamin House. Flynn stated that they spent the next number of hours at the property, where they played video games in his room and ate a chicken curry before leaving to drop Treanor to Crossmaglen PSNI station.

He told the PSNI that he then dropped Treanor off at his home and brought Aaron Brady to Concession Road. 'Aaron was supposed to be doing something but whatever happened he couldn't do it. I don't want to say what it was because it is nothing to do with me,' Flynn claimed. He told the detective that he then dropped his friend off at Colin Hoey's house sometime between 9 p.m. and 9.30 p.m. 'Aaron asked if I could come back and get him after an hour or so. I tried to get in contact with Colleen, my girlfriend, but her phone was off.' Flynn said he then visited two other friends living in Crossmaglen, Liam Crozier and Micky Leneghan, before returning to collect Aaron Brady an hour later and drop him to Jessica King's house. After returning home to shower, Flynn said he then went to his girlfriend's home for several hours, before later collecting Brady and driving back to Dunroamin House. He also told the detectives that he had received a call from his brother between 10 p.m. and 10.30 p.m. that night, informing him that there were 'garda everywhere' and that 'someone was shot at the credit union'. Call-data records showed that the brothers weren't in phone contact until over an hour after the robbery.

Five days after the murder, on 30 January, Flynn travelled to England to watch Manchester United play Southampton at Old Trafford. Gardaí also took a statement from Colin Hoey, who claimed that both Flynn and Brady were at his house around the time of the murder.

Brendan Treanor also gave a voluntary interview in Northern Ireland, recollecting a similar version of events from 25 January to those his two friends had given. He said he was dropped home after signing on at the PSNI station, where he watched TV for around an hour. An analysis of cell site data later showed that the eight unsuccessful phone calls made by Treanor to Aaron Brady an hour before the robbery pinged off three different phone masts, indicating that he may have been moving locations and not at home as he had claimed. He also told gardaí that he was at home at 10.30 p.m. when the PSNI called to his home to conduct a bail check. Further inquiries would determine that this bail check was not carried out until 11.10 p.m., with detectives suspecting that Treanor was trying to alter his timeline to create an alibi. In a statement his girlfriend, Charlene O'Callaghan, also accounted for his whereabouts at the time of the robbery saying he was at home when she arrived there at 9.15 p.m. that night. Explaining why his phone wasn't active anymore after that night, Treanor told the PSNI that he had dropped the device in the bath while washing his Bichon Frise. He also said: 'Last Friday between 7 p.m. and 8 p.m. the PSNI gave me a verbal [warning] of a death threat from the IRA or dissident republicans.' He added that police had received information of a threat to his life, saying: 'The Daily Mirror put a pixelated picture of me in the paper saying I'm a thug, someone mentioned there was a threat on my life even before I got the death threat. There was a picture on Facebook saying I'm the man who murdered the garda detective.' He also said in his statement: 'The only thing I've heard about the murder is what I've been reading in the newspaper.'

On 22 February, Mr C presented himself at Ardmore PSNI station with his father to give his own voluntary statement. Unlike the other men, he was far less willing to put forward any account of his movements at the time of the murder. One investigator recalled: 'He was shitting himself. He was at the station trying to smoke a cigarette and his hands were shaking, he was extremely anxious.' Mr C claimed that he was in Blanchardstown, County Dublin, on the afternoon of the murder, collecting a lorry trailer before returning to Crossmaglen at around 7 p.m. He said he carried out a few chores, including cleaning animals in his yard, and that between 9 p.m. and 10.30 p.m. he was with his brother and another man, travelling to McCaughey's garage in Castleblayney to buy cigarettes before going home to bed. Gardaí were aware that a serious road collision had occurred that night and a garda checkpoint was in place on the road for several hours. Mr C's brother also provided an alibi for him, claiming that his sibling jumped into the back of the van upon seeing the checkpoint. The garda manning the cordon that day later told investigators that Mr C, his brother, and the other man had not passed through, as they were all known to gardaí for involvement in criminality and their movements would have been noted. As investigators attempted to clarify his movements that night, Mr C became increasingly agitated and declined to give any more specific information. His father told the police officers that his son would not be speaking with them any further and the pair got up to leave, telling the PSNI that they would not be engaging any further with the investigation. Mr C also refused to sign the voluntary statement he had given.

Despite their attempts to shift the point of focus away from them, all four men were formally designated as suspects for the murder and robbery over the coming weeks. Explaining his rationale for making Brady a formal suspect on 18 February 2013, Detective Inspector Marry highlighted the inconsistent accounts he gave and his association with Brendan Treanor, the suspect in the previous credit union robbery. The senior officer also stated that he 'could not overlook the volume of intelligence that was being submitted in respect of Aaron Brady as a suspect'. Gardaí also noted that Aaron Brady used his girlfriend for an alibi by canvassing her to account for him being with her earlier than he actually had been that night. James Flynn, Brendan Treanor, and Mr C would soon join Brady on the list of formal suspects. Gardaí had also identified the gang's wider network, which included 20 people that were linked to each other through either socialising in the same circles or criminal activity. A formal assessment of the gang stated that, up until the murder of Detective Garda Donohoe, they were involved in a range of crimes including diesel laundering, creeper burglaries, stealing and dismantling stolen motor vehicles, and armed robbery.

The massive media interest in the investigation continued as the hunt for the gang went on. Details of the inquiry were also making their way into newspaper reports, with media leaks being discussed during one operational briefing. On 24 February, the *Sunday World* front page led with a story by investigations editor Nicola Tallant about the suspects in the murder. In large bold letters splashed across the front was the word 'WANTED', accompanied by the pixelated images of five people. The front page also referenced the €100,000 reward for information, while the teaser underneath read: 'We reveal Garda Donohoe's alleged killer's links to top GAA club Crossmaglen Rangers as gang of 5 splits under pressure.' In response to a series of questions about their connections to the suspected gang, the GAA club issued a statement to the newspaper through a lawyer that said: 'Garda Donohoe did not have any association with Crossmaglen Rangers football club. It was therefore not appropriate for the club to issue a statement of sympathy to his family. Crossmaglen Rangers has no knowledge of the prime focus of the Garda or PSNI investigation into the murder of Garda Donohoe, but if invited by either body to assist their inquiries will willingly do so.'

That night Aaron Brady was out partying in the Wright Venue in Swords, Dublin, when he got a frantic phone call from his mother telling him that he was on the front page of the *Sunday World*. The image of Brady had been taken from his Facebook page and heavily pixelated to avoid identifying him for legal reasons while he was still under investigation. The article, however, made reference to his association with Crossmaglen and his age. Friends of Brady's sister had also sent her the picture of the newspaper article, asking if it was her brother being referred to. The pressure on Aaron Brady and those around him from the media reports and local rumours was beginning to tell. The following week, on 2 March, Aaron Brady was back at the Swords venue, but this time he had been refused entry. Gardaí approached him and the group he was with because they had been loitering in the car park. The other men were Liam Crozier and Conor Nugent, also from Lismore Park in Crossmaglen, as well as a man who only gave his name as O'Callaghan. They were all searched, and while Nugent,

Brady and Crozier appeared in good form and chatty with the gardaí, O'Callaghan had a bad attitude and was exceptionally aloof with them. The men left a short time later in a car driven by a Crossmaglen taxi company up the M1 motorway and towards the border.

On 7 March Aaron Brady was back up before Dundalk Circuit Court for his ongoing case, which was once again adjourned. Gardaí noted that Brady came out of the court-house and walked down towards Rampart Lane and onto the Ramparts, where he entered a bookmaker's. He was on the phone the entire time during the walk and stayed in the bookie's for around 10 minutes before being collected by an unidentified female. Gardaí were keeping a close eye on Brady's movements.

7

SUSPECTS IN THE WIND

As in all modern investigations, CCTV footage would play an integral part in identifying those involved in the murder and robbery at Lordship Credit Union. The sheer scale of the task meant that over 30 gardaí and 3 sergeants were required at different points of the inquiry to trace, collect, and analyse footage from locations on both sides of the border. Gardaí had canvassed thousands of sites and would eventually secure video footage from 320 different premises, including businesses and private homes, in the collection of 416 CCTV exhibits. In all but one instance the data was voluntarily handed over, with gardaí securing with a court warrant the footage that was initially refused. The main zones focused on initially were the Ballymascanlon area, the cash route taken by the credit union escort, and the possible getaway route to the burn site at Cumsons Road. This was later expanded to include the footage relevant to the unauthorised taking of the Volkswagen Passat getaway car. Gardaí also focused on footage which could corroborate, or dismiss, a person's alibi, with six specific areas reviewed to assess the timeline given by Aaron Brady of his movements that night. Detective Inspector

Marry explained how a special computer system had to be developed to hold all of the footage:

The CCTV section of the investigation was scary, given the volume we had to collect and analyse. It came to a stage where I had eight people looking at footage, frame by frame, trying to identify the getaway car or indeed any cars linked to persons of interest. It was not an easy task, and early on it was clear that if a CCTV system became corrupted we would lose potentially vital evidence. I requested that Dell build an external hard-drive server to house all of the footage gathered. I put Detective Garda Gareth McKenna, a qualified CCTV examiner, in charge of being the exhibits officer for this. A more honourable man you couldn't find – he was dedicated and driven by Adrian's murder to do his best and missed nothing that was captured on CCTV. Any system seized was exhibited and put on the external hard drive, and copies were made to search for evidence. If the copy crashed, we still had the original, and each piece of footage was exhibited and accounted for. If one garda had to sit down on his own and view all of the CCTV collected throughout the course of the investigation, it would take them 40 years.

The persons-of-interest list grew in considerable size to 207 people, and I also had a team dedicated to following up on each person on this list, verifying their whereabouts on the night of the murder. In many cases CCTV footage that was gathered helped establish that certain people of interest were nowhere near the crime scene at the time of the murder and robbery. Aaron Brady and James Flynn said they were near Concession Road that evening, but footage taken from an electrical store nearby didn't support this claim.

The Volkswagen Passat used in the credit union robbery had been stolen in a creeper burglary from Hillcrest, Clogherhead, in the early hours of 23 January. The thieves had popped the door lock to gain entry to the house before taking the car keys and stealing the vehicle. Examinations of footage and phone data from that night indicated that Aaron Brady, James Flynn, and his brother Eugene were together and in the area that night. Phone records showed text messages being exchanged between James Flynn and Brady that night up to 00.28 a.m. Later Flynn's BMW was seen travelling to Dunroamin House, and at 01.44 a.m., Brady attempted to call Eugene Flynn Jnr. Gardaí believe this was to get him to open the electric gates to the property. There was no further communication from any of their phones that night, indicating that they were in each other's company when Flynn's BMW left Dunroamin House again at 01.53 a.m. One minute later the car was captured on CCTV at the Ballymascanlon service station, where the Flynn brothers got out of the car before returning and driving off. A third person was also visible in the vehicle, which gardaí believed was Aaron Brady.

Further CCTV footage showed the BMW travelling past the Monasterboice Inn near Drogheda at 2.16 a.m., and later at the credit union in Termonfeckin village at 2.24 a.m. James Flynn's BMW was seen passing by the same building on two more occasions, at 2.38 a.m. and 2.48 a.m., in what gardaí suspected was a scoping exercise for a car to steal. Footage from Corrs Pharmacy, located on Clogherhead Main Street, showed the BMW passing there at 03.17 a.m. in the direction of the Hillcrest estate and driving back away from the creeper burglary scene ten minutes later. Footage showed the stolen Passat and Flynn's BMW driving in convoy past the Glyde Inn in Annagassan at 3.24 a.m., and again heading in the same direction northwards at Cooley View House at 3.41 a.m. The BMW was captured passing through Dromiskin at 4.17 a.m., and CCTV footage near Dunroamin House showed that James Flynn's car didn't return until 4.51 that morning. Gardaí believe that after stealing the Volkswagen Passat in Clogherhead they parked it offside, possibly at Lough Road.

Other footage gathered indicated that the gang were involved in carrying out surveillance of the credit union the night before the raid and the day of it. Footage traced Flynn's car leaving Dunroamin House at 8.58 p.m. on 24 January and passing the Lordship branch three minutes later. They stopped outside a closed petrol station across the road from the credit union, giving them a line of sight to the premises as it was being locked up for the night. Gardaí suspected the two men were noting lock-up times prior to their plan to rob it the following night, before returning to Flynn's home at 9.11 p.m. Footage from the day of the robbery also showed James Flynn's BMW passing Lordship Credit Union with its passenger-side window rolled down at 1.46 p.m. It was a rainy afternoon and unusual that somebody would be driving along with their window open. Gardaí established that Flynn, Brady, and Treanor were in the car at this time, and believed it was another reconnaissance mission ahead of that night's raid.

Further evidence would be recovered linking James Flynn's BMW to the aftermath of the crime. CCTV footage was taken from Cortamlet Primary School in Newry, around 4 kilometres from the burn site, which showed two vehicles passing by a short time apart. The first vehicle, passing at 10.04 p.m., resembled a Volkswagen Passat while the second car, which drove by two minutes later, was a BMW 5 Series. Gardaí had also taken a statement from a farmer living on Chalybeate Road who said that on the night of the murder after 10 p.m. he saw what he described as a black BMW 5 Series car driving very fast by his house towards where the Passat was burnt out. He said that as the car approached a bend in the road it broke suddenly, skidded, and then paused for a couple of seconds before continuing along the road. Around 15 or 20 minutes later he heard the noise of a car exhaust coming from the direction of the burn site and believed it was the same vehicle. He also said he was certain of the exact vehicle make because he had a similar car. The BMW seen by the farmer was the car used to pick up members of the robbery gang from the burn site and pointed towards Flynn's involvement in the crime, at the very least after the fact in assisting those involved.

Gardaí later established that within weeks of the murder James Flynn had made efforts to get rid of his car, just months after purchasing it. On 1 March, a man from Mayo was searching through the buy-and-sell website Done Deal when he came across a metallic grey BMW 5 Series with the registration number W608 BDY. He rang the phone number on the ad and spoke to a 'James' about possibly buying the vehicle. The seller was looking for £13,500 for the car, and they agreed to meet the following day to inspect the vehicle and discuss the price. They met at the Texaco garage in Moy, County Tyrone, where the man took the sports car for a test drive before deciding he was happy with it. Ultimately, they agreed on a price of €15,150 in cash. James Flynn gave the new owner the keys, a service manual, and €50 for luck before heading off. The vehicle was subsequently flagged by gardaí, and months later Garda Hugh Egan was on patrol in Belmullet, County Mayo, when he came across the BMW parked at the Broadhaven Bay Hotel. He examined the vehicle and realised it was the car that gardaí in Dundalk wanted to seize in connection with the murder and robbery at Lordship Credit Union. The unfortunate new owner, who was unaware of the car's links to the serious crime, handed over the BMW to gardaí and it was brought away for examination at Santry Garda Station.

On 12 March, gardaí continued their efforts to gather more evidence against the gang, and Dunroamin House became the first property searched as part of the murder investigation. At 6.47 a.m. a team led by Detective Sergeant Mick Sheridan called to the home and were let in by Philomena Flynn. The operation lasted a number of hours and gardaí seized several items, including a walkie-talkie and scanner device. Her ex-husband's movements and his Mercedes car had also become of interest to the investigation team after gardaí gathered statements from witnesses who had been near Bellurgan at the time of the robbery. One such person was local woman Frances Malone who told detectives that she was driving near the Blue Anchor junction, close to the credit union, just after the murder. She said she saw two cars travelling from the direction of the credit union at high speed, one with its full headlights on. Moments later Ms Malone met another car which she said 'was absolutely flying'. She recognised the registration plate EU56ENE, which resembled the word 'Eugene'. Detective Inspector Pat Marry reviewed the footage from the credit union and noticed that after the getaway car sped off, the next vehicle that passed, 37 seconds later, 'strongly' resembled a Mercedes car. The senior officer believed that, with the information available, this vehicle belonged to Eugene Flynn Snr. In a report at the time Detective Inspector Marry noted that it was 'reasonable to believe it had something to do with the crime that had occurred given the manner of driving and the time gap it was travelling in behind the getaway car'. Gardaí put an alert out on the registration number of the car, asking for it to be seized if found. Frances Malone would make an additional statement to gardaí months later saying that she was 'one hundred percent sure' that the car she saw belonged to Eugene Flynn Snr, whom she knew well. Ms Malone told gardaí that she didn't want to mention names in her initial statement because she knew the Flynn family.

Garda Neil McGowan, a member of the divisional traffic corps unit in Louth, was on patrol on 31 March when he pulled into the northbound motorway service station at Whiterath in Castlebellingham. In the disabled bay beside the entrance of the service station he noticed a dark blue E-Class Mercedes bearing the registration number EU56ENE. Garda McGowan decided to check the car with the control room in Dundalk and was informed that it was wanted in connection with the murder investigation and that an alert had been put out for the car to be seized for technical examination. He was told to prevent the car from moving, and a short time later units from Dundalk arrived to take the vehicle away. Later that day Detective Inspector Marry was in Dundalk Garda Station with Detective Superintendent Christopher Mangan, then the head of the Garda Serious Crime Review Team, when Eugene Flynn Snr arrived to demand his car be returned. The senior detectives asked him where the vehicle was on the day of the credit union robbery, with Flynn Snr informing them that the seized Mercedes wasn't in Ireland at the time of the murder and that his old car, which used the same registration plate, was not in the country anymore. Asked if he was sure about this, he told them without being prompted that he drove past the scene at Lordship in his old Mercedes with the EU65ENE licence plate at the time of the shooting. In a note of the encounter Detective Inspector Marry said that Eugene Flynn Snr said he was coming from the Carlingford area and that afterwards he drove to the Roma café in Dundalk town centre for a sit-down meal. It was later established that the Mercedes he was driving at the time of the incident was sold five days after by an associate in the UK.

A report compiled by gardaí of the meeting also outlined how Eugene Flynn Snr was 'very anxious to know' if gardaí thought his sons were involved. When he asked gardaí if they believed James was involved, they replied yes. He then queried if gardaí believed Eugene Jnr was also involved. When gardaí told him maybe but not to the same extent, Eugene Flynn Snr replied: 'Well if you think Eugene had something to do with it, you have nothing.' Detective Inspector Marry also noted in his report: 'He stated he would talk to Jimmy and see what he would say. Eugene Flynn left the station but returned and he stated he rang Jimmy and that he would talk to the gardaí. I asked what was Jimmy's attitude, and he replied Jimmy said "They have not got a clue", Eugene Flynn then left the station.' Following this encounter, the senior detective also highlighted in his report that Eugene Flynn Snr did not protest James's innocence when informed that gardaí believed him to be involved in the crime. It was also stated that he admitted turning his Mercedes in to Dunroamin House after he passed the crime scene 'at this pertinent time'.

Unbeknownst to Eugene Flynn Snr, gardaí had also secured a warrant to secretly bug Dunroamin House. Using a legally planted audio device, gardaí recorded conversations between him and his ex-wife, during which they discussed the intense garda investigation, their son's car 'being out on the road' on the night of the murder, and about Eugene Snr hearing the gunshot as he drove by the scene. In one exchange he told her: 'I won't be taking the rap for it … because I won't because I can't, I won't be taking the rap for it … shoot the Guard.' Philomena responded by saying: '… whoever robbed that car …'

> **Eugene:** 'Wait till I tell you, don't talk shite because who robbed that car didn't shoot anybody, ok. Who robbed that car didn't shoot anybody … murder … listen till I tell you … use your brain …'
>
> **Philomena:** 'Fucking terrible …'

He told her how 'nothing was done about it' when he was shot in his house several years earlier and, recounting an interaction with gardaí, said he told them, when they inquired about talking to his Jimmy: 'You won't terrorise me and my family says I and you want me to accommodate you to talk to my son, he told me to tell you to go fuck yourselves.' Referring to Detective Sergeant Phillips and Detective Garda McGovern, Eugene Flynn told his ex-wife:

> Wait till I tell you, you don't understand, these fellas don't go home and go to bed at night and it all stops. They work 24 hours a day at this … people's place and numbers … they were able to tell your man that I was with today with that lorry, that his car was on that top road and what time would he come down the road and he told them he comes through the toll at such a time … toll bridges … How did

they know that, because he said he called his wife and told her what time he'd be home … and that was an innocent man, right … my car was … seen in the vicinity that night travelling down the fucking road …

Philomena: 'What one, the silver Merc?'

Eugene: 'Yeah, I come down that back road … I would say, I would think the boys had to go back in the south because I remember thinking what kind of fucking eejits is going on here … It was unnatural wet, pissin' out of the heavens, they put Jimmy's car on the road and it was stopped dead on the road with the right-hand indicator on and then they put on the left-hand indicator and I thought what the fuck's going on here … I can't go round them … I had to go past here and go to [an associate's] and I rang [the associate] and he wasn't there. I spun around up the road, I told them this, spun about the right way, these guards.

Philomena: 'Did he not talk back on the phone?'

Eugene: 'No, no answer, so I turned around and thought fuck it's half nine, think it was about half nine …'

Philomena: 'Don't mention that again …'

Eugene: 'What?'

Philomena: '… Don't tell them anything about that in Dundalk. Don't tell them anything about [his associate] not being there.'

Eugene: 'And I went into Dundalk and had something to eat.'

Philomena: 'Why did they question where you were?'

Eugene: 'Yeah, why wouldn't they? It was my car. I thought they were going to lift me.'

Philomena: 'Did you get involved?'

Eugene: 'No.'

Philomena: '... why didn't ... did you hear the shot?'

Eugene: 'Yeah, just as I was driving up to the back ... I tell you it hit me, and I thought it was over, I remember looking into the car park [sounds like] and thinking, now I was goin' to 'Blaney, whoever was on in 'Blaney that night, and I was thinking fuck me by the time I get something to eat over to 'Blaney it will be late, and I just drove about, back out there, up that way.'

Philomena: 'You didn't tell the Guards that you went up that way?'

Eugene: 'No, I told them I was going up to visit him and I changed my mind and turned around and drove back, eh, I went out there, up the road and met all the Guards at the roundabout.'

Philomena: '... to Dundalk. What time?'

Eugene: '... change me mind ... I can't remember but I can remember thinking by the time I get something to eat, if I go to 'Blaney it will be late, so if they tracked me in Dundalk they can track me in 'Blaney. I met all the Guards, I met the Guards, so did I do it? I couldn't have done it if I met the Guards.'

Philomena: 'I'm only saying, Eugene, you don't know what they had.'

Eugene: 'You don't understand – how can I be scouting if I met the Guards at the roundabout.'

Philomena: 'Coming after the thing?'

Eugene: 'Yeah, coming out.'

In a further exchange, Eugene Flynn Snr made reference to gardaí having 'circumstantial evidence', claiming that their son and Aaron Brady weren't involved, while also talking about Brendan Treanor signing on at the PSNI station. Philomena Flynn then made reference to two other relatives, with Eugene Flynn Snr responding: 'Let me tell you they weren't involved in the killing of anyone. Do you think Jimmy and Aaron was going out to a cold barn to rob the credit union for six thousand fucking dollars.'

Philomena: 'I know our Jimmy didn't kill anybody, but if they were involved then in any way ...'

Eugene: '... looking for most people involved because how could your man be involved after signing on in the barracks, he couldn't possibly take the risk that he wouldn't be in his house that night when they called three times in a row ...'

In a final excerpt of a recorded conversation, Eugene Flynn Snr stated: 'They wanted to know how the guard was shot, they wanted to know how he was shot. I said he got shot because the guards were never doing their job that's why. That fucking place was robbed a long time ago ...' A file later compiled on the taped conversations stated that gardaí believed Eugene Flynn Snr 'has knowledge of and took part in the murder and robbery as a lookout or scout'. Investigators also secured a court warrant to plant a listening device in the home of Brendan Treanor. However, the PSNI had placed the device in a location close to where Treanor's dogs slept. When gardaí attempted to listen back to the surreptitious recordings, they could only make out some conversations in which Treanor spoke about gardaí having his DNA. The rest of the audio was essentially useless, as his voice was drowned out by the sound of his dogs constantly barking.

On 8 April more searches were carried out in Northern Ireland as part of the murder inquiry. Members of the PSNI's Support Group gathered at Ardmore police station to parade before setting out for Aaron Brady's family home, located on New Road in Silverbridge. The police officers arrived there at 11.10 a.m. with a warrant signed by a local magistrate and spoke to Caroline and Laurene Brady. The suspect for the murder was not present and, during the search, the PSNI located a UK passport in Aaron Brady's name that had been issued just days earlier. The passport was given to his mother, and after several hours, the operation concluded at 3.45 p.m. with nothing of significant evidential value recovered.

The PSNI also searched an address connected to the Flynns, while another property searched was the home of Brendan Treanor at Slieve View in Silverbridge. The robbery suspect was not present, but his girlfriend, Charlene, was at home and let the PSNI into the house. The warrant allowed them to search the house and any vehicles registered or connected to the address. Nothing directly linked to the robbery was recovered, although the PSNI did recover a number of mobile phones and a box of SIM cards, as well as another SIM card from the mantelpiece. The other address searched was Lough Road, the Portakabin where Brady had stayed from time to time. Unfortunately for investigators, the premises had changed owners and another family were living there by the time it was searched. Investigators later established that Brady and his friends had cleared out the property within days of the murder and subsequently moved out. They did, however, find some partially burnt documentation that would later be linked to a creeper burglary some months earlier.

*

The gardaí were turning the screws on Aaron Brady and his associates, and the murder suspect was beginning to feel the pressure. Six people had to this point been formally classified as suspects, including Brady, James Flynn, Mr C, and Brendan Treanor. The fifth person was Eugene Flynn Jnr, although he was not suspected of involvement in the robbery itself. A female linked to the gang had also been formally categorised as a sixth suspect but would later be ruled out of having any involvement.

Four of the suspects had left Ireland while two, Treanor and the female suspect, were living in the North. On 13 February, Eugene Flynn Jnr boarded a flight to Australia, despite having business in Boston.

A month later, Mr C travelled to Dublin Airport for a flight bound for Sydney via Singapore. Gardaí were aware of his travel plans and were waiting for him in the departures hall when he arrived at the airport. The robbery suspect was terrified, believing he was going to be arrested in relation to the crime. However, gardaí did not have enough evidence at this point to detain him, despite the growing suspicion about his involvement in the credit union raid. Two detectives stopped Mr C and asked if he had anything he would like to offer to the investigation team before he boarded his flight out of the country. The suspect had absolutely no intention of offering anything and picked up his bags to pass through security. As he was about to walk off one of the detectives told him: 'You can go as far away as you want, but we will be right behind you.' It was an ominous warning for Mr C and the rest of the gang; international borders would not stop gardaí bringing Detective Garda Adrian Donohoe's killers to justice. Mr C arrived in Sydney on 14 March but left the New South Wales city and travelled to Perth in Western Australia where he acquired work with a gas pipeline company.

On 9 April, the day after the PSNI searches, James Flynn travelled to Boston, but despite being a green-card holder, his entry into the United States wasn't straightforward. Gardaí were notified of his travel plans and had to put a plan in place to have their suspect searched. Recalling that night, Detective Inspector Marry said:

We were working late one evening and information came into the incident room that Jimmy Flynn was on a flight to Boston. I thought, 'We have to get him searched' – what could he have with him that may be evidential? Detective Garda John Kissane was in the incident room and said that he knew a police officer in Boston with whom he had played football. We made contact with him, and the police officer said that the authorities would need good reason to stop and search any passenger. I informed him of our investigation, and I emailed him reasons which were sufficient to justify Jimmy Flynn being stopped and searched.

As he came through the arrivals terminal at Logan Airport, James Flynn was approached by a special agent from the Joint Terrorism Task Force of the Diplomatic Security Service. The official spoke to Flynn, who appeared nervous, and made inquiries about his plans while residing in Massachusetts. His phone and Toshiba laptop were seized and taken for analysis and, while the agent couldn't hold on to the devices, he could copy the information from them. The clothing Flynn had was also photographed before he was permitted to enter the United States. The information copied from the devices was downloaded and sent to gardaí for examination, which would later throw up significant information. Flynn's father followed him to Boston weeks later, and he was stopped before boarding his flight at Dublin Airport, with Detective Sergeant Phillips seizing his phone for examination, along with a satnav device. It would later emerge that this had been stolen in a creeper burglary in Mullingar, County Westmeath, some months earlier.

For Aaron Brady, it was also time to flee. On 13 April, he packed his bags and headed to Belfast International Airport to leave the country. He passed through security with his new British passport and boarded a United Airlines flight to Newark Airport in New Jersey. He was granted access to the United States after filling out an Electronic System for Travel Authorisation (ESTA) form, as part of the visa waiver entry programme. He listed his reason for travelling as being for pleasure and gave an address on 241st Street in the Bronx borough of New York as his place of residence. What he failed to disclose were his previous convictions and the fact that he was currently before the criminal courts for sentencing. The terms of the waiver programme meant that he would have to leave the United States within 90 days, but Aaron Brady had no intention of returning to Ireland in three months.

Over a week later, on 23 April, Sergeant John Moroney arrived at Dundalk Circuit Court for Aaron Brady's sentencing hearing, aware that he had already left the island. When the case was called Brady's solicitor informed the court that his client wasn't present and asked for the matter to be left over for second calling in the afternoon. The case was returned to after lunch and his lawyer said they had been in contact with Brady's father, who said he 'won't be here, he's not expecting him to be here'. Sergeant Moroney informed the presiding judge that the case was last on the court list in February and had been listed the previous week for a sentencing date to be fixed. He said Aaron Brady was aware of the matter and applied for a bench warrant to be issued, informing the court they believed he was in the United States. This was issued by the judge, who ordered that he should be arrested and brought before the court to be sentenced at the earliest opportunity. Aaron Brady, for the time being, was in the wind.

8

'IMGUNNA SHOOT A POLICEMAN HAHA'

While the suspects had fled to different corners of the world, gardaí continued gathering evidence that would link them to the murder and robbery. The material on James Flynn's laptop and phone had since been downloaded and reviewed, which showed further links to the credit union raid. One piece of data discovered on Flynn's phone contained messages joking about the shooting of a police officer. The text, from the early hours of 16 March 2013, read: 'Ur the Rulys ... imgunna [I'm going to] shoot a policeman haha.' The term 'The Rulys' is a colloquialism uniquely used in Crossmaglen meaning brilliant. The crassness of the comment that followed it, made less than two months after the murder and recovered on the phone of a man who knew he was a suspect, was telling. Gardaí also discovered videos and photos taken on Colleen McCann's phone that were saved onto Flynn's laptop. One picture from the early hours of 17 December 2012 showed Jessica King and Aaron Brady, dressed in a blue and white striped shirt, posing for the camera on a night out. Another photograph from that morning, taken at 4.14 a.m., showed two men in a house wearing balaclavas, with one wearing the same shirt Brady was pictured in hours earlier. Videos were also recovered from that night, one that showed a group in the sitting room of a house as 'The Green Fields of France' played in the background. A man wearing a balaclava and a dark Scania jacket could also be seen walking into the room and pointing a gun in the direction of Aaron Brady as the group laughed and joked.

Jessica King would give another statement to gardaí, this time about the people in the pictures and video. She identified the men in balaclavas as her boyfriend and James Flynn, saying the pictures were taken at the 'party house' in Lough Road. She also had more information to offer, telling gardaí that every time they went back to the house 'the boys were playing IRA music and sometimes wearing the balaclavas … I never questioned why they had them. I would never have taken it seriously until now. Aaron never said where he got them. I knew the balaclavas were in the drawers in the kitchen. There was two, max three balaclavas.' She said the 'wee handgun' James Flynn was holding in his hand appeared fake to her and looked more like a water pistol. What Ms King said next was of particular interest to gardaí. 'I remember that night earlier on. I'm nearly sure it was that night. I saw a black handgun in the top drawer with the balaclavas. This gun was more human' sized like a standard gun you would see on T.V. I can't say if this gun was real or not, but it looked more realistic than the one in the picture that Jimmy was holding. I think I asked what it was for and I think one of the boys said it was for shooting birds. I'd say most likely it was Aaron or Jimmy who answered.' A few weeks later she said they were back at the house when she noticed that the balaclavas and gun were no longer in the drawer. Ms King told gardaí that, when she asked her boyfriend about them, she was told: 'It's gone, or long gone, dumped or something to that effect.' She said this conversation took place before the murder because after that day 'everything changed and nothing like this stuff, like parties, happened again'.

She also told gardaí of a conversation she had with Colleen McCann prior to Christmas 2012 in which their boyfriends having a shotgun was brought up. 'There was talk of either Jimmy or Aaron having a shotgun. Me and Colleen were briefly talking about it. She said it to me. As far as I recall she said it was Aaron that had it. I didn't think it was true ... Colleen just passed a remark like "Sure Aaron has a shotgun". I can't remember discussing this with Aaron,' Ms King told the gardaí. Detective Garda Joe Ryan was later asked to look at an image of the balaclavas and identified them as being similar to the masks worn by the robbery gang. He also said the accents in the video matched those of the raiders at Lordship Credit Union.

Another photograph was also recovered from Flynn's device, which had no time or date stamp, showing a man posing with a single-barrelled shotgun, similar to the shotgun used in the credit union raid. This, investigators stated in one report, was evidence that James Flynn had 'access to firearms and other material used by criminals in the commission of crime, a number of weeks prior to the murder'. Gardaí added in their report that the device's contents 'show communication that directly makes reference to the shooting of a policeman'.

By July the investigation had seen 3,460 jobs issued, 1,853 statements taken, and 1,163 reports generated, after just six months. Detective Inspector Marry was also considering targeting the persons connected to the investigation under a 'serious organised crime group setting'. Gardaí had carried out

24 searches, 9 of which related directly to the murder while the rest were connected to the commission of creeper burglaries. Several arrests had also been made in relation to offences not directly linked to the credit union robbery. One person detained was the girlfriend of Eugene Flynn Jnr, who was found to be in possession of a motor vehicle containing stolen parts taken from another car during a creeper burglary in Kells, County Meath, in December 2012. Later examinations discovered that Eugene Jnr's phone was also active in Kells on the night of this unauthorised taking. A separate search of a yard in Faughart led to a stolen motor vehicle, 25,000 litres of laundered diesel waste, and burnt documents being found.

In another operation in the area on 4 May, officers recovered over 1.1 million contraband cigarettes, 403 kilos of tobacco, six litres of counterfeit Smirnoff, and €34,000 in cash. On 27 May, on foot of information, investigators recovered clothing that was worn by culprits involved in the armed robbery of Sheelan's Post Office in Riverstown on a grass verge just north of the border. Gardaí were also continuing to disrupt the activities of dissident groups, and that month detained two men on suspicion of IRA membership and possession of explosives. The operations, while not directly relating to the murder, highlighted once again the knock-on effect the increased garda activity was having on criminality in the border region.

While the investigation was progressing, gardaí noted in one report that the 'departure from this jurisdiction of a number of the suspects has hampered the close examination of each of these suspects'. To counter this, gardaí began liaising with international colleagues including the Federal Bureau of Investigation (FBI) and the Department of Homeland Security in the US, the PSNI and Border Control Agency in the UK, and Australian police. The PSNI had launched its own murder inquiry based at Geogh police station and conducted familial DNA testing to establish any potential links to suspects with unidentified DNA profiles. In one request for assistance from law enforcement in Australia and the United States, gardaí said that six persons had been 'firmly established' as suspects in the inquiry and that 961 items of intelligence were recorded at the incident room in Dundalk, 150 of which 'have provided a direct nomination or indication that the suspects named in this report were involved in the organisation and carrying out of the armed robbery and the murder of Detective Garda Adrian Donohoe'. Gardaí sought the assistance of police forces in the United States to covertly monitor Aaron Brady and the three Flynns, and help from agencies in Australia to carry out similar inquiries with Mr C.

James Flynn, investigators established, was residing with a relative on Oxford Road in Norwood, Massachusetts, where he was portraying himself as a construction and paving specialist. Investigators noted that a perusal of the company online was 'not complimentary' and that reviews 'alleged poor work-manship and indicated difficulty in contacting the firm'. His brother, Eugene Flynn Jnr, had been in Melbourne, Australia, for three months but departed the country on Qantas Airline flight QF93 for Los Angeles on 19 May. On leaving Australia, he was stopped by police officers there and said that he intended to stay in the United States for three months before returning.

*

That year's annual delegate conference of the Garda Represent-ative Association (GRA), which represents some 11,000 frontline gardaí, saw the ongoing frustrations at government cutbacks brought to the fore. It came to a head when Justice Minister Alan Shatter was not invited to address the conference, a rare snub, while Garda Commissioner Martin Callinan also received a damp reception when several members refused to applaud his address to delegates. It emerged during the conference that Detective Garda Donohoe had spoken out against Minister Shatter attending that year's event, just days before he was murdered, at a meeting about issues for gardaí within the Dundalk district

Speaking at the conference, Garda Robbie Peelo, a colleague and close friend of the detective, said: 'At that meeting, it was decided that Alan Shatter was not to be invited to this conference and that, if he attended, I was to get out. Adrian spoke at that meeting, and if he were alive today, he would demand that he not be here, because of the way Alan Shatter and the Government are so out of touch with ourselves and everyone else in this country. It was hugely attended in Dundalk. There was only a small proportion, who were on duty, who couldn't attend the meeting – everyone else was there. Adrian was very vocal at the meeting,' Garda Peelo said. It highlighted the growing anger among rank-and-file gardaí at the government over the continuous slashing of their resources.

The investigation into the Lordship murder and robbery was also not exempt from staffing shortages. On the afternoon of 22 July, a colloquium conference was held at Dundalk Garda Station to review the status of the investigation and strategies going forward. In a note on the meeting, Detective Inspector Marry described several areas 'causing great angst' and apprehension regarding the availability of resources to progress the inquiry. It was noted that the 'main area of concern was without doubt the volume, workload and size of the investigation and the requisite manpower to maintain the progress and advancement of the inquiry'.

On 30 July, senior investigators held an operational briefing with garda management at headquarters in the Phoenix Park, Dublin, on the progress of the inquiry along with recommendations going forward. Garda management suggested that the PSNI and gardaí identify all of Mr C's relatives who had legally held firearms, particularly shotguns, with a view to seizing them and potentially matching them against the cartridge found at the murder scene. Detectives had also established that Eugene Flynn Snr had an apartment in Estepona, Spain, and that they should contact a garda liaison officer based in Spain with a view to looking at possible opportunities there. Gardaí had identified a Volkswagen Passat being driven by a close friend of Aaron Brady who they believed was the getaway driver in the murder but was still only categorised as a person of interest. His car had been subject to monitoring by the NSU, while it was suggested that the PSNI also conduct surveillance on the vehicle in Northern Ireland. Detectives had also been reviewing creeper-style burglaries in the border region and, through analysis of phone data and CCTV footage, linked the gang to around a dozen such crimes in Counties Louth, Monaghan, Cavan, and Westmeath.

Following an intense seven months of pursuing thousands of lines of inquiry, gardaí knew they were in for the long-haul. Of this Detective Inspector Marry said:

Adrian's case was complex, and we were always looking for the big break. We thought at first when we discovered the culprits had left the hammer at the scene that their

DNA could be our saviour here. The hammer recovered at the scene was a very used panel beater's hammer with a red handle and it was described as a soft-faced hammer. We did not delay in putting the hammer into the forensic lab to see what evidence we could glean. I could not believe it when I was told it was forensically cleaned by the culprits, with no DNA recovered. The handle was made of rubber and it had 50 to 70 pin holes in it for grip. I returned the hammer to the lab and instructed them to dig deep into each hole for DNA. There was again no result – it had been well cleaned before being used by the culprits. I was sure that something would have shown up, but you have to accept when there is nothing there.

I was fearful of not solving the case. There would be cold-case reviews looking at how the case was handled, and I was more than determined to run an honest and professional investigation. We got very little comfort or encouragement from senior management. I remember one man of rank rolling up his sleeves and banging on the conference table, shouting to those around him: 'We have to solve this case.' He had good intentions, but I knew we had to rely on our own resolve to get justice for Adrian.

The Lordship murder and robbery inquiry wasn't the only major investigation continuing in Dundalk, and Detective Inspector Marry was the SIO for a number of other ongoing probes. This included the fatal shooting of Seamus McMahon, a former dissident republican, in March 2010 and the gun murder of drug dealer Paul Rea in November 2006. There was also the murder of Irene White in 2005, the allegations of sexual abuse against Dr Michael Shine, and the ongoing cold-case investigation into the disappearance and murder of 17-year-old Ciara Breen. It was a significant workload for Detective Inspector Marry and his team in Dundalk.

Not only did I have to juggle these investigations, but I also had divisional responsibility for other areas of policing within the divisions. I was in charge of family liaison personnel, the specialist interviewers, subversive activity, divisional search teams. The list goes on. But Adrian's murder was something that shocked us; it was an insult to his colleagues and an affront to everything good about the gardaí. We had to ensure that every effort was made to catch the killers. I always made it clear that if one of us were shot Adrian would be fighting for justice for us and would be sitting around the conference table. I was under a lot of stress and I knew it. To help me cope I moved into a bed and breakfast across the road from the garda station. It allowed me time to rest and be in the station by 4 a.m. to brief teams and searches. I always had operational orders and risk assessments completed before any operation. I would finish work by 10 p.m., even midnight some days, and get a quick rest before starting early again the next day. My working hours were well outside the European directive on working hours, but we had to progress the investigation.

In the autumn of 2013, the toll and pressure of the mammoth investigation was beginning to show. For Detective Inspector Marry it also began having physical effects. That August he began feeling a pain in his right calf, similar to a sensation he'd experienced ten years earlier when he developed a clot in his ankle that spread to his right knee. He was operated on at the Mater Hospital in Dublin and spent four weeks as an inpatient while doctors tried to dissolve the clot.

I knew in August 2013 that I was in trouble and I went to the Beacon Hospital in Dublin. They confirmed I had a clot in my right calf which they needed to dissolve. They did this over a day or two and released me, only to have me come back in for an operation to remove veins from my leg. I duly obliged and went into hospital at the end of that month, having the operation and being released the same day. Three weeks later my surgery wounds became infected and I attended my GP who was, given my history, very concerned that I wasn't on blood thinners. He was so concerned that he rang the surgeon there and told me that if I took antibiotics, I would be fine.

About three days later I was in Naas with my wife and began feeling poorly; I had a pain in my chest and was having difficulty breathing. My wife, seeing how terrible I looked, instructed me to go to Caredoc in Naas. The doctor put a heart monitor on me and I could tell from the reading it was bad; it was one slow curve with no lines peaking up or down. I said to her: 'That doesn't look great,' and she swung the monitor away from me. She had urgency in her eyes and sprayed something in my mouth. The nurse held my hand and I knew I was dying – the feeling was consuming. The nurse shouted to the doctor: 'He thinks he's dying' and told me that the ambulance would be here in a few minutes. I remember the white light – I was gone. Yes, I died but I was revived by the paramedics in the ambulance.

I was rushed into A&E where I was given an oxygen mask, blood tests, the whole lot. The next morning the doctor came into the ward and told me that I had a bilateral multi-embolism. I had a blood clot an inch long in the bottom of my right lung. Professor O'Connor who tended to me told me that I was very lucky to be alive. I spent six weeks in Naas General Hospital trying to get better, and the care I got was second to none. I was in no fit state to return to work and my head was in a mess knowing I'd had a close brush with death. I knew it would be several months before I could return to work.

While he was out on sick leave the investigation was taken over by Inspector Brian Mohan, who would be running the case conferences in his absence.

*

Having spent several months lying low in Australia, Mr C returned to Ireland in August 2013. Intelligence from that month indicated that he was back living in Crossmaglen and was spotted driving a four-by-four with a trailer, while on 27 September gardaí became aware of an incident involving Mr C in the North. He had been pursued by the PSNI and abandoned the car he was travelling in. The vehicle was seized but intelligence indicated that Mr C later arrived at the lock-up facility where the car was stored with a spare key and removed it. Despite being under scrutiny by security agencies on both sides of the border, he continued to be involved in fuel smuggling and other forms of criminality.

That October, Eugene Flynn Snr had also spoken to

investigators and invited them to the United States to conduct an interview with him and his sons. He commented that they would tell gardaí 'about people and things in the investigation which they knew nothing about'. Gardaí surmised that this was indicative of Eugene Flynn Snr having possession of information relating to the murder and robbery. The proposition was accepted, and two months later Inspector Mohan, Detective Sergeant Phillips, and Detective Garda McGovern travelled to Boston to speak to the family as part of the investigation. Unbeknownst to gardaí, within two hours of touching down at Logan Airport, James Flynn was on a plane heading in the opposite direction back to Ireland. The three investigators, along with local police officers, attended the address given to them by Eugene Flynn Snr, who met them as they approached the front door.

While he appeared helpful when extending the invitation to come to Boston, his demeanour had changed by the time they arrived. One investigator described him as going 'ballistic' while also sniggering and laughing at the gardaí. Eugene Flynn Snr began shouting abuse at both the detectives and the American law-enforcement officers present, asking what they were doing at his house and why they were there. He told the gardaí: 'The boys aren't here, the boys are gone. You'll never get them,' and also stated that gardaí 'did not have the full story and that he wasn't interested in telling it'. It was another indication that he had information or knowledge about the events at Lordship Credit Union. After several minutes the investigators decided to withdraw from the premises and no interview took place. While he sniggered at the gardaí as they departed with their tails between their legs, Eugene Flynn Snr's mood was about to change.

Just a week after leading gardaí on a fool's errand he was back in Ireland. Unfortunately for him, the High Court in Dublin had endorsed a European arrest warrant issued for his return to England, where he was to be prosecuted for absconding from prison. He was detained while in Dundalk town centre and brought before the courts in Dublin. Garda Niall Smyth gave evidence that Flynn Snr had left an open prison less than two months into his jail sentence for fuel laundering and that UK authorities wanted to prosecute him for escape from lawful custody. Eugene Flynn Snr was later extradited to England to serve his prison sentence.

*

On the first anniversary of Detective Garda Donohoe's murder a press conference was held in which Commissioner Martin Callinan vowed that they would work tirelessly to ensure the killers were brought to justice:

> It is almost a year since the callous murder of our colleague Detective Garda Adrian Donohoe, who was shot dead while carrying out his normal day-to-day duties as a member of An Garda Síochána. His murder had a profound impact not only on his colleagues in Dundalk, but also on the wider An Garda Síochána family. It had an impact not only on the lives of those he positively affected in Co. Louth through his work, or through his involvement with the GAA community, but also country wide. Most importantly, his senseless, cold-blooded murder led to the bereavement of Caroline and their two children. It is Caroline and the two children who are uppermost in my

mind at this time, as we remember a man who involved himself wholly in his family, his community, and in his job, and who ultimately gave his life in the service of them.

Commissioner Callinan also revealed how in the previous 12 months gardaí had taken over 2,100 statements, gathered 400,000 hours of CCTV, collected over 1,200 exhibits, and carried out more than 30 searches. He confirmed that gardaí had travelled to several countries to gather intelligence and evidence, thanking the FBI and PSNI for their help.

Detective Inspector Marry had taken several months off work and in March was ready to return to his role as the SIO of the murder investigation, but his superiors had other plans:

I returned to work with enthusiasm and on my first day back I paid a visit to my superintendent's office. He welcomed me back but informed me that I would not be running Adrian Donohoe's case now that the stand-in inspector was in situ. He informed me I would be helping him out. I said: 'No, I was appointed SIO on the case and now you want me to be some sort of stage-door Johnny.' I told him I was taking myself off of Adrian's case and that I had other cases to solve. I was not going to be degraded by management and that was it. I got stuck into the double murder of Joseph Redmond and Anthony Burnett, and it took me three years to solve it but I did. It involved some outside-of-the-box thinking which would help down the line in Adrian's case. I worked hard on Irene White's murder and I was so close to securing a charge on the suspect for Ciara Breen's murder. I also sought to be promoted but, yet again, despite having an impeccable record I was being overlooked.

On making inquiries as to why I was being overlooked for promotion, I was made to understand that my face didn't fit what they were looking for higher up the line. What do you do after hearing that? I thought to myself that it may have been how I had taken myself off Adrian's case and perhaps it didn't sit well. I was always honest in my approach to any job given to me.

Meanwhile, the suspects continued residing outside garda jurisdiction, believing they were safe from the reach of the investigation team. Aaron Brady also began building a nice life for himself in the United States.

9

LYING LOW IN NEW YORK

After arriving in America to escape the garda pressure and domestic charges, Aaron Brady spent his first weeks in Woodlawn, a predominantly Irish American community in the north of the Bronx. The working-class neighbourhood is steeped in Irish culture and a home away from home for the thousands of Irish ex-pats who reside there. Sitting at the northernmost point of the New York borough, it also extends into the suburb of Yonkers in Westchester County. One of the most popular streets is Katonah Avenue, a strip dotted with Irish bars and restaurants, making it the centre of nightlife in the area. Informally known as 'Little Ireland' in some quarters, the pubs, restaurants, and shops in the neighbourhood are decked out with Irish and American flags. Families with Irish heritage have been residing there for generations, while, unlike other areas in New York, it continues to see Irish immigrants move there to live and work.

Garda intelligence indicated that the fugitive had been staying at a property on East Street in the Bronx until 1 June, before renting a room on Woodlawn Avenue. Gardaí also had information that Aaron Brady would board an early morning bus on Katonah Avenue every day to go to work on a building site in Manhattan spreading concrete, while Jessica King also travelled over a number of times to visit him. Two months after arriving in New York, Aaron Brady was convinced by James Flynn to travel north to Boston and work with him in his various businesses. He agreed, and for several months he stayed at Oxford Road in Norwood, living with the Flynns while working in their snow-clearing business in the winter months. Things were going well initially and Brady, who had overstayed his visa departure date of 11 July, was working away despite living in the country illegally.

The relationship soured, however, in early 2014, and the two robbery suspects had a falling out. This happened after Brady had been entrusted with looking after the business while the Flynns travelled to California for power-washing work. Brady had decided to head to New York, where Jessica King was visiting, taking Eugene Flynn Snr's car. In his absence heavy snowfall hit the Boston area and he was uncontactable, the car he had taken was damaged, and the business suffered as a result of him going missing. It was the last time he spoke with the Flynns.

He resettled in Woodlawn and for the first few weeks was couch-surfing, being put up at different places while looking for more permanent accommodation. Brady, having played intermediate football with Crossmaglen Rangers, also began searching for a Gaelic team to play with in New York. Because of the large number of Irish immigrants living in the city, it has around 30 football teams that play in senior, intermediate, and junior competitions at Gaelic Park in the Bronx. Brady initially began training with Cork New York, before moving to Sligo New York, where he played and trained during the rest of his time there. He posted one picture on his Facebook page of him celebrating with teammates after winning an intermediate football championship.

Despite not being certified, he also began working as a heavy machinery driver and in late 2014 got a job with Structure Tech in New York City, where he started off earning $32 an hour. He began by driving Bobcats, four-wheeled machines with a box bucket used for moving building material, and would be given the nickname 'Bobcat' among associates there. It was a more endearing sobriquet than 'Butterfingers Brady', which had been given to him by criminal associates back home after he allegedly dropped the shotgun during the Dundalk racecourse robbery. He worked his way up to operating large diggers and rock drills, with one of the properties he worked at belonging to a famous artist called Jeff Koons. Brady also found more permanent housing, moving into an apartment on 1st Street in Woodlawn with a young woman from Donegal and an Antrim man that had spent time in Australia with his sister.

Brady's social media accounts remained publicly accessible despite his status as a murder suspect and fugitive. He would often post images of himself socialising in New York with friends he knew from Armagh and others he had met in the city, while his family regularly travelled over to visit him. An avid Liverpool supporter, he also shared pictures of himself attending one of the club's games during a pre-season match in New York. Brady living openly stateside and publicly gloating about how he was enjoying life would also be the subject of several newspaper articles. The *Irish Daily Star* printed one story about his attendance at the Liverpool match using a pix-elated image taken from his Facebook account, stating that the suspect in the murder of Detective Garda Donohoe was 'living it up' in the Big Apple.

Much of Brady's wages were spent in the endless line of pubs along Katonah Avenue, including the Coachman's Inn, which would be packed most weekends with the Irish diaspora. It also had a reputation as having rowdy clientele, with physical violence often breaking out inside the bar. Other pubs that Brady and his circle socialised in included Behan's, Ned Devine's, and the Rambling House, and gardaí had information that Brady himself would often enter into aggressive confrontations when drunk. He was earning good money and enjoying his life in the United States while, in his eyes, remaining far away and out of the reach of the garda investigation back in Ireland.

In February 2015, Jessica King had plans to travel to Australia with her new boyfriend, but gave gardaí another statement before departing. She recalled being told a story about Aaron breaking into a woman's home in the countryside and robbing her jeep, and that she confronted him about this. Ms King said that Brady had admitted to it but blamed it primarily on Treanor and Flynn. She added: 'This happened long before, this was years ago before he was with me. I would never tolerate that from him, and he knew that.' Two days later she set off for Australia with her new partner.

Detectives in Dundalk were continuing to keep an eye on Brady in New York through the assistance of the FBI. Their interest in Brady would be stepped up in late 2015, but in the interim the investigation would focus on other suspects.

Eugene Flynn Snr had been jailed after being extradited back to England and was imprisoned in HMP Haverigg in Cumbria, a low-security facility where inmates can participate in full-time employment. On 9 June 2015, Detective Sergeants Mark Phillips and Ciaran Clancy travelled to the jail in another bid to get him to account for his movements on the night of the robbery. The detectives also wanted to inquire if he had any other information regarding the murder of Detective Garda Adrian Donohoe and the robbery at Lordship Credit Union. To their surprise he agreed and, at the outset, Eugene Flynn Snr said that he refused to speak with investigators when they travelled to Boston previously 'on a point of principle' because gardaí had not returned his seized Mercedes to him. He outlined how he held no animosity against gardaí for executing the arrest warrant, as he had been diagnosed and treated for cancer in his ear while in prison. In a report of the meeting, investigators stated: 'Eugene Flynn enquired did Gardaí know who had carried out the robbery at Lordship Credit Union in 2011. Detective Sergeant Phillips indicated that a person had been arrested [referring to Brendan Treanor]. Eugene Flynn stated that he could tell Gardaí about the exact denominations of money stolen at the time.' He also claimed that his sons were making large profits from their business in Boston, and that James had purchased a new house in Boston for $700,000 and bought his girlfriend a new BMW 3 Series.

Eugene Flynn Snr went on to say that he felt he and his family were treated unfairly during the investigation, alleging that his sons were harassed by gardaí in Dundalk and that he should be compensated for the seizure of his vehicle. The report of the meeting continued:

> He stated that he would give an account of his knowledge surrounding the murder of Detective Garda Donohoe and the robbery at Lordship Credit Union to investigating

gardaí in Ireland and would appreciate if An Garda Síochána could help expedite his transfer to Ireland. Detective Sergeant Phillips stated clearly that the matter concerning his transfer to a prison in Ireland would have to be dealt with by senior management at Dundalk and that he could not give any indication as to a decision at this time. Detective Sergeant Phillips reminded Eugene Flynn of his comments made on the telephone in October 2013 where he stated that following a discussion with his sons Eugene Jnr and James that he was extending an invitation to travel to the United Stated where he would tell investigating gardaí about people and things in the investigation that they knew nothing about. Detective Sergeant Phillips also reminded Eugene Flynn about his comment in the driveway of [the] house in Boston where he told investigating gardaí that they did not have the story and that he was not interested in telling it. Eugene Flynn acknowledged.

The detectives asked him if his account to them would include his knowledge of the events at Lordship Credit Union and any other information he had relating to the crime. Eugene Flynn Snr told them that he would speak with investigating gardaí in Ireland but did not elaborate any further. At the end of the meeting he told the gardaí that he wanted them to expedite his transfer to an Irish prison, that he would be compensated for the seizure of his car in 2013, and that property seized from him and his family would be returned. Then, he said, he would give an account to investigating gardaí in Ireland. He added that once he was released from prison he would be moving on with his life and putting the matter behind him. Despite the lengthy conversation, he had again declined to account for his movements on the night of the murder.

In Louth, despite the support from most of the local community, gardaí were at times subjected to taunts and insults about the murder of their colleague. On 1 September 2015, Detective Sergeant Kirwan had just left a shop and was driving in the Carlingford area when he noticed he was being followed by a Mercedes. The driver told Detective Sergeant Kirwan: 'You're harassing my girlfriend, you yellow bastard. Get out of the car and we will see how big you are.' He later asked him: 'By the way, how's Adrian?' It was a direct and cruel reference to his murdered colleague and a sign of the attitude of certain people in the area to gardaí.

*

Gardaí had been making further inroads with American authorities to tighten the net on their suspects living there. Detective Superintendent John O'Reilly, in charge of serious crime in the northern region, had been given contact details for the deputy chief of police in the New York Police Department (NYPD), Paul Ciorra, and initiated contact with him. He inquired if the NYPD could provide any assistance to gardaí in connection with the murder investigation and was invited to brief the department on their ongoing probe. On 3 August 2015, the senior garda travelled with Inspector Brian Mohan to New York where they presented a briefing to their international counterparts. It outlined how Aaron Brady was a prolific criminal in Ireland linked to an organised crime gang who specialised in armed robberies, residential burglaries, and theft of high-value motor vehicles, while he also had access to firearms and was a cocaine

user. It also included his links to an individual who, according to
PSNI intelligence, was listed as a dissident republican in
Northern Ireland and his links to a family in Crossmaglen who
were described as 'predominant republicans'. It asked the NYPD
to 'identify the present location' of Brady and establish his mode
of transport and telecommunication devices.

At that point gardaí had 32 persons of interest, and two men
who remained on this list were residing in the United States,
including a friend of Aaron Brady's from Crossmaglen who was
living in the Bronx and played football with him. The briefing
also listed him as providing an alibi for James Flynn, that he had
been in phone contact with Brady around the time of the murder,
and that he was uncooperative with investigators. The detectives outlined how in Ireland they had conducted evidence and
intelligence gathering while utilising lawful telecommunications
interceptions and authorised technical surveillance aids. The
scope and nature of the assistance they were seeking from the
NYPD included intelligence-gathering techniques, use of undercover operatives, and conventional and technical surveillance.

At the meeting Detective Superintendent O'Reilly also
inquired about the possibility of obtaining a DNA sample
from Aaron Brady for comparison with an unidentified DNA
profile taken from the door pillar of the unmarked garda car.
He asked if American investigators could obtain evidence
lawfully that would assist the garda investigation. A report of
the meeting stated: 'Deputy Chief Ciorra undertook to help
us in any way possible and offered the possibility of NYPD
considering the use of an undercover police officer to develop
or obtain evidence to assist us. We made it clear that we were
not formally requesting this option and that it was entirely a
matter for him and the NYPD.' It was a further example of

international cooperation and boosted the garda investigation in keeping surveillance on their suspects and other persons of interest in New York.

Members of the NYPD's undercover unit were assigned to the task force on Aaron Brady. Inquiries at the address gardaí had for him in New York established that he wasn't living there anymore. Using the intelligence provided by gardaí, which included that he regularly togged out for New York Sligo at Gaelic Park in Yonkers, Detective James Walsh decided to attend one of the club's games taking place at the park. He paid his entrance fee and sat in the stands, blending in with the other spectators, while taking pictures of the game. Through his long-lens camera Detective Walsh was able to snap a number of pictures of Brady, whom he identified from a picture supplied by gardaí. From this point the undercover unit were able to place surveillance on their target, eventually following him to the apartment in Yonkers where he was living at that time. On weekdays he would also be covertly tracked into Manhattan where investigators established his place of work.

Undercover agents also attempted to interact with Brady and befriend him in the hopes of obtaining a confession. This involved approaching him in Woodlawn or as he was returning home from work in Manhattan. The task force monitored his social media accounts, too, and decided they could perhaps interact with him at the many social and sporting events Brady attended. One plan involved attempting to approach him after he posted that he was going to an Irish bar in Manhattan for an event featuring former Liverpool players. However, he abandoned his plans at the last minute and instead went to Madison Square Garden to watch an MMA fight involving UFC star Conor McGregor.

The murder suspect was also security conscious in many ways and when sober kept to a close circle of friends. When agents attempted to engage him in conversation on the Metro train or in public, he would be cordial but refuse their attempts to speak with him. Detectives also established that Brady appeared forensically aware and would bring his own water bottles to Gaelic Park and dispose of them at home, rather than discarding them in public bins where they could be recovered and examined for DNA for comparisons with the crime scene at Lordship. Speaking in an interview with the *Irish Sun* about the tactic, Detective Walsh said:

> We bought tickets for the event in lower Manhattan, but he didn't show up. By that stage, we had watched him quite a bit and we thought we'd try and get to know him. We knew he was someone who was arrogant, someone who enjoyed a drink. We were just going to see if he would strike up a conversation and we could try to get to know him better, earn his trust and then see if he said anything about the cowardly murder. There were other times when our guys approached him on the subway, but he pretended to be asleep and other times just smiled. We never got to know him, but his arrogance contributed to his demise because he was boasting how much of a gangster he was.

On another occasion, Detective Eddie Gonzalez was attending a street festival in Woodlawn when he came across an individual who matched Brady's description. He took a number of discreet pictures of the subject, who was in the process of setting up a bouncy castle for children at the fair, and the hundreds of families in attendance were oblivious that a murder suspect was among them. From the pictures gardaí determined that his appearance hadn't changed much in the previous two and a half years, although he had grown facial hair and bulked up considerably. With the investigation into the murder of one member of An Garda Síochána continuing, that year the nation would get yet another stark reminder of the dangers gardaí face on any given day.

*

Garda Tony Golden, stationed in the Dundalk sub-district at Omeath Garda Station, had been on the initial cash escort on the night Detective Garda Donohoe was murdered. Originally from Culleens in Ballina, County Mayo, he was married with three young children and had ten years' service with An Garda Síochána. On the evening of 11 October 2015, he was assisting a victim of domestic violence to leave her abusive ex-partner who had subjected her to a lengthy and violent cycle of harm. He accompanied Siobhán Phillips, a young mother of two, to the house in Mullach Alainn in Omeath that she shared with Adrian Crevan-Mackin so that she could safely gather her belongings from the home. The previous day she had given a lengthy statement to Garda Golden in which she outlined the horrific abuse Crevan-Mackin had subjected her to, including a brutal and sustained attack hours earlier. Garda Golden never made it out of the house alive.

Inside the property Crevan-Mackin opened fire, fatally wounding Garda Golden and seriously injuring Ms Phillips, before turning the gun on himself. The 24-year-old criminal was facing serious charges before the non-jury Special Criminal Court after being accused of being a member of the IRA and had been released on bail. It later emerged that he had admitted being in possession of guns to gardaí nine months before the murder, but was never charged with firearms offences. A subsequent report by the Garda Síochána Ombudsman Commission found that Crevan-Mackin had breached the conditions of his bail 10 times in the lead up to Garda Golden's murder. The report also found that the Special Criminal Court had relaxed his bail conditions four months before the fatal shooting and that transcripts from those court proceedings indicated that the court was not informed of the bail breaches and no objections had been made by gardaí.

Four days after the murder, in a display of unity tragically similar to that for Adrian Donohoe in Dundalk, thousands of mourners gathered in Omeath for Garda Golden's state funeral. Father Pádraig Keenan, parish priest of Haggardstown and Blackrock, described him as 'one of life's gentlemen', a 'big gentle giant', and a 'lovely man'. Fr Keane said that he had 'a charisma that was calm, gentle and polite'.

With the death of Adrian Crevan-Mackin, nobody would ever be brought to justice before the courts for the serious harm caused to Siobhán Phillips and the murder of Garda Golden. He is the 88th member of An Garda Síochána to lose their life in the line of duty. Detective Inspector Marry described the impact yet another murder of a garda in the Dundalk district had on gardaí there:

It was hard enough getting to grips with Adrian's murder, but for a second member to lose his life at the hands of a madman was another blow. I was walking the Camino when I heard of Tony's death and made immediate arrangements to return to Dundalk to help with the workload. Tony, in my mind, was another garda who, if management were doing their job, should not have lost his life. I say this because manpower levels were so bad in the Louth division and several requests were made to acquire more resources, but these requests fell on deaf ears.

That station party were livid at Tony's murder and a meeting was held, addressed by Garda Commissioner Nóirín O'Sullivan. One particular member stood up and asked the commissioner why manpower was so bad in Louth, why it was like this, and why nothing had been done about it. In fairness to the commissioner, she was totally unaware of any manpower issues in the division. She turned to the regional commander, who said it was not his problem but a matter for B Branch, which looks after manpower, allocating members to stations and that.

If manpower was at normal levels and Tony Golden had a partner on that fateful night, he might well have been alive today. Tony was on his own, a brave man doing his job without fear or favour, when he was gunned down. I had met Tony Golden most mornings while on the dig for Ciara Breen's body at Balmer's Bog in Dundalk. He did the graveyard shift and said it suited him as he had children to get to school and the family life. Just from meeting him those few times you could see he was a decent guy, a family man, and a credit to An Garda Síochána.

Tony's murder was a sucker punch and we all felt deflated, upset, and vulnerable. The blue uniform is no protection against what's out there and what we could encounter on any day at work. Questions and concerns were raised at the time about how a lone, unarmed garda would be sent to the home of a known violent terrorist, suspected of importing and selling guns, and why he was still in possession of illegal firearms and ammunition while on bail for terrorist charges, and even why he was on bail at all.

*

In New York, believing enough time had passed and that he would never be prosecuted, Aaron Brady began building a more permanent life for himself. In late 2015 he met a young woman from Kerry and they began a relationship. Originally from Tralee but having dual Irish American citizenship, Danielle Healy worked in the Heritage Bar in Yonkers, another of the many pubs Brady frequented. The couple began dating and went on several romantic outings together, which included going to a New York Knicks basketball game in Manhattan. A short time after they began going out, Ms Healy fell pregnant with the couple's son.

In March 2016, Detective Superintendent O'Reilly and Inspector Mohan once again travelled to New York to receive an update on the investigation. This included determining if any evidence had been secured to assist the murder investigation. The NYPD confirmed that Aaron Brady was living at an apartment on Sterling Avenue in Yonkers and that he was in a relationship with a young girl from Kerry who they believed was pregnant. Gardaí were also informed that an undercover officer had been deployed but at no time had Aaron Brady engaged with him in any manner: Brady only socialised with persons he knew and no evidence had been obtained in any form. He had also moved employer the previous month and got a job with Empire Pile Construction in Manhattan. Despite not having a licence to operate heavy machinery, Brady would regularly post images on his social media accounts of himself operating large excavators. While many who interacted with Brady in New York would have been unaware of his dark background, others were all too familiar with what he was suspected of back in Ireland. One person who spoke to the authors stated:

> There were always rumours that he had shot a guard in Ireland. I never spoke to him about it, but his friends would openly say it. He seemed like a bit of an eejit, I wouldn't have taken it too seriously, but I also didn't know him too well. It was certainly discussed, though, by his own circle, who seemed fine to be hanging around with him even though they were aware of what he had done. One time we were drinking in the back garden of a house in Woodlawn and one of his friends turned to us and said: 'That's the guy who shot the guard in Ireland,' pointing at Brady. It was said very casually – this was only a short time after we arrived in New York.

Despite the comprehensive investigation continuing with the assistance of the NYPD and the FBI, there was still insufficient evidence to bring charges against Brady over the Lordship Credit Union murder and robbery.

10

ENTER HOMELAND SECURITY

On 22 September 2016, Detective Garda Adrian Donohoe was posthumously awarded the Gold Scott Medal for valour in recognition of the sacrifice he made that night at Lordship Credit Union, while his colleague Detective Garda Joe Ryan was awarded the Silver Scott Medal. Adrian's wife, Caroline, accepted the award on behalf of her late husband to a standing ovation of more than 300 people at the ceremony at the Garda Training College in Templemore. The garda commissioner of the day, Nóirín O'Sullivan, said that they were determined to get justice for their murdered colleague who had 'made the ultimate sacrifice'. Commissioner O'Sullivan also defended the length of time the investigation was taking, saying that gardaí needed help from the wider community to bring Adrian's killers to justice.

Later that year, on 7 December, Detective Inspector Marry was formally reappointed as SIO of the investigations into the murders of Detective Garda Donohoe and Garda Tony Golden. He had requested an official written report for the formal handover process and to be briefed fully on how the investigation had been conducted in his absence. Detective Inspector

Marry also met with the investigation team for a strategy meeting and for them to voice any concerns they had.

> I took my place at the top of the conference table and looked around at the team. Their faces were pale, drained of energy and any enthusiasm to continue. I hadn't received the briefing document I'd requested, and it was an open discussion to find out the state of play. I asked what progress there had been since I departed. I went through the investigation over the past three years and all I can say is it was at a standstill. There was no strategy in place to move the investigation forward. There was no strategy around the suspects, and the person-of-interest team had been incorporated with an inquiry team. I had to motivate this team and decided to have each and every one of them come into my office on an individual basis over a three-day period to get their views and thoughts on the best way forward.

One avenue presented itself that Christmas when Danielle Healy returned to her home in Kerry with her and Aaron Brady's son. Brady decided not to risk travelling back to Ireland, where a bench warrant was in place for his arrest over the Dundalk ramming incident. In the New Year, Detective Sergeants Darren Kirwan and Kieran Reidy travelled to Tralee to visit Ms Healy and speak to her about her partner's involvement in the murder. The visit to the south-west of the country, however, didn't result in any progress, with Detective Inspector Marry saying:

> Danielle Healy was a potential witness and someone who I thought may want to cooperate. I dispatched a team to

go to Kerry and interview her. They informed me that they were invited into the Healy house but that was the end of it. They explained to the family the stance of the gardaí and their suspicions of Aaron Brady. It became quite clear Danielle Healy had nothing to offer and that, in their mind, her partner was an innocent man. Her parents were not sympathetic to the gardaí and believed in their daughter and her commitment towards Brady. That was that. The garda team left the Healy house knowing they would not be back and would not be welcome back. It was an avenue of inquiry that had to be looked at all the same.

Later that month the SIO met with Garda Commissioner O'Sullivan, on 30 January 2017, to discuss the progress in the case and what the investigation team needed. He identified several points, which included placing Detective Sergeant Phillips and Detective Garda McGovern back on the investigation team full-time, as they had been moved to a different investigation in the interim. A request was also made to assign a member of the Criminal Assets Bureau to the investigation, that Detective Garda Bobby Ogle be brought onto the investigation, that there would be flexibility to travel to the United States, and that another temporary detective inspector with SIO skills be appointed. The fact that their chief murder suspect had continued to live freely across the Atlantic for so long was also a major point of contention for Detective Inspector Marry:

I could not understand why Aaron Brady was allowed to live in New York while there were domestic bench warrants in Ireland. I was told there had been contact with the FBI and they were doing inquiries. When I asked if there was a paper trail, I was told that that the FBI were 'keeping an eye on him' and that was it. This reflected the state of what had happened with the investigation over the previous three years. Nothing. The FBI route was not one I wanted so we had to look elsewhere. I was informed that the Department of Homeland Security may be in a better position to help so I began making inquiries with them. I was clear on what I needed to do and that we had to look more closely at America and the three suspects that were in New York and Boston.

*

In response to the September 11 terror attacks that claimed almost 3,000 innocent lives, the US federal government had moved to develop a framework that would protect the country against similar atrocities from abroad while also enhancing its own capabilities to prevent such attacks internally. The key aspect of this revamp was the establishment of the Department of Homeland Security, which brought together 22 separate agencies and offices, including the US Customs Service and the Immigration and Naturalization Service. Beginning operations in 2003, it is now tasked with a broad remit including investigating terror threats, border security, and immigration and customs offences, as well as disaster prevention and management. Over the years it has also grown in size to over 240,000 employees, making it one of the largest cabinet departments in the United States and having one of the most critical roles within the government.

Its principal investigative arm is Homeland Security Investigations (HSI), which is responsible for carrying out

inquiries into transnational crime and threats, with a particular
focus on criminal gangs that exploit the country's infrastruc-
ture through which international trade, travel, and finance is
moved. Its mission is to investigate, disrupt, and dismantle
terrorist and criminal organisations that threaten to exploit
the customs and immigration laws of the United States. The
array of international crimes its some 9,000 agents investigate
include terrorism, drug and weapons smuggling, child exploitation, money laundering, and human trafficking.

In 2017, the new target of the investigative superpower
became the suspects for the murder and robbery at Lordship
Credit Union. That year alone, the Department of Homeland
Security had apprehended more than half a million individuals nationwide and conducted over 450,000 removals and
returns. They would now be asked to help gardaí in tracking
down the three suspects living in the United States: Aaron
Brady, James Flynn, and Eugene Flynn Jnr. Of the HSI's
significant staffing level, some 2,800 task-force officers are
assigned internationally to help combat transnational crime,
anchored by 250 special agents based at US embassies and
consulates. The London base, one of the larger international
hubs, has responsibility for Northern Europe including the
UK, Iceland, and Ireland. It is only smaller in size to the
likes of the Colombian office, which requires significant
resources due to international drug networks operating in
South America.

The purpose of these foreign offices is to develop partnerships with the host countries and governments so operations
including surveillance, undercover meetings, and interviews
can be facilitated. In 2016, Special Agent Scott Crabb was
based in the London office and supervising seven other agents.

Outlining the remit of the foreign-based agents he explains:

> Our primary responsibility as diplomats is to serve both
> the US mission that falls under the ambassador, but also
> the missions of the Department of Homeland Security
> and HSI. We're pulled in multiple directions but really it's
> all about developing contacts and international partner-
> ships, people we could talk to and tap for support and
> resources. Oftentimes you'll have a situation where your
> foreign partners need something in the US and we're
> there for that as well, so if someone comes to us and says:
> 'We're needing to run an operation in the US – we want
> to meet with someone or talk to an informant,' we will
> help facilitate that with our domestic offices and host
> them under US authority. In the same way we don't have
> foreign authority in Britain or Ireland, or wherever we're
> covering, we would rely on counterparts to execute their
> authority to facilitate our case. And then a lot of that
> is because we have police-to-police sharing agreements
> between our countries – we can share police matters or
> non-state classified activity on an informal basis. Then,
> if we needed to use that in court and procure evidence
> or submit that as evidence, we would go through a more
> formal MLAT [Mutual Legal Assistance Treaty] process
> which would allow us to obtain that information from
> another country and use that in a US court.

Around that time their main targets were criminals operating on the darknet, with the agency utilising proliferation and
undercover operations relating to the purchase of firearms.
One of the key agents involved in this was Special Agent Matt

Katzke, an expert in counter-proliferation, who was involved in facilitating controlled deliveries of purported illegal commodities sought by foreign nationals. These stings were being primarily conducted in the UK and Belfast. One of the most significant operations undertaken by the HSI London team at that time was an investigation into a man Special Agent Crabb described as the 'worst child exploitation and blackmail offender I have ever seen'.

The four-year manhunt for university lecturer Dr Matthew Falder involved security services from the United States, Australia, New Zealand, Israel, and Europe. On the surface Falder appeared to be a Cambridge-educated academic living a normal life, but beneath the façade he operated on the darkweb, obtaining images of paedophilia through blackmail before sharing them with other offenders. Officials estimate that Falder had over 50 victims in an eight-year period from 2009. He was arrested and subsequently pleaded guilty to 137 offences against 46 people and is now serving a 32-year jail term. After the sentencing, Special Agent Crabb described Falder as a 'monster' and 'pure evil', adding: 'There's some closure to be had with a sentence like this. I've just never seen anything like this, where someone is willing to go to these lengths to torment people.'

It was one of the HSI's success stories in terms of international cooperation, despite the London office facing cuts in that period. Initially, it had several agents pulled due to a number of factors, including financial measures, but the cuts were quickly reversed. Special Agent Crabb and Jim Mancuso, the London attaché at the time, were selected to oversee the UK office and hand-pick a team of special agents to work with. They then reviewed the landscape from the HSI's point of view and how their international partnerships worked. While the connections in the UK were strong, their links to Ireland were minimal, with Special Agent Crabb saying:

In Ireland we had very little partnership with the Irish garda. We had one agent that had been left behind from the older regime and he had good connectivity with Ireland – he was Irish himself, so it was easy for him to have that connectivity and he'd established some pretty good relationships with the Irish government, but we weren't doing very much work with them. I think they had partnerships with different US agencies, the FBI primarily, and we just weren't connected; we couldn't get into Ireland and make a call to get something done quickly.

We had to navigate different avenues because a lot of people just didn't know who we were, what our authorities were, what we were capable of, and I can understand that from a foreign law-enforcement perspective, as you see what you see on TV and you know what you know. So, we really put a lot of effort into developing relationships in Ireland, specifically in Dublin and the garda. We had good relationships in Ireland with Customs but they're not the investigative agency in Ireland, so we could get stuff done in a Customs to Customs perspective because HSI has a significant customs investigatory remit.

The HSI agents set about conducting trips to Dublin to establish new relationships and contacts with Garda Headquarters. Their partnership with the PSNI had been hugely beneficial in carrying out their proliferation operations around the darknet, and they wanted a similar connection with An Garda Síochána.

Having been informed of the potential assistance the Department of Homeland Security could offer, Detective Inspector Marry also wanted to forge a strong relationship between the two agencies. He set about arranging an appointment with the HSI and was put in contact with their London office, meeting two of their agents weeks later.

> The first time I met Matt Katzke and Scott Crabb was in the foyer of the Ashling Hotel in Dublin. Two absolute gentlemen. It's hard to explain but I could see they were utterly professional. They were neatly dressed in their suits, and you could see they meant business. They were very interested in the story I had to tell, and they were engrossed in the murder and the fact that three of the suspects were now in America. I wanted to go slowly at first, as I needed to know what Homeland Security could offer us. It took time but I had regular contact with Matt Katzke, and over time our relationship grew, we got to a stage where we understood each other and what we were about. It was not long before our relationship strengthened and both Homeland Security and An Garda Síochána were singing off the same hymn sheet. We both wanted to see justice for a fellow colleague.

Special Agent Crabb also recalls the immediate interest he had in the case, given the fact that the 'triggerman' and other alleged members of the robbery crew were living openly in the United States. While no criminal offence had been committed in America, the HSI carried out enquiries and soon established that they had authority to become involved in the case. 'Once we identified there were some Irish nationals in the US who had overstayed their immigration commitments, we realised we had authority at that point, even from an administrative, non-criminal perspective,' Special Agent Crabb says.

> Even though we're not an immigration or administrative specific agency – we're a criminal investigative agency – we have that authority revolving around immigration and customs. And when I say administrative, that would be someone illegally in the country but we don't have a crime associated with them, or them committing some type of crime other than just being in the country without authorisation, but we can apply our authorities to that. There is another agency which actually handles that, and we overlap on authority, so we looked at it and said we can probably help the Irish with this case.

While the initial stages were slow, with both agencies trying to understand the other's position, any trepidation soon disappeared and the garda investigation team formed a strong connection with the HSI agents. Both were also cognisant of the different laws and investigative powers in each jurisdiction. Of this Special Agent Crabb says:

> Throughout that process we also had to respect the differences between US and Irish laws in terms of what can and can't be done, and the method at which you would proceed through certain aspects. So in the US we can move pretty quick on things – we're fairly dynamic in terms of how we can operate, specifically HSI. We don't need lots of permissions from the judicial side, which is the end of the case. You do the investigation, and you

present it; you don't ask them for permission to do undercover meetings and interviews, that kind of thing. They
don't provide any authority, in other words. That was a
new learning experience in how Irish law worked versus
the way US law worked and making sure whatever we did
on our side had no impact on the real criminal investigation – the one that mattered was the Irish one, so that's
kind of how we approached that.

Over time the HSI agents would accommodate dozens of
trips by gardaí to the United States to assist in the criminal
investigation. Once the HSI team were given Aaron Brady's
name and details, they began looking to confirm his whereabouts and the circle he associated with. Surveillance was placed
on the previous address he had been residing at on Wakefield
Avenue in Yonkers, but it soon emerged that he had moved
out of there. Investigators were aware of the pubs he regularly
frequented, which were also placed under watch, while HSI utilised a wide range of databases available to them. Special Agent
Crabb says that they began to run Brady's name through their
systems, which would have put him on the map in New York:

He was not on anyone's list as a criminal, he wasn't
committing any crimes, he was going to work, he was just
kind of blending in with society in the US even though
he wasn't legally in the US, he was just doing his thing. I
think he got into fights or something like that but there
was nothing where he was really popping up heavily on
anyone else's radar. Ultimately, though, he needs electricity and water and things in his house, and he needs
other aspects that put himself out there, so we were able to

identify a general area he was in. Then we had some work done around the local community.

The HSI team then set about pinpointing his exact movements and locations. They confirmed that he was living in an apartment on Sterling Avenue in Yonkers with Danielle Healy and their son, who was born the previous October. He was still working at Empire Pile construction in New York City, having only left briefly for other employment before returning. Despite living in the US illegally, Brady was being paid good money, earning around $65 an hour in his role as a machinery driver. By February 2017 Danielle Healy had returned from her visit to Kerry back to Yonkers, and intelligence indicated that a christening celebration for their son was held at the Rambling House Bar. Members of the Brady family had also flown to New York for the celebration.

A key aspect of the inquiry, like in any investigation, was relying on informants or people in the locality to provide accurate information. However, this proved difficult at times within the Irish community of Woodlawn where Brady had been effectively hiding out for several years, and where he had made a name for himself as someone to be feared. Special Agent Crabb says:

It's a fairly tight-knit community; it's Irish based and an area not very easy to penetrate from a law-enforcement perspective. We did have some people who had access to that area, and we just identified people who knew of him and where he was, and that he hung out in certain establishments, so we started watching some of those places where he was hanging out and what he was doing. Once

we knew where he was and where he lived, now it's time
we can make decisions on what we do; do we want to go
pick him up and bring him in on immigration charges or
do we want to leave him in place and let investigations
unfold? We just took our time from there and worked
in unison with Pat and his team to make sure that every
step we made was in support of what their case in the
investigation was.

There was some emotion around the case as well
because, in international law enforcement, a police officer
detective is a police officer detective – it's a unique family,
whereas, say, opposing militaries wouldn't collaborate
necessarily like law enforcement does across the world.
And so, it's unique. If you go as a law-enforcement officer
to another country, with the exception of a few, you are
welcomed with open arms, brought in, and make immediate friends that you're a part of. That's done all over the
world – I've worked all over the world and that's what
I've seen.

In terms of what Matt [Katzke] brought to this case,
he had a lot of emotion attached to it as well. He said,
'Look: these guys lost a brother, and he's a police officer
and he was doing his police duties. What can we do?'
And we said we'll throw everything at it because, as
time went on, Adrian became one of our own. And the
people that knew Adrian and worked with Adrian, we
saw what it meant to them, and we became very close
with those guys as well, so there was nothing that was
really stopping us in the desire to help and what needed to
happen. We would do this if any police came and said it
was a non-law-enforcement officer this happened to, if it

was a regular civilian was killed. If the police wanted that support and that help, we'd do it because that's the way [the] international law-enforcement community works.

To give some context, why we put so much effort into it was multifaceted. We considered Adrian as one of our own, part of that big law-enforcement family, so it was not a hard thing to get support for. We went to our HSI New York office, a huge office, they've got so much work so they're massively busy, and we go to them and say we need some help with surveillance, we need some help tapping some of your informants, to find out where this guy is and what he's up to, [to find] anybody that surrounds him that we might be able to talk to, any people that might know him. And that's kind of how we end up developing the case even more, getting more information ...

You go to our HSI office and I might have had to make some calls to people at my level to get support because they're doing a lot of work and moving around, but we'd go in and say: 'Hey, there's allegations that this subject in your area of responsibility, he killed a police officer in Ireland' – most people didn't bat an eye at it, especially in New York where there's a heavy Irish community and a lot of our agents are of Irish descent. So our agents just said: 'No problem, we'll go out there and do it.' So those teams in the US put a lot of work into it as well and pretty much held nothing back in terms of what support and resources they could give. We got very little pushback in terms of the late-night deploying of informants or under-covers, agents being on hand for surveillance aspects – we didn't have any issues with that.

The HSI agents would later also assist gardaí in speaking
to members of the local communities and identifying people
with whom Aaron Brady associated in New York. Detective
Inspector Marry praised the assistance given by the HSI in the
investigation, particularly Special Agent Matt Katzke:

> I have to say, of all the police I have ever worked with
> during my career, Matt Katzke is without a doubt the most
> clued-in, helpful, understanding, and professional. I could
> not talk highly enough of him as a police officer, special
> agent, and downright good guy. All my correspondence
> concerning Adrian's case with Homeland Security was
> guided through Matt Katzke. Daily we would email or
> speak on the phone. I was informed a lot of what Aaron
> Brady was doing in New York, where he was working,
> where he socialised, and who he hung around with. Matt
> and his team were invaluable to us and our team when we
> descended on New York to make inquiries.

In one strategy meeting, the idea of placing an undercover
officer into Aaron Brady's environment with the hope that
he would befriend the suspect was again discussed. Gardaí
believed that Brady had already confided in people close to
him about his role in the murder but was surrounded by a
circle who were either too loyal or too afraid to speak out.
There was also an understanding between the agencies that
they had to operate within the parameters of both legal
systems, with Special Agent Crabb saying: 'Nothing we did
was outside of our authorisation or allowance based on police
procedure or law. I know some of the stuff we can do in the
US is not anything remotely close to what we can do in other

Detective Garda Adrian Donohoe, Reg Number 26222F, who was murdered at Lordship Credit Union on 25 January 2013.

Detective Garda Adrian Donohoe speaking with children at Bellurgan National School.

The crime scene at Lordship Credit Union near Dundalk, County Louth.

The Volkswagen Passat, used in the murder and robbery, burnt out at Cumsons Road, Newtownhamilton, South Armagh.

23/1/2013 03:17:59

James Flynn's BMW 5 Series on the main street in Clogherhead, County Louth, the night the getaway car was stolen from a house nearby.

Eugene Flynn Jnr captured on CCTV at Bellurgan filling station on the afternoon of the robbery.

Aaron Brady and James Flynn pictured socialising together while living in the United States in 2013.

Aaron Brady pictured by an NYPD surveillance team setting up a bouncy castle at a street fair in Woodlawn.

James Flynn (l) and Aaron Brady wearing balaclavas and posing with a firearm weeks before the murder and robbery.

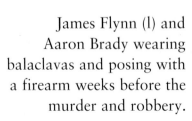

A tattoo on Brendan Treanor's back, drawn in 2018, depicting imagery linked to the murder and robbery which prosecutors claimed was a 'pictorial admission'.

Aaron Brady being arrested for immigration offences in Woodlawn in May 2018.

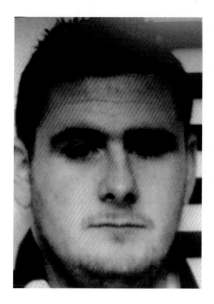

Brendan Treanor, identified by the Special Criminal Court as a member of the gang, but acquitted of robbery charges.

The Garda investigation team with members of Homeland Security after Aaron Brady was charged with capital murder.

Detective Inspector Pat Marry holding the capital murder charge sheet and his own retirement papers.

Senior counsel Michael O'Higgins who led Aaron Brady's defence team during the eight-month-long capital murder trial.

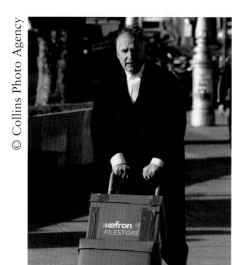

Senior counsel Brendan Grehan who oversaw the prosecution's case into the murder and robbery.

The garda investigation team, senior gardaí and officials from the Department of Homeland Security.

Homeland Security Special Agents Scott Crabb, Matt Katzke and Alex Hagedorn at Adrian Donohoe Pairc in 2018.

The grave of Detective Garda Adrian Donohoe.

countries. But everything we did we were allowed to do within our own authorities.'

By early 2017 the cooperation was in full flow when Colleen McCann was extradited from the United States to Ireland over the fatal road crash she'd been involved in five years earlier. James Flynn's fiancée appeared before a sitting of Carrickmacross District Court where she was charged with dangerous driving causing the death of Ciaran McKenna. Detective Garda John 'Bobby' Ogle objected to bail, alleging that McCann was a flight risk and that several previous attempts to interview or charge her were unsuccessful. In a tactic similar to the one employed by the Flynns in Boston, the detective said that on one occasion a relative of McCann said she would be available on a specific date when in fact she had already gone to America on that date. Evidence was also given that her father had tried to block access to the family residence and ordered gardaí to stay away. Colleen McCann was remanded in custody but was later granted bail.

*

That year the fourth anniversary of Detective Garda Donohoe's murder passed and, despite the in-depth garda investigation spanning the globe and generating thousands of lines of inquiry, the suspects were continuing to live outside the jurisdiction and no arrests had yet been made. The media interest had also dwindled in the intervening years, but there were sporadic press reports that covered the continuing garda inquiry. On 6 February 2017, *The Journal.ie* published an article on its website with the headline 'It won't be over until there's justice: Four years on from the murder of Adrian Donohoe'. The author, journalist

Garreth MacNamee, had spoken to members of the local community in the Cooley Peninsula about the lasting impact the murder had in the area. Local Sinn Féin councillor Antóin Watters was also interviewed for the article and spoke out about how there would never be closure in the case until there was justice for the murdered detective. 'It's something which will always be raw for people, and you can understand that completely,' he was quoted as saying. 'He was a man of the community, someone everyone who knew him would have looked up to. He was everything you'd want not just from a guard but from a local. I know the guards are doing all they can to catch the people who did it. I'm urging anyone who has any information to come forward as it might be the smallest detail which does it for the guards.'

After the article was published, Mr Watters shared a link to the story on his Facebook page. He was connected to thousands of people in the community through his role as a local representative but would have had little hope of his appeal striking a chord with those harbouring the gang and supporting them. Across the Atlantic in New York, the link popped up on the Facebook feed of a young man whom the councillor went to school with, and he scrolled down through the article. The man had some vital information about the case, having encountered Aaron Brady in New York, and decided to message Antóin Watters. Gardaí were about to get a significant breakthrough.

11

THE BREAKTHROUGH

Christopher Morton was born in Meigh, County Armagh, where he lived with his family of three brothers and two sisters. In 2009, at the age of just 20, he decided to emigrate to America where he began working as a barman in the Bronx, before moving up in the industry to become a manager. On the day Antóin Watters's news article was shared, he decided that someone finally had to speak out about the murder, typing up a message to the councillor and pressing send. On the other side of the Atlantic, Antóin Watters opened the unexpected mail from his former schoolmate, carefully reading the lengthy text.

Mr Morton wrote: 'How're you boss. Here the lad that's on the run for that gardas murder is living in the Bronx. If you can get in touch with the authorities that deal with it I can find out where he lives. He's a scumbag. Everyone knows who he is and where he is. I think the nypd would be more than happy to help if someone reached out. I'm not "touting" I'm just being responsible, and it'd be nice to have some justice for the mans family.' Having read the extraordinary message, the councillor rang Dundalk Garda Station and asked to speak with someone from the murder investigation team. Detective Inspector Marry was informed of the development by Detective Garda James Doherty and both discussed the potential value of the information.

James was excited, as he more than anyone else had generated thousands of lines of inquiry which often would not develop into any result. He knew the value of this type of information and he wanted it assigned with my blessing. I told James to assign it to me and I would deal with it. I had to be very private about this lead and keep my cards close to my chest. After several years of hard graft, this could be the break we were looking for. With the carry-on of senior management in the early days, and the leaking of information in newspaper reports, I could not trust any of them. I spoke with Antóin Watters, and he was very upfront, stating that Christopher Morton wanted someone from the investigation to contact him.

On the afternoon of 16 February, Detective Inspector Marry rang the number he had been given for Christopher Morton. The barman answered and relayed to him that the person who had shot the garda was in the United States, and spoke about an interaction he had had with him in a bar some years earlier. He also told the investigator that this individual admitted carrying out the murder to him. This man, Mr Morton said, was Aaron Brady. Despite the explosive revelation that Brady had confessed, the potential witness was reluctant to give a formal statement about the matter. However, Detective Inspector Marry believed that he could convince him to make a statement.

I kept in touch with Christopher Morton and my objective was to get him to make a statement, because the suspect had relayed to him his involvement in the murder of Detective Garda Adrian Donohoe. I just knew from talking to him that he had a conscience and that I just might make him see the value of putting what he knew on paper. Believe me, I appealed to the inner depths of his good nature to do the right thing. I got to know a good many personal details about Christopher, and we spoke openly about life in general. I found him to be a decent bloke with a sense of duty that I appealed to.

While efforts to convince Mr Morton to give a witness statement were ongoing, gardaí continued focusing on other avenues to target the gang. On 2 March, gardaí met with members of the Criminal Assets Bureau, the state agency that investigates the assets of criminals derived from illegal activity. Gardaí had already identified different assets linked to the suspects in Ireland, the US, and Spain, and were hoping to deprive them of their wealth from ill-gotten gains. That month a strategy meeting was also held with the HSI team to devise the next steps in terms of the US suspects. Detective Inspector Marry feared that his opportunity had passed after hearing no more from Christopher Morton, who in their last conversation had again stated his opposition to giving a statement:

There was a three-week period where I heard nothing from Christopher and his phone was off. I resigned myself to believing that I had lost this lead and that he had simply gotten fed up of me appealing for him to do the right thing. Out of the blue one evening, while I was walking my dog on Mornington beach, I received a phone call from Christopher, who apologised for the loss of communication. We had a lengthy call and he told me that he had difficulty because he was a member of Sinn Féin and, as far as he was aware, he could not make a statement to the gardaí without their approval. I assured him that would not be a problem and I would straight away try to resolve that issue for him.

Christopher told me that there were two people in particular whose opinions he valued, and he had asked both what they would do. The first person told him to forget about the gardaí, that they can't be trusted and not to cooperate. The second person, thankfully, told him to be a man, to stand up and do the right thing. Christopher had decided to go with the advice of the second person and, if he could get confirmation that the party was OK with it, wanted to make a statement. I introduced the reward but he shot me down and told me not to mention it. 'I don't want money, I am doing this for Adrian Donohoe's children, that's it,' he told me.

The next hurdle was to deal with the idea that Sinn Féin would for some reason prevent him from giving a statement. Detective Inspector Marry made contact with a sitting Sinn Féin TD and arranged a meeting, during which he explained his predicament to the politician, who didn't believe this would be a problem:

Two weeks passed before the TD made contact and we met again. They informed me that Christopher Morton was one of them and that word had been relayed to him

to go ahead and cooperate with the gardaí. This Sinn
Féin TD told me that, from the top, if Sinn Féin could
do anything whatsoever to assist in bringing the killers
of Adrian Donohoe to justice they would. The TD was
genuine and I informed them I may need their help in the
future. We shook hands, and it was a handshake of understanding and it was genuine.

In early May, Christopher Morton informed the senior
investigator that he was willing to make a statement, which
would have to be done on camera in a police station. He was
agreeable to this, and 15 May was set as the date that they
would meet in New York to listen to his story. A further obstacle Detective Inspector Marry faced was getting approval from
garda management to travel to the United States for this. The
investigation had progressed significantly to a point where that
month he was in contact with the DPP's office about Aaron
Brady's arrest and deportation back to Ireland.

One of Homeland Security's remits is that, when they
arrest a person for deportation, that person is given an
opportunity to confess to any crime they were involved in
either within or outside the United States. This was a strategy
that gardaí were considering deploying for Brady's arrest
for immigration offences, but potential legal difficulties this
could cause meant it had to be reviewed with state prosecutors. After speaking with the DPP's office, and consulting
HSI's strategy, Detective Inspector Marry was assured that
all was legally sound. He then made a case application to his
superiors seeking permission for him and Detective Garda
Bobby Ogle to travel to New York. It would cause issues that
they had previously experienced.

Within hours of sending this application up, I was hauled into the office of a senior garda and berated as he sat in his chair in front of a very large oak table opposite me. My chief superintendent was there, as were all types of senior management. I got a grilling and was asked if I could trust this witness and if he was a plant. I explained that I had all the checks done on him, including through our own Crime and Security branch, that I was a detective, and that I knew how to do my job. He then asked why I hadn't told my chief superintendent. I thought to myself how can I trust my chief superintendent, a man I didn't have respect for. Senior management had prevented my team from going to Australia and solving the Irene White murder. We had previously made good progress in the White murder investigation in 2016, and I wanted to send two of my detectives to Australia to take a statement. At a case conference I updated management about the need to send two detectives to Perth and was asked to put it in writing. I told them that everything was arranged for the trip the following week and that we only needed management approval. What happened next still to this day defies logic and common sense.

I got a phone call saying that the trip was being denied because the costings were out by €500. I explained the costings are approximate and can never be to the penny as the flights were booked at the best price available. I was told that if the witness was not there we would be ruined. I relayed this message to my team and they were equally devastated and upset at the attitude and stupidity, especially given all of the hard work that went on. Two months had passed and there was no change in the stance despite repeated requests. It was suggested by one high-ranking official whether the two highly professional detectives I had picked to go to Perth, a male and a female, might have an affair. I was stunned and shocked by this, and it was the straw that broke my resolve to listen to more incompetence.

I took the bull by the horns and told management that I would inform the families and the media that I was being prohibited from solving the murder of Irene White. The next day I was informed that the trip was sanctioned. Just like that. We had to put back in place everything we had in place two and a half months earlier. The statement subsequently resulted in us getting two murder convictions. Now, years later, I had the same issue with the Adrian Donohoe investigation.

By pure coincidence, just weeks prior to requesting permission to travel to the United States, the man suspected of physically carrying out the murder of Irene White was arrested on foot of the statement that had been supplied to detectives in Australia. But, once again, there was pushback from garda management to sanction a trip abroad for the purpose of taking a critical witness statement. Detective Inspector Marry took the decision to repeat the same threat he had made years earlier with the White case: if his application to travel to the United States and take a statement was refused, he would report to the media that garda management were preventing the solving of Adrian Donohoe's murder. The next day he got the go-ahead to fly to New York with Detective Garda Ogle.

*

On 15 May, they flew into JFK Airport and were collected by agents from Homeland Security before being brought to their offices in Manhattan. The meeting was arranged for that afternoon, and Detective Inspector Marry patiently waited on the street corner near the Federal Plaza building, praying that Mr Morton hadn't changed his mind. After waiting for several minutes, he saw a man he recognised appearing from the crowd and walking towards him. They shook hands before taking the short walk to the HSI office. They were brought into a large room with a conference table and black leather chairs, and a camera was also ready to record the interview. The room had been set up by HSI Special Agents Katzke and Mary Anne Wade, who were facilitating gardaí in any way possible to gather the crucial statement.

Christopher Morton began to talk, recalling how he had heard about the murder of Detective Garda Donohoe on the news the day after he had been shot dead. He then outlined his encounter with Aaron Brady in the early hours of the morning after a wedding in 2013, as he was drinking in the Tombstone Bar in the Bronx. Recalling the incident, he told the detectives: 'I went up to the bar to get a drink after I got there, there was a fella sitting next to his girlfriend. I asked him who he was, he gave the name Brady. I said I was Chris. I had heard stories of who was accused of shooting the garda and Aaron Brady was the name mentioned.'

Detective Garda Ogle was writing down his statement, and Mr Morton continued:

I had heard the name previously in different circles, but I didn't know him. I asked him straight out are you the lad that's on the run for shooting the garda, and he said:

'Yeah that's me I am the one that shot him.' He spoke [with a] normal demeanour, kind of scoffed it out. He didn't go into any detail. I laughed for a second, he didn't laugh back. I then felt uneasy, I was getting drinks and I bought him a Jameson. I joined my own company. I felt uneasy, we talked a bit about construction, and I moved on to my company.

Mr Morton said there was a lot of noise in the bar and he wasn't sure if Brady's girlfriend had heard the comment. He said that Brady didn't seem drunk to him and that he himself was tipsy. The bar manager said that the comment was on his mind and that he had thought about it several times over the next few years. He also went on to state: 'I thought about it a few times, then I seen the article on Facebook, it was around the anniversary of Detective Donohoe's murder. I then contacted Antóin. I had originally heard Aaron Brady's name from people in Woodlawn, the Bronx, and when this fella gave me his surname I then asked the question of him.' Having taken the statement, the detectives then undertook an identification process, showing the witness a mugshot of Aaron Brady to confirm it was the same individual he had spoken to. After looking at the image he said: 'I recognise the person in the photograph as Aaron Brady, the same Aaron Brady who when asked by me was he the lad on the run for the shooting of the garda he said: "Yeah that's me I am the one that shot him."' Mr Morton would also later clarify that the admission at the bar happened after the wedding of a couple from Crossmaglen at a hotel in Orange County. The wedding itself took place on 20 September, with celebrations continuing the following day in the Bronx bar. Detective Inspector Marry thanked the witness for his integrity and they chatted generally about how it was well-known in the Irish American community what Brady had done.

He said one thing to me that changed the focus of the investigation. He said that Aaron Brady was mouthing all over New York about the murder and there were other people who heard him talking about it. He said he knew some of them but he would not break confidence and would not tell me any names. I accepted this and I respected his stance. We parted with a solid handshake and a commitment to keep in touch.

Bobby Ogle and I needed to unwind and Homeland Security wanted us to visit an Irish pub in New York before we flew home. Well, the pints of Guinness were creamy, and they just kept flowing. We were on our fourth pint when Homeland Security stated that we had to go if we wanted to make our flight. We snuck in one more and headed off at high speed, lights and sirens blaring to get us to JFK. Bobby and I ran like hares to departures, where a worried-looking cabin-crew member shepherded us onto the flight. I can still see the people on the plane looking at us with curiosity.

The trip was the making of the case against Aaron Brady. On that flight back to Dublin Airport I thought about what Christopher Morton had said and came up with a plan. I turned to Bobby Ogle and told him: 'I know what my next step is, I'm going to get myself a burner phone and get posters drawn up asking for information with the number attached. I will get Homeland Security to put them up in pubs, coffee shops, electricity poles, and stores around Yonkers.' That was my next plan once we dealt with the deportation of Aaron Brady.

*

After arriving back in Dundalk, Detective Inspector Marry tasked the investigation team with assisting in the deportation process, including arranging emergency travel documents and sending over the arrest-warrant details to American officials. By the end of May 2017, undercover agents in the US had been watching Aaron Brady for several months. Speaking on the length of time and the circumstances surrounding this, Special Agent Crabb says:

It was a lot longer than we had hoped. It was a unique situation because we didn't have any cause or reason to remove him because we weren't aware of any crimes he was committing. We were also waiting on the Irish case. While we were watching him, we were also talking to people that were around him or connected to him or associates. People who had been around him and had heard him say things or had spoken to him about the incident … we often do this from an investigative standpoint, we leave the main player in place and develop some people around those subjects for additional information with willingness to support our efforts. That's what we were doing in that time.

The HSI agents decided to pounce on their target on 18 May. Shortly after 5 a.m. that morning, Brady left his home on Sterling Avenue where he was living with Danielle Healy,

whom he had married a month earlier on 12 April, and their
son. He reversed his black Audi out of the driveway and began
the journey to work in Manhattan that Thursday morning.
Unknown to Brady, he was being watched by the HSI team,
supported by US marshals and officers from the Immigration
and Customs Enforcement (ICE) office as he drove through
Yonkers. A suspect profile of Brady stated that he could try and
escape if cornered, and that he 'will use force to evade capture',
given his previous form for ramming gardaí in Dundalk.
This assessment, along with the fact that he was suspected of
shooting dead a law-enforcement official, meant the American
agents were taking no chances. After watching their target for
several minutes, the police convoy swarmed around Brady's car
and forced him to a sudden stop. Initially, he thought it might
have been a traffic stop, but the reality of what was happening
soon dawned on him: his time in America was coming to an
end. The agents asked him to identify himself and to hand over
any identification documents he had. Brady was then detained
and placed into the back of a police car before being driven
back to his home.

Special Agent Mary Ann Wade, a key member of the HSI
team in New York, knocked on the door and informed Danielle
Healy that her husband was being detained for immigration
offences and asked for his passport. The convoy of police cars
then drove to downtown Manhattan where they entered the
underground car park for the Federal Plaza Building. Brady
was placed into a holding cell for a short period before being
brought up to an interview room with Special Agents Wade
and Katzke. A camera was used to record the process as Brady
was questioned about the murder of Detective Garda Adrian
Donohoe, with him denying any involvement. Brady was then

taken through documentation relating to the immigration offences, before being asked if he understood it. Brady signed the papers and was then asked again about the murder and robbery at Lordship Credit Union, which again he denied, before speaking with an immigration attorney. His phone had been confiscated but it was briefly returned so he could speak to his wife, while his passport, wallet, and wedding band were also seized. The special agents placed him back into a holding cell before he was transferred to the Hudson County Correctional Center in Kearny, New Jersey, where he was held in custody for several days.

The minimum-security facility is where persons detained for immigration offences are brought to before their deportation. The centre has also been the subject of several critical reports over the quality of medical care as well as the poor quality food given to inmates being served on unwashed or dirty dishes. For Brady, it was a far cry from the life he had built for himself and which was now coming crashing down.

Back in Dundalk, gardaí were getting the paperwork in place for Brady's repatriation. Homeland Security needed travel documents in order to deport Brady, so Detective Garda James Doherty sent an email to the Irish consulate in Washington in relation to the repatriation efforts, which included a copy of the suspect's passport and details of the outstanding arrest warrants from Dundalk Circuit Court. A day later, emergency travel documents were issued for Brady.

The following Tuesday, 23 May, Brady was put on a prison bus with other detained persons and brought to the HSI building on Varick Street, New York, where he once again met the US agents. As part of the formal procedure, he also had to sign a document stating that he would not cause any trouble on the plane back to Ireland. The agents transported Brady to JFK Airport, where he was escorted in handcuffs through a security entrance. He knew what was awaiting him in Ireland and protested that he wanted to be brought to the UK, but he was placed on a flight back to Dublin Airport, where gardaí were waiting for him.

Sergeant John Moroney was informed that Brady was due to arrive in Dublin the following morning, and he travelled to the airport with gardaí Dave Buckley and Paul Connolly. They went into Terminal 2 and through the security area, where they waited for the fugitive to be brought in by the American agents. Brady walked in front of the HSI officials, who were closely behind, and made his way up the escalator, where he was arrested at 7.23 a.m. by Sergeant Moroney on foot of the bench warrants issued four years earlier. The gardaí and Brady were escorted out of the terminal by airport police before driving up the M1 motorway to Dundalk.

Appearing before a judge that morning, Brady was asked why he had gone to America, with his barrister stating that Brady had family there. There was no mention of the fact that he was also a suspect in the murder of Detective Garda Donohoe. No application for bail was made, and he was remanded in custody to appear in court again the following week for sentencing. Another man present in the court building that day was Eugene Flynn Snr, who had not been listed for any hearing. When gardaí approached him and asked if he was on the court list for a case, he told them: 'No, do you want to put me on it?' Gardaí noted of the encounter that he was not impressed at being spoken to and that he was well disguised, wearing a blue shirt, jeans, paddy cap, and a pair of sunglasses – not attire usually worn in a courtroom.

Investigators believed he was there to check on the progress of the case against Brady.

On Wednesday 31 May, Aaron Brady was back before Dundalk Circuit Court for his sentencing hearing. A character reference was handed in by his former coach at Crossmaglen Rangers, who described him as 'a prodigious player' as well as 'reliable and trustworthy'. They were characterisations of Brady that gardaí investigating the murder of their colleague would disagree with. Aaron Brady's family were also present at the hearing to support him, including his father Tony, sister Sonya, and his wife Danielle, who had returned from New York to be with her husband. His defence barrister claimed that his client was 'a different person' from the one shown on the CCTV footage from the day of the incident. In evidence, Sergeant Moroney said that Brady had a number of convictions for road-traffic and public-order offences, adding that he believed he used cocaine. Brady's barrister said his client had tested negative for drugs in a test required for US citizenship, for which he had applied. The judge directed that €400 be given to the Golf owner and €500 to the taxi driver forced on to the pavement. The judge handed him a sentence of one year's imprisonment, with the final six months suspended, for dangerous driving, using a stolen car, and criminal damage.

The DPP subsequently appealed the sentence given to Brady on the grounds that it was unduly lenient. The state argued this on the basis of the number of people that were put at risk of injury, the extent of the damage to property, and the persistent nature of the offending over a short period of time, in addition to the existence of relevant previous convictions. The Court of Appeal found that the seriousness of the offences was beyond question, with the sentencing judge seeing the CCTV footage and witnessing 'first-hand the carnage inflicted on the town of Dundalk over a relatively short period of time'. The court also said that the gap between the date of the offence and the sentencing date were considerable but were 'entirely caused by the respondent'. The three presiding judges agreed with the state's application and resentenced Brady to two years' imprisonment, suspending the final 12 months of the term.

Some weeks later Christopher Morton gave an additional statement to gardaí about Aaron Brady. Mr Morton told Detective Sergeants Phillips and Clancy that he had heard from about 15 to 20 people that Brady had shot a guard in Ireland before his early morning conversation with him. Talking about that interaction, he also said:

> I didn't mention it in my earlier statement because I was a bit nervous but about twenty minutes after I left Aaron Brady's company I saw him taking cocaine in the bathroom. I saw him with a wee Ziploc bag of white powder. He took out some of the white powder on a key and sniffed it with both nostrils. Then he handed the bag to a fella standing behind him. I don't want to say who he was. The bag was roughly 3 inches x 2 inches in size … I want to say that I had never seen the fella at the bar who said he was Aaron Brady before that night. I never saw him after that night. When Aaron Brady was arrested in New York in May 2017, everyone thought it was because he had shot the guard. It was only when it was on the RTÉ news website that I knew that it was for something different.

The ruling by the Court of Appeal meant that Brady would spend several months behind bars and was not due for release until the following February. It also gave gardaí more time to compile further evidence to arrest and charge him with the murder. He had left the country once before, and if he wasn't detained upon his release, there would be nothing stopping him from fleeing again. The clock was ticking.

12

THE MOST FEARED
MAN IN IRELAND

Gardaí believed there were many others that Aaron Brady had confessed to while living in the United States, and the process now began of identifying more people who could assist the investigation. Detective Inspector Marry put plans in place for the poster campaign he'd thought of while on the plane back to Ireland, and he tasked his team with drawing up the placards. The posters contained information about the murder of Detective Garda Donohoe, the €100,000 reward in place for information, and the number of the burner phone that the senior investigator had purchased specifically for the campaign so that he could be contacted in confidence.

Detective Inspector Marry also did an interview with the *Irish Central*, a newspaper catering for the Irish diaspora in New York. The article highlighted the appeal for information and detailed how the chief suspect, referring to Brady but not naming him, hadn't kept a low profile while living in Woodlawn but instead used his given name and maintained a circle of friends. It also stressed that the suspect was not part of a paramilitary gang or larger criminal network that could lead to any reprisals. HSI agents assisted in placing the posters in shops and pubs around Woodlawn in the hope that people who knew first-hand of Brady's involvement in the Lordship murder and robbery would come forward. Detective Inspector Marry kept the plan confined to only a small number of people, and in the initial stages it seemed that it was a futile exercise. However, two weeks later, in the middle of June, he received an unexpected phone call.

I was driving home from work and the burner phone started ringing. I pulled into the side of the road and answered. A guy on the other end of the line asked: 'Are you the buck looking after the murder of the garda?' I told him I was and he responded: 'I will tell you every-thing there is to know about Aaron Brady when he was out here.' I rustled around the car for a notepad to write down what could be significant information but couldn't find one. I had to rip a Strepsil box down the middle to jot down what this guy was telling me, and this would become an exhibit in the case.

The anonymous caller didn't ask about the reward or have any interest in giving a statement; he simply wanted to tell the investigation team about the life Brady had been living in New York and who to approach. The caller said that Aaron Brady had been working with Empire Pile construction, and he had bragged to his co-workers that he was involved in diesel laundering back home, having worked for the Border Fox. This was the moniker given to the dangerous dissident terrorist Dessie O'Hare, from Keady in Armagh, who has previously been linked to both the IRA and the INLA. In 1988

he was sentenced to 40 years' imprisonment for kidnapping
and mutilating a Dublin dentist, Dr John O'Grady, but was
released early under the terms of the Good Friday Agreement.
O'Hare continued to be involved in cross-border crime, but
whether Aaron Brady worked for him, or if this was just a
delusional boast, was never established. The anonymous caller
also gave the names of two people who had worked with Brady
on site in New York and whom he was close to – one of whom
was a man called Tommy McGeary from Armagh. It was the
only phone call that Detective Inspector Marry received on the
burner phone as a result of the poster campaign but it would
yield significant leads.

> The names given by the caller meant nothing to me, and
> they were not names we knew to be associated with Aaron
> Brady. I didn't delay in putting together a team to travel
> to New York to liaise with Homeland Security and iden-
> tify these people who had befriended Brady while he was
> living there. The team were also tasked with contacting
> his employers and making general enquiries about him,
> while myself and Detective Garda Doherty concentrated
> on two other suspects who were living in Boston.

James Flynn was continuing to reside openly between Boston
and Northern Ireland in 2017, working in his snow-clearing
and tarmacking businesses, while staying out of the garda's
jurisdiction. But he was within the reach of HSI agents based
in London, who attempted to speak with him on 6 June 2017,
at Belfast International Airport. As Flynn walked through the
arrivals terminal with his fiancée, Colleen McCann, he was
approached by Special Agent Katzke, who asked him about

giving a statement about the shooting of Detective Garda Donohoe. The couple agreed to speak with him, and they all convened to a nearby coffee shop. During the conversation, Flynn outlined the dangers associated with speaking to authorities in the border region, telling the agent that people 'get a bullet for talking'. He also asked Katzke during the encounter about the possibility of a deal, saying that he needed protection and that, once he had this, he could possibly offer something if he heard anything.

Flynn also moaned about the gardaí investigating the murder and robbery, telling the US agent: 'They don't want to offer people anything, they just want to terrorise people.' Special Agent Katzke suggested he could help Flynn's brother with an outstanding issue in the United States, while emphasising that he wanted information in relation to the prosecution of Aaron Brady. Flynn appeared amenable to meeting the agent again, and they parted company. Any possibility of Flynn turning on his former best friend, however, was short-lived. Two days later, he sent the agent an audio tape of their conversation via WhatsApp, which had been surreptitiously recorded, along with an image of a recording device. It was clear from the communication that Flynn was playing games with the agent and had no intention of making a formal statement, sticking to the Armagh code of omertà.

*

Further plans were being put in place to advance the American angle of the investigation with four gardaí travelling to the United States on 28 August 2017. Detective Sergeant Kieran Reidy and Detective Gardaí Paul Gill and Padraig O'Reilly would go to New York to speak with one of Aaron Brady's associates identified by the anonymous caller, while Detective Inspector Marry and Detective Garda Doherty travelled to Massachusetts to brief local prosecutors on their investigation into the Flynns. On arrival in Boston, they gave a presentation to the Massachusetts State Police and the Norfolk County district attorney, outlining their case against the Flynns while asking for support from local agencies. Recalling the meeting, Detective Inspector Marry says:

> I remember going to a government building in Boston and the district attorney had assembled a representative from each arm of law enforcement as well as revenue, customs, intelligence, and so on. It was a daunting task but we nailed it with our PowerPoint presentation. The district attorney assured us that he would help in any way he could to bring the murderers of Detective Garda Donohoe to justice. His name was Morrissey, and he told us his ancestors came from Ireland.
>
> We were exhausted and found a craft beer bar to go to. As we sat outside my phone rang – it was Detective Sergeant Reidy, who was in New York. He informed me that they had no joy with some of the people on the list they were given and were making efforts to locate an address for another associate of Brady who had worked with him in construction. Homeland Security managed to get an address for his girlfriend's house and Detective Sergeant Reidy said they went there in an attempt to locate Brady's associate, Tommy McGeary, who was living illegally in the United States.

That afternoon Molly Staunton opened the door of her grandmother's house in New York. A US citizen, her parents are of Irish heritage, and she had been raised in the Bronx but often travelled to her ancestral home in Mayo. The detectives told her that they were there looking for her boyfriend, Tommy McGeary, but she informed them they had broken up. The gardaí were initially dejected, but their mood quickly changed when the young woman told them that she had information about the crime they were inquiring about. She said her boyfriend had shared a house with Aaron Brady and that she herself had heard him confessing to the murder. She agreed to go to the police station and make a statement, sitting down with Detective Gardaí Gill and O'Reilly to outline what she had heard.

The detectives started by saying they believed she had information to assist their investigation and reminded her that she was free to leave at any stage, as this was a 100 per cent voluntary process. Detective Garda Gill then asked her to tell them in her own words what she knew about the murder. Referring to Brady, she told them: 'Well, he definitely said himself that he murdered a cop or a detective.'

She recalled one incident when she went back to the house that her boyfriend shared with Brady:

Aaron came out of his room and he was crying, he looked very distressed. He was talking about how he shot a cop in Ireland and how there were cops in Ireland looking for him. This happened at Aaron Brady's house. When I walked into the house Tommy was in the house and Ronan Flynn was sitting on a different couch. Then Aaron came out of his room and said all this, Ronan told him

to calm down. Aaron was drunk. [He said] they were the
biggest gangsters in Ireland. I was in total shock by this.

The young Irish American woman was wearing a Mayo
Gaelic football top as she sat in the interview room, recalling
how Brady had spoken about the murder 'a few times' in front
of her. 'There was one time he just exploded when he was
talking about how he needed money and that he killed a cop
and that I can't tell anyone, he would try not to talk about it
too much, but he definitely said he killed a cop over there.' She
also told gardaí that Brady bragged that 'he's the most feared
man in Ireland' and that 'they were the biggest gangsters in
Armagh'. Ms Staunton recalled seeing a news article about
Brady referencing a 'cop murderer' but couldn't remember if it
was shown to her by him or McGeary.

The information was highly significant and boosted the case
against Aaron Brady as the triggerman. According to Detective
Inspector Marry:

We all knew this was another breakthrough in the case.
I told Detective Sergeant Reidy we would fly down to
meet him and discuss tactics. By this time we had a new
divisional officer in Louth: Chief Superintendent Christy
Mangan, a gentleman, an investigator, and a man's man.
He is someone you could trust and by far the best chief
superintendent the Louth division has ever had. I informed
him of our breakthrough, and he congratulated the team.
In New York I evaluated what had been achieved and
what was left to do. I decided we would return home and
make a further application to travel to back again, as I
could see an ocean of work to be done. There would be

several more trips to the United States as part of the investigation, and I would make sure all members of the team had an opportunity to travel there and get the experience of working with Homeland Security. It would stand to them as investigators long after I retired.

Gardaí had learned from Molly Staunton's statement that, on at least one occasion, the other two men he was living with had heard him confess to murder. Given that the three men were all friends, and because of Brady's volatile nature, they assumed there were other occasions too when he'd confessed to shooting Detective Garda Donohoe. Ronan Flynn, originally from County Louth and a cousin of the Flynns, had known Brady before they met in New York and had himself arrived in the United States around 2012. Ronan Flynn also had something in common with Aaron Brady: he too was being sought by gardaí.

On 6 August 2011, Tommy Eccles was handing out anti-drugs literature at John Long's pub in Carlingford, County Louth. Eccles and a fellow member of the local Sinn Féin branch in Cooley were distributing the leaflets when he asked for a poster to be put up in the pub. He got into a heated exchange with a customer before he was grabbed by his coat and subjected to a violent assault. Eccles was kicked in the head and had a pool ball smashed into the side of his face, spending several weeks in hospital recovering. Eccles himself was no stranger to violence and bloodshed – he had previously been sentenced to 40 years' imprisonment for the murder of Detective Garda Frank Hand during an IRA robbery at Drumcree post office in County Meath on 10 August 1985. However, he'd been released early from his sentence under the terms of the Good Friday Agreement.

Gardaí investigating the assault on Tommy Eccles identified two suspects, Ronan Flynn and a male relative of his,
with the DPP directing that Flynn should be charged with
assault causing serious harm, the highest level of assault, which
carries a maximum sentence of life imprisonment on conviction. However, Ronan Flynn had already left Ireland, and a
European arrest warrant was issued by the High Court for his
removal back to the country. Over the following years Flynn
lived on the East Coast of the United States, residing in New
York and working as a barman, despite living there illegally. In
late October 2017, he was detained by HSI agents in relation to
immigration offences and, after being processed, was asked if
he wanted to speak to gardaí about the Lordship murder and
robbery. On 25 October 2017, Detective Sergeant Mark Phillips
as well as Detective Gardaí Paul Gill and Padraig O'Reilly sat
down with Ronan Flynn in an interview room of Yonkers Police
Station and took a formal witness statement from him.

Fidgeting with a plastic bottle as he sat in the chair, the
witness relayed to gardaí what Brady had told him. 'He said:
"I shot him, so what" in our house in Yonkers. He admitted
it, man. On more than one occasion he admitted it himself
right in my face, in front of Tommy as well, he just said it.' The
detectives asked the witness what his reaction was to being told
by someone that they had shot a policeman, reassuring him
that, if it was negative, he wasn't insulting them and that they
weren't concerned with what he thought. The witness couldn't
recall his reaction but said that he believed Aaron Brady. When
pressed on why he believed him, he said: 'Because I know what
he's like, I lived with him. He'd do something stupid like that,
he'd act before he'd think.' He also went on to say that he was
'100 per cent sure' that Aaron Brady and Brendan Treanor

robbed the car in the murder and, in a damning remark on his cousin's intelligence, said that James Flynn wouldn't 'have the brains to rob the car'.

He told gardaí that one of Brady's closest friends from Armagh, who was now living in the US, had also told him about Brady's role in the murder. The witness went on to say that Aaron Brady would 'try not to talk about' the murder but that when he was drunk, he would 'spill the beans on everything, saying that he shot him and all this'. The details within the statement were similar to Ms Staunton's recollection of the confession and corroborated her version of events. Ronan Flynn also told gardaí that Brady said he was involved in the armed robbery of a service station in Castlebellingham, County Louth, in January 2011.

The detectives left Yonkers Police Station with another critical statement implicating Aaron Brady as the shooter. In a later development, Tommy Eccles withdrew his complaint over the assault, while the other suspect in the attack had already been acquitted following a trial. Given these factors, the DPP decided to drop the charges against Ronan Flynn and withdraw the European arrest warrant.

*

Other witnesses who came forward were more disingenuous and had their own reasons to assist the investigation. As part of the inquiries made in America, one individual approached gardaí and said he had information relating to Aaron Brady. However, when gardaí met the man, he told them that he would say whatever they wanted him to. Gardaí immediately stopped the interview and didn't take a statement from the individual.

One detective said of this: 'There was no chance of taking a statement from this person after this proposition was made. Gardaí only wanted the truth from people.'

Aaron Brady's alibi on the night of the murder was also broken that autumn. Colin Hoey, who had been living with Brady in Lough Road at the time of the robbery, had originally told gardaí that both his housemate and James Flynn were at the house on the night of the raid between 9.15 p.m. and 10.45 p.m. Four years on, however, Hoey had a change of mind and walked into Carrickmacross Garda Station with his father. He told gardaí that he wanted to withdraw his initial statement, as he could not stand over what he had said at the time, and was now stating that he had not seen either suspect 'at all' on the day of the robbery. This crucial development meant that the alibi put forward by Brady for his whereabouts at the time of the murder and robbery was clearly false.

The HSI team continued identifying and tracking down witnesses for the garda investigation team, with teams of detectives regularly flying to New York and Boston to gather more witness statements. Almost 100 people were identified as potentially having information pertinent to the inquiry, with the majority of these based in or around Woodlawn while 18 were based in the Massachusetts city. Special Agent Scott Crabb says that his colleague Special Agent Katzke was 'phenomenal' in dealing with potential witnesses and bringing some emotional aspects into the equation when there were doubts about cooperating and stepping up against Brady. 'But there was a massive apprehension,' he says.

People were afraid of [Brady]. I do recall people saying they were afraid of him and his connections – there were times where maybe there were confrontations previous to our involvement with Aaron Brady and so there was still that lingering impact. And I do recall Matt and Pat and the team having trouble trying to get people to cooperate, but there were some people who came forward after some conversations that happened. I'd gone on the initial occasion with Pat, his team, and Matt to New York to pitch this effort to our officers there.

On 28 November, gardaí tracked down Tommy McGeary, who agreed to go with detectives to the HSI building at Federal Plaza in New York. He had initially travelled to the US in 2014 on a three-month visa and got a job with Eugene Flynn Jnr, working for their snow-ploughing businesses and earning good money. In January 2016 he wanted a change of scenery, though, and decided to move down to New York. While working in Boston he had gotten to know Ronan Flynn, and he moved in with him and Aaron Brady at 1st Street in Yonkers. He recalled hearing about the murder of Adrian Donohoe before he'd left Ireland through news articles and reports on RTÉ, but said he didn't know who was responsible until he got to America. Not long after arriving, he said, he had read an article which stated that two suspects were brothers who were living in the United States and running a tarmac business. A relative of the Flynn brothers later told him that the article was about them. McGeary told gardaí that Aaron Brady was trying to 'suss him out' about his time with the Flynns and asked if the brothers had enquired about him. McGeary told him they hadn't and that he had his own problems with them.

In his statement to Detective Sergeant Phillips and Detective Garda McGovern, the Armagh man said that about three weeks after moving into the apartment he was playing darts and drinking with Brady.

It was on my mind to ask Aaron Brady about what people were saying about him and his involvement in the murder of Garda Adrian. It had been on my mind since I had moved in with him. Ronan Flynn had never said to me that I would be living in the same apartment as Brady. I knew that I would probably bump into Brady around the area but not actually be living with him. I said to Aaron Brady that 'I want to address the elephant in the room'. These were my exact words to him – the elephant in the room was with regard to what the papers were saying about the murder of Garda Adrian Donohoe, what people in the Woodlawn area were saying about Aaron – that Aaron had killed Garda Adrian, every man, woman and child in the Woodlawn area were saying it about Brady – that he killed Garda Adrian ... when I told Aaron Brady that I wanted to address the elephant in the room I also said to him at the same time 'Was it true what the papers were saying and what other people were saying in relation to the murder of Garda Donohoe' and he said to me 'Yeah I was there and you know the man capable of it – Benny'. Brady said to me 'They are never going to get me, I am here that long'. I remember him saying this to me at the time. I understood this Benny to be Benny Treanor who I have heard numerous stories about in the past.

McGeary continued relaying the interaction with Brady, saying he was 'shocked' by what he had heard. 'I didn't quiz him about what he had said – I was concerned about what he had said to me as I was living in the same apartment as him, and he was in the room next to me.' He said he told his father about this, who advised him that living with Brady was 'bad news'.

McGeary recalled another incident during a house party in their apartment attended by six people, including Aaron Brady, who he said was 'doing his party piece stuff' and mixing songs including rave tunes and the Wolfe Tones. McGeary stated that a 'random fella from Cork' was also present and asked Brady out of the blue if it was true what the papers were saying about him. 'Brady was sitting on the couch and he replied to the random fella: "Yeah. What are you going to do about it." I was standing playing the darts and I heard this. Again I was shocked by what Brady had said,' he told gardaí of the nonchalant confession. He added that the only articles he had read referred to Brady as the shooter and that 'Brady himself often said this to me that they were accusing him of being the shooter in the murder of Garda Adrian in the newspapers.' He added that after the Cork man had left, another person in the group asked Aaron Brady if he had shot the guard, to which he responded: 'Yeah, I shot him.' In his statement, McGeary said that he was standing on the countertop when he heard this and that there was an awkward silence afterwards. 'I was shocked when he said this; I remember saying in my head "Holy fuck". A couple or more songs were played, Brady was singing and shouting out loud ... it was either during or after this song that Aaron Brady got very emotional and he started crying in front of us.' After that, the party fizzled out and everybody left.

McGeary told gardaí about another occasion weeks later in which he discussed stolen cars with Aaron Brady while they were on a lunch break from work. A friend of his had had his car stolen in Tyrone, and he was enquiring if Brady had heard who stole it. He said Aaron Brady told him about how he used to steal cars – either by taking a vehicle for a test drive and not returning or by carrying out a creeper burglary.

Brady said his crew used to travel into the South of Ireland, not on their own home patch, where they would steal cars. During this same conversation, Brady told me that the only car he robbed close to home was in Clogherhead. Brady told me that this car was a Volkswagen Passat and that they kept this car for a while and that this car was the one that he used in the Lordship [robbery] when the Garda was killed. Brady told me that there was stuff in the Passat that he fucked out, just threw out … Brady also told me that in relation to the Passat which he stole in Clogherhead that as well as what he threw out, he also changed the number plates on the Passat like he always did with all the other cars he had stolen.

Later on in his statement he told the detectives:

Aaron told me that him and his crew were doing and had done robberies like the Lordship incident, he told me that they robbed cars and that he was one of the best in the business at stealing cars and that they used to break them up for parts and get good money for the parts. He also told me that they were doing burglaries, that they had stolen red farm quads and trailers.

Tommy McGeary named four of Aaron Brady's friends in New York who had told him that Brady was the shooter in the Lordship robbery. He recalled another incident when an Irish American man confronted Brady in Moriarty's Bar on McClean Avenue. The man asked Brady if he'd done it, referring to the murder, to which he responded: 'Yeah, I done it.' The two men had a fight later that night, resulting in Brady being barred from the pub. Detectives later attempted to speak to these people about the chief suspect's admission, but they refused to cooperate and were categorised as persons of interest in the investigation.

McGeary also told gardaí that, when he informed James Flynn of Brady's arrest, Flynn responded by saying: 'Sure doesn't he deserve it, wasn't he there.' Eugene Flynn Jnr, he added, responded similarly and told him: 'Sure didn't he do it.' As gardaí were finishing taking his detailed statement and vivid recollection of events, McGeary told them: 'I just want to add that in any of the times I've spoken to Aaron Brady in relation to what Aaron Brady told me he had done regarding the shooting of the guard Adrian; he never showed any remorse or regret for what he had done.' He also said that his reason for giving the statement was because it was the right thing to do, adding: 'I want to help in any way I can now and in the future and I want to help Adrian's wife and two children. I am coming forward because of the information that Aaron Brady told me about what he did at Lordship on the night Garda Adrian was killed. That's why I am here telling you this.' After giving his statement, McGeary voluntarily agreed to be deported back to Ireland, having overstayed his welcome in the United States.

13

'KEEP YOUR MOUTH SHUT'

Two days after their interview with Tommy McGeary, which secured yet another crucial statement implicating Aaron Brady as the gunman, the garda investigation team were given the name of a person who could also possibly assist the inquiry. Detective Sergeant Phillips and Detective Garda McGovern met with Anthony Maguire, from County Armagh and a cousin of Christopher Morton, at his house in New York. The carpenter said he was initially scared to come forward, as he had been warned to keep his mouth shut about an interaction he had had with Brady. 'I have been scared but they shouldn't be getting away with it,' he told the detectives, before going on to recount the events of St Patrick's Day 2015 in a witness statement.

Anthony Maguire said he'd gone to the Coachman's Inn in Woodlawn to cash a work cheque at around 9 p.m. that night and ordered a glass of water. While waiting for his money in the bar, which was packed with people, he said he noticed a 'blocky fella' wearing a green Irish soccer jersey sitting with three other people, including a tall guy and a man with ginger hair.

These guys were having a conversation. The nature of the conversation was 'Do you think you have what it takes to kill a man'. The blocky man in the green jersey said those exact words. The other three of his friends were saying 'I don't know' or 'Maybe'. These four guys were right beside me. The blocky fella was right beside me. I was listening to this conversation. I'm saying to myself 'Who are these guys talking about, what it takes to kill a man'. The ginger fella whispered something in the blocky fellas ear. Immediately the blocky fella in the jersey turned to me and said: 'Well, do you think you have what it takes to kill a man?' I replied 'No, why do you?' He said, 'Yes that's the reason I'm over here, I shot that guard in Louth'. I automatically linked his comment to the Guard who had been shot in Dundalk a couple of years earlier.

Anthony Maguire recalled that he was drinking his water as he heard this and got a lump in his throat, becoming angry at the blocky man's attitude, as if 'he didn't care'. Mr Maguire said he asked the man: 'Do you think you're cool bragging about shooting a Guard, you're a scumbag.' He said this was the last thing he said to the man, and he took his money from the cashed cheque and walked out of the bar. Unfortunately for him it wasn't the end of the matter.

Just as I got onto the street, I felt two hands push me very hard into my back, it moved me along the street a good bit. I turned around and saw the blocky fella in the green jersey standing there on the street. He immediately hit me with his right fist just over my left eye. He bursted me open, there was a lot of blood. He then hit me with his left fist and right fist. I fell to the ground. He knelt down and put his right knee to my neck. He said, 'Keep your mouth shut or you know what will happen you'. I saw the ginger fella coming from the bar a bit up the street. I heard him say 'Cmon Aaron, cmon Aaron'. The ginger fella lifted Aaron off me and broke up the fight.

Mr Maguire told the detectives that the fight was over quickly, and he used his T-shirt to stem the blood oozing from his head wound, before getting a taxi home. He knew the man who assaulted him had a Crossmaglen accent and began searching on Facebook for people with the name Aaron from the South Armagh village. He came across a picture of a Crossmaglen Rangers team and the person who had attacked him was in the photo. A name underneath the picture identified this man as Aaron Brady. 'I didn't report the assault to the Police. The only thing that people knew was that I had been fighting. I did not tell them anything about who had assaulted me out of fear and because I had been threatened not to open my mouth. Up until now I have been keeping this in because I didn't know what these guys are capable of,' Mr Maguire said.

The carpenter had a scar over his left eye from the attack carried out by Aaron Brady, and he allowed gardaí to take a photograph of the wound. After recounting the assault and confession, Anthony Maguire told the detectives: 'I want to add that I had told you this today because I don't feel that Aaron Brady should get away with it. I was scared to step up but now I am willing to do all I can to help. I'm 100 per cent happy with what I have told you and I will have no problem meeting you again if you need.'

He later gave an additional statement to gardaí, saying that he bumped into Aaron Brady at a bar called St Pats on 22 June 2016, when he was going to watch the European Championship football match between Ireland and Italy. Mr Maguire said Brady was with an older man and woman, who he assumed were his parents, and that the murder suspect looked at him as they walked by one another before looking away. He added that he had told Christopher Morton in a conversation in 2017 that it was Aaron Brady who had assaulted him after confessing to shooting a guard in Ireland. The account given in this conversation was also corroborated in an additional statement by Mr Morton to gardaí.

Aaron Brady's release from jail over the dangerous-driving incident was approaching, and gardaí began making preparations to arrest him for the murder and robbery. In a report to the DPP on 3 December 2017, Detective Inspector Marry outlined the evidence pertaining to Brady up to that point. This included that Brady, and his criminal gang, were linked to 12 creeper-style burglaries through mobile-phone analysis, while the statement from Ronan Flynn linked him to the armed robbery of the Apple Green service station in Castlebellingham, County Louth, in January 2011. The crime involved a similar modus operandi to the Lordship raid, with the getaway car also stolen in a creeper burglary before being burnt out after the robbery. Detective Inspector Marry noted Brady's close association and interactions with suspects James Flynn and Benny Treanor, and that they were in Flynn's car driving past and 'casing' the credit union on the afternoon of the robbery.

There was also the evidence relating to the theft of the jeep and shotgun from Kingscourt, County Cavan, on 9 September 2012. Call-data analysis identified that Treanor and Brady were in phone contact near this location around the time of the burglary, with Treanor's phone pinging off a phone mast in Kingscourt that night. Gardaí suspected this weapon was the shotgun used in the murder. However, despite the best efforts of investigators, the owner of the jeep refused to make a statement about the theft of his vehicle and the shotgun. Detective Garda Joe Ryan also watched the footage of Brady and Flynn in balaclavas and identified the masks as being similar to the ones worn by the raiders, providing another potential link to the robbery.

Other evidence included the phone blackout during the robbery, statements from Jessica King and her family, who said that Brady didn't arrive at their home until after 11 p.m. on the night of the murder, discrepancies in Brady's own statements, his alibis that were broken by witnesses retracting previous claims, and his own admissions to people in the United States.

Gardaí had also taken another statement that showed that Aaron Brady had previously been at the remote laneway on Cumsons Road where the stolen Passat used in the Lordship raid was later found. A man who lived in the area told gardaí that in the early hours of 16 June 2012, he had been awoken by the noise of a van driving up the laneway, around 150 metres as the crow flies from the burn site. At the time a lot of laundered fuel waste was being dumped in the area, and he believed the van was there for this reason. He said he got out of bed and into his car to confront the suspected diesel waste dumpers. As he reached the van at a junction near Chalybeate Road, he saw two young men pushing a diesel waste cube out of the back of the vehicle. The van fled but he gave chase and contacted both the PSNI and gardaí as he did so.

The witness also noticed the registration of the white Ford Transit van, which he relayed to authorities: 01-D-92824. It was the same van model and registration plate as that of a vehicle previously photographed at the diesel-laundering yard at 155 Concession Road. These images had been recovered from the mobile phone of Eugene Flynn Snr and were, by coincidence, taken on the day of the Lordship robbery.

The farmer told gardaí that he followed the van, which had a flat tyre, past Cortamlet Primary School and onwards in the direction of Castleblayney. As he pursued the van, just before the border crossing, a silver Peugeot emerged on the road and pulled out in front of him, swerving so as not to let him past. He believed the car was linked to the van and preventing him from getting closer to it. The pursuit continued for another few miles in the direction of Cullyhanna until the witness said he got cold feet, as he wasn't familiar with the area. He pulled back and again contacted the authorities. Gardaí had also previously received intelligence that the same van described by the farmer was being used by Aaron Brady and James Flynn. It was another piece of evidence linking the pair to the rural location where the raiders had abandoned the getaway car.

Other potential witnesses were uncovered by going over previous lines of inquiry, with Detective Inspector Marry explaining:

One of the strategies was of course to recap all of the jobs generated, and my incident-room coordinator, Detective Garda James Doherty, brought to my attention a job that was generated when I was not running the investigation. The job referred to a garda member in Cork who alleged his friend had encountered Aaron Brady in New York

and had socialised with him. The report associated with
the job revealed the garda member would not give his
friend's name, as he did not want to get involved. This was
certainly a job that, in my mind, was not bottomed out
and should have been pursued.

I spoke to the garda in Cork and he relayed to me that
he did not want to give his friend's name, as he had asked
not to be identified. I was furious and told him: 'You
contacted the incident room with this information and
don't for one minute think I will not follow this through.
A potential witness, your friend, may be in a position to
help.' He still declined to give the name and I went to my
superiors, asking that this garda's chief superintendent
be informed of his unwillingness to cooperate with the
investigation into the murder of a colleague. I did hint
I would arrest the garda for withholding information.
Anyway, the guard saw sense after being spoken to by his
seniors and he rang me with the name and phone number
of his friend.

On 19 January, Detective Inspector Marry spoke to the
man, who stated that he had previously been living in an
apartment on Katonah Avenue in Woodlawn with another
guy and a girl. They had been asked to put a guy up on their
couch for a few days, with the request made by people from
the Carrickmackross and Crossmaglen areas. The witness,
who was from Cork, said that he played for the New York
Cork GAA team and that there was an understanding between
Carrickmacross and Crossmaglen GAA and the club from his
home county. The man went on to tell Detective Inspector
Marry that the person they were asked to put up was Aaron

Brady. He said he knew nothing about him prior to housing him and that they socialised nearly every night for two weeks when he stayed with them. In that time there was no mention of the garda murder, and the housemates had no reason to suspect there was anything untoward about their lodger.

However, he told the senior detective that later on 'one of the Armagh boys let it be known that Aaron Brady had a violent streak and he was involved in the garda murder'. Brady had told them that he had come from Boston where he had been staying with Travellers. The witness said that him and his friend confronted Aaron Brady about the murder, during which it was put to him and asked why he shot a garda. The witness said Brady became upset and told him he was there and that he got caught up in it. Detective Inspector Marry asked the witness to relay once again what he had heard Brady say for the avoidance of doubt or confusion. The man once again repeated that Brady had told him: 'I got caught up in it … I was there.' The witness agreed to meet with the investigation team to give a formal statement about the murder. On 22 January, just three days later, Detective Gardaí James Doherty and Paul Flynn met the witness to take a formal statement.

> Arrangements were made to travel to Cork and I brought the two detectives with me to take the statement from him. I did this as I wanted him to relay in his statement to two others what he had said to me. However, when it came to it he could not remember the conversation with Aaron Brady or what was said. It was put to him about our telephone conversation, but he said he was now unsure what he had said. This man would not back up what he'd said to me and he didn't want to cooperate. Was he intimidated

in the interim possibly? The bottom line was that he didn't want to stand over what he'd told me three days earlier and did not want to cooperate. His flatmates were tracked down and they said they had heard nothing. That's the way it unfortunately is with witnesses, I guess. I believe he was got to, and he might have been a good footballer, but he was not going to be a good witness.

*

On the fifth anniversary of the murder, senior gardaí gave a media briefing to provide an update on the progress of the investigation while appealing for the family and friends of the gang members to come forward. Chief Superintendent Christy Mangan said that he knew there were people out there with information about the murder who had not yet spoken to investigators. He also said that suspects for the murder were both in Ireland and abroad, and that gardaí would 'follow them to the end of the earth' in order to bring them to justice. 'The persons involved in this murder have no doubt received logistical and emotional support from their families and friends. And I'm speaking to you in particular, the families and friends of the people who were involved in the murder. Your mind will never have peace until you tell the truth of what happened to Adrian. It's not too late to do the right thing,' Chief Superintendent Mangan said.

That same day, members of the Homeland Security Investigation team visited Dundalk to pay their respects to the detective whose killers they were helping to catch. Special Agents Scott Crabb and Matt Katzke were brought to the murder site as well as the Adrian Donohoe Memorial Park, located across the road from Lordship Credit Union and named

after the late detective. Recalling that visit, Special Agent
Crabb says:

> We went to the site of the crime scene and we stood behind
> the wall where the subjects jumped out from. And you
> talk about chills and feeling, like, now it all kind of makes
> sense, looking at the crime scene. It was pretty emotional.
> We then went over to the Adrian Donohoe Memorial Park
> – I was proud to be standing there. It shows you the impact
> on the community, the loss of not just an Irish detective, it
> was about much more than that. It was a family impacted,
> a community impacted. It was a unique sort of experience
> and it really solidified the reason and support, helping
> me as a manager and leader of an office to continually be
> pushing that theme and message to our own leadership.
> It's easy for someone to look and question how much
> we're spending on travel and trips when there's been no
> criminal violation in the US. But we just pre-empted that
> with the emotional aspect of it, the importance of inter-
> national relationships and partnerships, and what [effect]
> potentially our support in this investigation could have on
> future relationships with each other. What if an American
> detective or special agent was killed in the line of duty
> and the suspect fled to Ireland, what would we want from
> them? Across the board we didn't have any real pushback
> on it which was good. We went to Dundalk and visited all
> of his people – it was a surreal and unique experience to
> see it first-hand.

The Homeland Security Agents were also brought across
the border and shown around Crossmaglen to get a sense of

the location where many of the suspects were from and the dynamics of the border. Special Agent Crabb says:

> Pat and his team had driven us to Crossmaglen, a tough little spot, and brought us around where these guys are based and where they are from. It was a real history of the area, smuggling fuel and all the different things people were involved in. For me as an American having seen this on TV I knew where it was, but actually standing there was pretty surreal. As we're driving around they were pointing out certain people associated to the Flynns and Brady that were in town. We didn't stay too long though and bounced out.

*

Weeks before his expected release, gardaí began focusing on prison calls Aaron Brady made while in custody. In an eight-month period Brady had made 458 phone calls – he was permitted three phone calls a day because of his enhanced prisoner status, for which inmates are given privileges as a reward for good behaviour in jail. Detective Sergeant Brian Hanley of the NBCI requested copies of the recordings from the Irish Prison Service, with gardaí initially listening to these calls after they were seized to uncover any evidence relating to Brady's role, or anyone else's involvement, in the murder and robbery.

Later, Detective Sergeant Darren Kirwan applied for a court warrant to obtain the recordings and copper-fasten their lawful retention by gardaí, after they established that the phone calls included conversations identifying witnesses and attempting to contact them. The warrant was applied for under Section 41 of the Criminal Justice Act, 1999, relating to conspiracy to interfere with or pervert the course of an investigation or course of justice. In one phone call with his father on 17 November 2017, Aaron Brady spoke about contacting his close friend in New York as well, Tommy McGeary, who had given a statement to gardaí that month implicating Brady in the murder. Later in the phone call, Brady said: 'Sure they asked them would I, did I say anything to them drunk at a house party. Sure even if, how would that stand up in a fucking thing. Even if it's … you know what I mean.' It was a clear sign to gardaí that Brady was identifying people in New York who were talking to authorities about him.

At the beginning of February, gardaí were finalising their plans to simultaneously arrest three suspects as part of the investigation. The three men to be detained were Aaron Brady, Eugene Flynn Snr, and his son James, with all arrests to take place as soon as Brady walked free from prison. Meetings were held with the Level 4 garda interviewers – the highest training specification in the organisation – who would oversee the interrogation and the strategy to be implemented for each prisoner. Several members of the NBCI would also be brought in to both monitor the interviews and carry out the interrogation of the suspects. In a meeting on 20 February, less than a week before the planned arrests, Detective Inspector Marry and the investigation team discussed the strategy again to ensure that all evidence gathered to date would be available to be put to the suspects. Security and safety protocols around Brady's arrest were discussed, including:

- Be mindful of property handed into prisoner – newspapers etc.
- No hoodies/clothing which can cover face in interview room. No clothing to be worn which could be a danger to himself.

- Will other prisoners go to Drogheda? Cells closed? Drunk prisoners at night – Brady may not get proper rest – consider this.
- Consider prisoner communicating with Brady – being arrested purposefully to get into garda station.

On Sunday 25 February, the garda arrest team had a final briefing at 3.45 p.m. before Detective Sergeant Kieran Reidy travelled to Dublin with a unit to detain the murder suspect. Due to Brady's previous form for forcefully resisting arrest, and the fact that he was suspected of murdering a detective, members of the heavily armed ERU were requested to secure the prisoner. Shortly before 7 p.m. Aaron Brady walked out of Wheatfield Prison in West Dublin a free man and made his way out of the gates onto the Cloverhill Road. His freedom was short-lived, and as soon as he was on the public road the ERU team pounced and detained him. Once he was secured, Detective Sergeant Reidy approached Aaron Brady, identifying himself and producing his Garda ID card. At 7 p.m. he detained Brady for an arrestable offence, to wit the murder of Detective Garda Adrian Donohoe with the use of a firearm at Lordship Credit Union on 25 January 2013. It was the first arrest in the long-running investigation.

Brady was handcuffed and taken to a garda van, where he was searched by Detective Gardaí Paul Gill and Padraig O'Reilly before being transported to Dundalk Garda Station. The arrests of Flynn father and son had not happened as planned, as both men were outside of the jurisdiction. Aaron Brady arrived in Dundalk shortly after 8 p.m. and was booked in by Garda Leonard Clarke, who was the member in charge that night. This role is also referred to as the prisoner's friend, to ensure that the rights of a person detained are looked after as set out by regulations. Aaron Brady was being detained under the provisions of Section 50 of the Criminal Justice Act, 2007, meaning gardaí could question him for a period of up to seven days. Detective Inspector Marry then requested authorisation to have Aaron Brady fingerprinted and photographed and a DNA swab formally taken to compare with forensic evidence recovered at the murder scene.

At 9.52 p.m. the first interview commenced with Detective Sergeant Mark Phillips and Detective Garda Jim McGovern, while Brady's solicitor, Neil Manley, was also present. They were informed that the interview was being video recorded by two cameras in the interrogation room and that a microphone on the table would audio record the interview.

D/Gda McGovern: 'Aaron, do you want a drink of water, tea, coffee? Just ask – any request made will be acceded to if possible, do you understand?'

Brady: 'Yes.'

D/Gda McGovern: 'Have you had any issues regarding your treatment since your arrest?'

Brady: 'No.'

D/Gda McGovern: 'Just to explain to you, Aaron, you were arrested at 7 p.m. on 25 February at Cloverhill Road, Cherry Orchard, Dublin 22, on suspicion of murder with a firearm of Detective Garda Adrian Donohoe. Do you understand why you were arrested?'

Brady: 'Yeah.'

The detective then outlined and summarised the detention times and periods under the act to Aaron Brady and his
solicitor.

D/Gda McGovern: 'Aaron, I think since you came in here
you had access to a solicitor by phone and in person. Any
issues?'

Brady 'No.'

D/Gda McGovern: 'I think, Aaron, you obviously met
myself and Mark before.'

Brady: 'Yeah. It's a while back, I think. Yeah, I gave yous
a statement of my own accord, ya.'

D/Gda McGovern: 'I think the start of February in 2013?'

Brady: 'I can't remember dates.'

D/Gda McGovern: 'The start of February 2013, I think
it was, here.'

Brady: 'Yeah.'

D/Sgt Phillips: 'It was here, Jim, yeah, in this room.'

Brady: 'Ya.'

D/Gda McGovern: 'Do you recall that?'

Brady: 'I remember being here, ya, and giving a statement
and anything other than that is going to be no comment
unless there's anything incorrect or that shouldn't be.'

The voluntary statements given by Aaron Brady five years
earlier were then read to him and, while he signed them, he

didn't give any comment as to their contents. On the evening of Monday 26 February, gardaí also located Eugene Flynn Snr in Dundalk, and he was arrested for questioning in relation to the investigation. In an operational plan drawn up, gardaí assessed that there was a medium risk of aggressive driving or obstruction when detaining Flynn, and as part of control measures put in place it was decided that at least one armed garda should be present. The operation passed off without incident and Flynn Snr was brought to Balbriggan Garda Station, where he was detained under Section 50 of the Criminal Justice Act, 1984. The grounds for his arrest included the fact that his car was spotted passing the scene at the time of the robbery, that he never fully accounted for his movements that night, and the belief of gardaí that he was in possession of information relating to the murder. This suspicion was further bolstered by his comments to gardaí during their unsuccessful trip to Boston when he told them 'they did not have the story and that he was not interested in telling it', as recorded by investigators in a report of the meeting. Detective Inspector Marry also stated in his grounds for the arrest that the recorded conversation at Dunroamin House 'would make me believe Eugene Flynn Snr has a knowledge of and took part in the murder and robbery as a lookout or scout'. He was questioned for several days but was eventually released without charge while a file was prepared for the DPP, which later directed that he should not be charged in relation to the crime.

On 2 March, Brady's sixth day in custody, Detective Garda Gill and Detective Sergeant Phillips put the statements given by Molly Staunton to Aaron Brady, which included confessions he made about shooting a garda. After certain extracts from it were read to Brady, Detective Garda Gill asked him: 'So who is Molly Staunton?' The murder suspect deviated from his 'no comment' stance and replied: 'I do not accept any conversation took place with Molly Staunton in which I confessed to the offence I am arrested for.' During several other rounds of interviews Brady only commented on the evidence put to him by denying any involvement in the murder and robbery, while also denying making any confession of his own free will.

As the interviews wore on and the deadline for his release from custody came closer, it was put to Brady that he had said on a number of occasions that he was acting on the advice of his solicitor, and he was asked if he had anything to say about that. He replied that his actions were his own and that his approach to the questioning had been his own decision. Later that day Detective Garda McGovern informed Aaron Brady that they were applying a provision under Section 19(a) of the Criminal Justice Act that allows for inferences to be drawn from an accused person's failure to answer certain questions. Detective Sergeant Hanley explained this to the suspect in simple language, outlining how if he failed to answer any questions or mention a fact that he later relied on in court as part of his defence, then this failure could be used to support other evidence against him. Brady was also informed that inferences from any failure to answer a question could not be used on their own to convict him of an offence. Detective Sergeant Hanley then asked him if he had anything he wished to say, to which Brady replied: 'I strongly deny any involvement in the murder of Detective Garda Adrian Donohoe and any other offence put to me to me.' He also once again denied making any confession in relation to the murder.

Asked if he wished to make any changes to his statement, Brady responded: 'I strongly deny any involvement in the murder of Detective Garda Adrian Donohoe. I strongly deny any confession to the murder of Detective Garda Adrian Donohoe and any other offence put to me here in interview.'

Throughout the week of Brady's detention period, Detective Inspector Marry was in constant contact with the Office of the DPP. At 6.13 p.m. on 4 March, he rang Deputy Director Barry Donoghue and informed him that inference provisions were being put to Brady and that this would be completed within the next 25 minutes. He was told to call back once the final interview was finished. Forty minutes later, at 6.53 p.m., Detective Inspector Marry called Mr Donohoe again, informing him that it had been completed. During that conversation he was given the direction to charge Aaron Brady with capital murder.

At 6.57 p.m., the senior investigator told Brady that he was releasing him from garda custody. He then told him that he was arresting him for the purpose of charge. At 8.05 p.m. he cautioned Brady and told him that he was being charged with the murder of a garda in the course of their duty under Section 4 of the Criminal Justice Act, 1990. In response Brady said: 'I strongly deny any involvement in the murder of Detective Garda Adrian Donohoe.' Recalling charging the chief suspect, Detective Inspector Marry says:

I remember going to the cell, the jailer opened it, and Aaron Brady walked out as cocky as you like – he was looking for the exit sign. I told him he was being released from the terms of this detention and was free to go. One second later I put my hand on his shoulder and told him I was now arresting him for the murder of Detective Garda Adrian Donohoe. I informed the jailer of his new arrest for the purpose of charge and a new custody record was completed. There are few members of An Garda Síochána that charge someone with capital murder, the murder of their colleague. As I read out the charge to Brady I couldn't see a man but a snivelly, pathetic little creature full of his own importance, but empty at the same time. I honestly believe he felt he would beat the rap and that gardaí were wasting their time. Most murderers underestimate the gardaí and the power of the investigating they do. When put to him, Brady denied any involvement with a confidence and smugness – it was like he had it all worked out. But we were confident too. We had all worked so hard to get the investigation to the point of an arrest, we had invested everything. We used up every ounce of our energy and our skills to get this man. Looking into his face as I charged him with murder is something I will never, ever forget. Brady's arrest meant so much to us all – in fact, it meant everything.'

After 9 p.m. that night Aaron Brady was brought before a special sitting of Dundalk District Court to be formally charged with the murder. A large press pack of journalists, photographers, and camera crews had gathered at the court-house ahead of the hearing and were joined by dozens of local people who came out to watch the scenes unfold. Brady, wearing a black coat, blue jeans, and red runners, was brought handcuffed into the court and didn't speak during the hearing as Detective Inspector Marry outlined the charge. Also in the packed courtroom was Caroline Donohoe, members of the garda investigation team, and Homeland Security personnel, including Special Agent Scott Crabb, London Attaché Jim Mancuso, and their team. After his brief appearance, Aaron Brady was taken away in a garda van to prison, where he would spend his time awaiting trial.

14

GUILTY CONSCIENCE

While it was the first charge in the long-running investigation, it would be Detective Inspector Marry's last act as a member of An Garda Síochána, having served in the force for 32 years and worked on many high-profile investigations.

Charging Aaron Brady was a bittersweet affair for me. I had decided some one year beforehand that I was leaving the job. I'd had my bellyful of management, and when I was rejected for promotion the final insult had been delivered. I had discussed the prospect with my wife and told her that they had no intention of promoting me and I wanted out. I would stay on to solve Adrian's case. I told her I knew we could do it and if the investigation progressed the way I wanted, it would be solved. I myself, being Adrian's inspector, felt I owed him nothing but the best. His murder was an affront to everything good about a person of his standing and to the general public. I observed the day of Adrian's funeral the throngs of decent people from Dundalk who lined the streets and applauded the hearse as it passed, identifying a mark of respect for Adrian and what he stood for. I was not going to let those people down. I owed nothing but the best to the Irish people. I informed my wife that the day I charged the culprit with the murder I would hand in my retirement papers. That day came on 4 March 2018 after my consultation with the DPP's office. I prepared a charge sheet to reflect the capital murder charge for Aaron Brady.

I had also prepared my resignation letter, which I was going to hand in after charging him. I returned to my office and handed in my resignation to the chief superintendent's office. I said: 'That's it, lads, I am out of here.' I kept my word and I didn't let anyone down. I was leaving the job with a clear conscience and I had plans for my future. I remember standing in my office, charge sheet in one hand and retirement papers in the other. I was photographed and told: 'You will not do it, you love the job too much.' Little did they know my feelings towards the job and certain people in it. After I retired they appointed two detective inspectors to oversee serious crime in the Louth division. It was what I had asked for during the inquiry but wasn't given, and it showed the amount of work to be covered.

Following Detective Inspector Marry's retirement, the reins of SIO were passed to Detective Inspector Martin Beggy, a well-respected investigator who had almost 40 years' policing experience in the border region. While a murder charge had now been preferred, the investigation was still gathering evidence against Brady and his accomplices. Gardaí were also continuing to liaise with the Department of Homeland Security on the US side of the investigation. After Brady was charged, Acting Deputy Executive Associate Director of HSI Alysa D. Erichs said: 'The United States will not be a safe haven for cop killers. When it comes to cop killers, there are no boundaries between us. The Garda is remaining true to their promise to the Donohoe family and to the Irish people. It is an honour for HSI to have worked alongside our Garda partners to investigate, locate, arrest and deport Aaron Brady to Ireland.' Detectives believed there were more people who he had confessed to while living in New York and continued to undertake regular trips across the Atlantic to track down more potential witnesses they hadn't yet spoken to. One of these journeys, in the summer of 2019, would eventually prove fruitful.

Daniel Cahill was born in Dublin in July 1992 and grew up in the suburb of Donaghmede on the city's northside. His father lived close to a well-known Dublin family, the Ryans, with whom Daniel Cahill hung out growing up. One of the siblings was Alan Ryan, who had become the leader of the Real IRA in Dublin before being shot dead in 2012.

Daniel Cahill was friendly with Alan's younger brother Vincent Ryan, a hairdresser who was also suspected of involvement in dissident republican activity and was shot dead in Dublin in March 2016. Another friend of Mr Cahill growing up was Dean Evans, who was his age and from the nearby area of Raheny. While in his younger years Daniel Cahill had been acquainted with people who went on to become major players in the city's dissident republican movement, gardaí did not suspect he was himself involved in any illegal activity. In August 2013, with no job and wanting to get away from Dublin, Daniel Cahill decided to travel to New York, where he initially got a job in construction before working as a barman in various pubs around Yonkers, including the Coachman's Inn on Katonah Avenue, which Aaron Brady and his friends frequented while living in the Bronx.

In the months before Mr Cahill crossed the Atlantic, Dean Evans carried out the IRA murder of Peter Butterly at the Huntsman's Inn pub in north Dublin. He was charged but later fled Ireland after being granted bail. While Mr Cahill was living in New York, authorities arrived at his home looking for Evans, but the pair had not had any contact in years. Evans was later extradited from Spain and is currently serving a life sentence for the murder of Peter Butterly. Authorities would later call to Daniel Cahill's door once again, but this time for different reasons.

At 7 a.m. on 25 July 2019, a HSI team led by Special Agent Mary Ann Wade, supported by an enforcement removal officer, arrived at the apartment where Daniel Cahill was living with his wife in Yonkers. The agents waited outside the house for around an hour before knocking on the front door. They had no warrant or cause to search the house, but were there to inquire if Cahill would speak with gardaí who were in the area. His wife answered the door and allowed them into the house, saying her husband wasn't home. During a search of the house the agents discovered a small amount of suspected cannabis plants, along with light bulbs and fans in a shared communal area of the property, while local police officers who called to the house later found a quantity of steroids. When the HSI agents searched the attic, they found Daniel Cahill hiding in a crawl space, where he had been for several hours.

He was taken down and asked if he wanted to speak to the gardaí who had travelled over from Ireland, which he agreed to. The police convoy travelled to Yonkers Police Station where Detective Sergeants Phillips and Paul Gill, who had been promoted, as well as Detective Garda Padraig O'Reilly, took a lengthy statement from him in relation to his various encounters with Aaron Brady. Over the course of two and a half hours he outlined how he was first introduced to Brady in the pub one night and detailed various interactions he had with him over the following years. Mr Cahill said he first became aware of the rumours relating to Brady in a conversation with Ciara Wilson, a friend of the suspect, during a gathering at a house in Woodlawn. 'Ciara told me not to try and aggravate Aaron because he was involved in the shooting of the Garda in Ireland,' he told them. 'She told me he had come here to get away from the Guards in Ireland. She told me this when she came back from the bathroom. Ciara put me wide to the situation that Aaron was out here to get away from the situation in Ireland where he had shot a Garda.' The fact that Brady was on the run, he added, would be brought up frequently by his friends in New York.

Mr Cahill then told the detectives of the first time Aaron Brady directly admitted to him that he had shot a guard in Ireland. Brady had been in the bar and was struck in the face by another man, Shane Farrell, suffering a gash to his eye and leaving a trail of blood to the bathroom where he went to clean himself up.

At this time, I was under the impression that Aaron was a hardman but at that time I thought he was a coward. I went into the bathroom to see if Aaron was okay. Aaron is looking in the mirror at his eye and there's a lot of blood. I asked if he was okay. He seemed to be trembling and upset. When he spoke his voice [was] trembling. That was when he was trying to reaffirm who he was within the bar. He was ranting about how that was the last thing Shane Farrell would do and he was going to get revenge. He wouldn't get away with what he had done to him. Aaron then proceeded to say he had done it before. He went on to say he would do the same thing to Shane as he had done to the Garda in Ireland. I asked him why he did not retaliate. He told me: 'I've done this before and he won't get away with this.' Aaron said to me that Shane Farrell was going to get it, [he said] 'I'll do the same thing that I done before to the Garda in Ireland.' He was ranting ... He was very volatile.

It was the first of many encounters Daniel Cahill would relay to gardaí in the interview room of Yonkers Police Station. He recalled another incident several weeks after the bar fight when Aaron Brady was drinking in the pub for several hours. 'Aaron seemed to be emotional, he was resting his hands on his head and his face in his hands. I walked over and asked him what was going on and was he alright and he asked me had I ever killed somebody. I said no and he said to me "Well, you wouldn't understand." He then told me that he had a lot on his conscience.' Mr Cahill told the detectives that he returned to Brady ten minutes later when the conversation continued.

His eyes were watering. He told me that the guard in Ireland that he had shot was something that was constantly on his mind. I didn't really know what to say. I'm pretty sure I asked him was he gonna get caught for it ... on this occasion I asked him what way this had gone down. He told me that him and his friends were going to commit a robbery. They were all tooled up and had got a car. The cops came and he produced a gun and he fired at the cops to try and escape. I kind of left it at that. He was nearly in tears when he was telling me this.

The witness said that, at this point, he didn't know the garda's name and wouldn't have known about the investigation. The detectives continued to listen intently and noted down what Daniel Cahill was telling them while the audio-visual devices recorded the interview. He recalled another time where he was in an apartment on 234th Street in the Bronx after work where a group of men, including Aaron Brady, were exchanging stories. Mr Cahill told gardaí:

Aaron tells us that none of us know what it's like to kill somebody. He says he has nightmares where he hears people shouting and gunshots from the day where he shot the cop. And he was very emotional and saying he never gets it off his conscience and it's with him every day ... Aaron said: 'This follows me everywhere I go.' Towards the end when I was leaving he was saying how he was on the run. This would have been around the summertime of 2014.

Daniel Cahill later got another job at a pub in White Plains but would have further encounters with Brady, including one time when he was driving home in the early hours of the morning. He was passing through Katonah Avenue when he was stopped outside Behan's pub, and Aaron Brady walked over to him. Mr Cahill recounted the interaction to Detective Sergeant Gill.

Cahill: 'I was trying to get away from him and then he was like, "Aw, did you see this" and he pulls out a picture of him in the newspaper. He's at a soccer game. Then he's like "Aww I'm worried."'

D/Sgt Gill: 'Go back, he pulls …?'

Mr Cahill: 'He shows me, he's like laughing, "Did you see this picture", on his phone, it's from a page of a newspaper and I read the caption like "Garda …" some bullshit. He was like "This is all papers from home and they're really out to get me." I said, "For what" and he said "For that whole thing shooting the cop". I said, "Oh yeah" and he said "Oh yeah like I said to you before". It looked like a football game. I couldn't believe it.'

D/Sgt Gill: 'Can you describe the article?'

Cahill: "[In] the picture he was wearing some sort of jersey […] at a sporting event. [It said] "living it up in New York". And I'm pretty sure "murder suspect" or "cop killer". It was the first newspaper I've ever seen, I think the only time I've seen it in a newspaper. At that point I, that's the only article I've ever seen of him. I've never looked into it. I was under the impression [it was] to try and intimidate me or my friends or get a message across.'

D/Sgt Gill: 'What way would you describe?'

Cahill: 'To try and get a point across of like "This is who the fuck I am". I think he knew I never really, I think he kept playing this up because I knew of the time he got hit [in the bar fight]. He was ranting about what he was going to do and what he's done. He was like "Ah it'll be grand, it'll be grand" and I was like "I'm blocking traffic". I went on my way.'

Mr Cahill also said he couldn't recall if the image in the article was a clear picture or blurred, but that Aaron Brady separately showed him the same unpixellated image on his phone, which had been taken from his Facebook account. He added that his impression from the encounter was that Brady was worried gardaí were coming to get him and that he was scared. When Detective Sergeant Phillips later read notes of the statement, he recalled previously reading an article as described by Mr Cahill, and he searched through newspaper articles held on file. The story the witness referred to was an article printed on 25 August 2014 in the *Irish Daily Star* by journalist Michael O'Toole, and the details contained in it matched the encounter described by Mr Cahill.

At the police precinct in Yonkers, the witness also told gardaí that Brady revealed that he and his friends had got a car and that four of them carried out the robbery. Brady, he stated, told him that two of the gang went to Australia and two of them went to Boston. He continued: 'Aaron told me that it didn't go to plan and to escape from the cops that he shot at the cops and found out one of them was dead. He told me he had a gun and that he shot at the cops. He never told me what kind of gun it was.' The witness told gardaí that he had encountered Aaron Brady between 30 and 40 times in New York, recounting another time when he went to Brady's house, where around five others had gathered. 'I recall that they got a measuring tape and measured out a line of cocaine or white powder that I presume was cocaine. They were all taking cocaine.' Explaining why he made the witness statement as part of the investigation, Mr Cahill said that it was 80 per cent because he has friends in the cops, which is why he wanted to step up, and 20 per cent because of a moral code that everyone in society should have to get justice.

He would give another statement to gardaí over the course of nearly five hours on 29 July at the HSI building in New York City, further clarifying points to his previous statement including persistent cocaine taking from Brady and his associates. Mr Cahill told gardaí he believed Brady's friends would also boast about his involvement in the murder 'so he could establish a dominance over me of some sort. I feel like he used the reputation from his actions to manipulate people in situations.' Mr Cahill also told gardaí of another encounter he had with Aaron Brady at Tara's Deli on Woodlawn Avenue in 2017:

> We only had a general conversation, he told me he had just had a child and I think he said he had just got married or was about to get married. I can't recall for sure. At this time, he told me that the cops had been out investigating him and that they had tried to get Micky Leneghan to speak to them. He said that he did not think that anybody would speak to the police and that he thought that that would be the end of it – that there was not much more they could do.

In the conference room of the HSI building, Mr Cahill also revealed how he wished he had come forward sooner, that he was 'not trained to detect a murderer', and that he could have 'made this a lot easier on the family of Adrian Donohoe by shedding light on this person' sooner. Daniel Cahill added:

The things that Aaron Brady told me in relation to the murder and robbery are not speculation by myself or anybody else. In terms of myself these are the words Aaron Brady gave to me. I think I should rephrase the 'gave'; these are the words Aaron Brady used to tell me on different occasions what actions he chose to take in relation to committing a murder and a robbery; the actions that he tried to escape by moving to America where he continued to hurt and intimidate the community that he lived in.

The bravery shown by Daniel Cahill in providing his witness statement would lead to him coming under threat down the line.

*

While awaiting trial, Aaron Brady was additionally charged with the robbery of approximately €7,000 in cash and assorted cheques during the credit union raid. As his trial date neared, gardaí were targeting another cross-border crime gang. In the first eight months of 2019, more than 30 thefts of cash machines had taken place in Northern Ireland and the Republic. Security services suspected that as many as three criminal gangs were operating independently in the crime and that associates of Brady were involved in targeting ATMs south of the border. The incidents all involved the same modus operandi: heavy machinery, normally a JCB or excavator, would be stolen and parked offside along with stolen cars before the gang would target ATMs in rural towns in the middle of the night. The machinery would be used to rip cash machines from a bank's wall and place them onto a flatbed trailer before this was driven away. Some of the more lucrative robberies for the gangs were reported on 16 December 2018 in Ballybay, County Monaghan, 10 March 2019 in Kingscourt, County Cavan, 3 April in Castleblayney, County Monaghan, and two on the same night of 19 April in Kells, County Meath. The audacious raids had netted the crime gang hundreds of thousands of euros and were becoming a major political embarrassment. The justice minister of the day, Fine Gael TD Charlie Flanagan, ordered that gardaí spare no resources in tracking down the gang involved.

Garda intelligence led them to a cross-border crime group that included Danny O'Callaghan, an All-Ireland club winning footballer with Crossmaglen Rangers, who was also an associate of Aaron Brady. The pair had even partied together in New York, with Brady posting a picture of them celebrating in a group on New Year's Eve in 2014. O'Callaghan was a person of interest in the Lordship robbery in the early stages of the investigation because of his association with the gang, while his sister Charlene had been going out with Treanor at the time of the raid. However, gardaí later ruled him out of having any involvement in the robbery.

A major investigation was put in place to bring down the ATM-theft gang involving the garda's Drugs and Organised Crime Bureau, the National Surveillance Unit, and the Emergency Response Unit, as well as local and regional garda units. In the early hours of 14 August 2019, after watching the criminals for almost three months, the gardaí's patience paid off when they intercepted the crew as they targeted an ATM on Main Street in Virginia, County Cavan. A jeep belonging to the raiders was rammed by heavily armed gardaí, and several gang members were arrested as they tried to rip another cash

machine from a building. Five men would later be convicted
for their involvement in the ATM-theft gang, including Danny
O'Callaghan, who was sentenced to ten years in jail, after the
Special Criminal Court found that the crime group had stolen
around €800,000 in a series of raids in an eight-month period.
While gardaí suspected that Brendan Treanor was a leading
member of the crime network, he wasn't prosecuted as part of
that garda investigation.

*

Aaron Brady's murder trial was due to begin in October but was
adjourned to the following January as legal teams dealt with
significant pre-trial arguments. Since being charged he had been
held on remand in Mountjoy Prison in Dublin and had never
applied for bail on the murder charge. On 21 November 2019,
Detective Garda Padraig O'Reilly travelled to Blackrock in
County Louth to serve a witness order on Tommy McGeary. He
was aware that the witness, who resided in the North, was
carrying out work in the area that day and approached him as
he was unloading furniture from a truck on Main Street.
Detective Garda O'Reilly asked the man if he could speak with
him for a moment and informed him that he had a witness
order for the trial due to commence the following January
before the Central Criminal Court. However, McGeary's attitude had changed in the two years since he had given a detailed
statement outlining how Brady had confessed to his involvement in the murder and robbery. He refused to engage with the
detective, simply telling him: 'Get off me truck.' There was
clearly little hope that the man would come to court and testify
to what he had previously told gardaí.

Aside from the murder inquiry, investigators and legal teams also had to conduct the significant task of disclosing thousands of documents to the defence ahead of the trial. Many of these were redacted after being reviewed by a judge for various reasons, including that they could reveal garda tradecraft secrets and because of a threat to life if the information was released. Speaking on the process, Detective Inspector Marry says:

It is often perceived that once the accused person appears before the district court charged that your job is finished, you got your man, and now you have to wait for the trial, but often the large bulk of administrative work is just beginning. In criminal cases the prosecution must disclose to the defence all the relevant evidence that it has gathered during the investigation. The disclosure must include everything the prosecution will rely on at the trial as well as all materials that will not be relied on. The disclosure in the Adrian Donohoe case was colossal – for example, each written statement taken was provided to the defence as well as all typed versions, all reports generated, all CCTV footage, forensic reports, questionnaires, and every document generated over the five-year span of the investigation. Also, all emails generated between myself and Homeland Security and any external police force.

I knew that disclosure would be a big task, and I had delegated four detectives to compiling all the paperwork, having it properly accounted for and in a professional filing system for handing over to the DPP for onward disclosure to the defence. It was calculated that there were over a million pages of disclosure.

I often thought about this and, in fairness to the justice system, to prevent any possible miscarriage of justice, it is best practice to see justice being served. It is so important to conduct your investigation with honesty. I always believed you had nothing to fear at a trial if you conducted your investigation in an honest and professional fashion. An SIO must keep in mind during an investigation that his decisions and his skill of managing and controlling an investigation must be seen as fair to any suspect. I could not emphasise enough to investigators the values that honesty, accountability, responsibility, and professionalism play in any major investigation, as these qualities will be reflected in any trial process, and any lacking in those qualities will be found out and it may well lead to a collapse of a trial or an acquittal.

What an investigation must be aware of is that an accused has a right to a fair trial. It is one of the most fundamental constitutional rights afforded to a person and is deemed a superior right. The trial is a big deal, and it is where the garda's investigation is hung out for all and sundry to see. It is a nervous and daunting time for any senior investigating officer. I was always anxious that things would run smoothly.

By December 2019, a month before the trial was due to start, Aaron Brady had had well over a year to review all of the evidence in the case against him. While he was granted a laptop to review a lot of the material, he also had hundreds of printed out documents to study. One official remarked to the authors that Brady's jail cell in Mountjoy Prison was 'like a library' because of the amount of material and folders stacked up. That month, the State Solicitor's Office received an email from Brady's legal team that set out his alibi on the night of the murder. He stated that when giving his voluntary statement in February 2013, he 'was not at all convinced' that he wouldn't be prosecuted for his involvement in diesel laundering. Therefore, he said he was only at the yard for 15 minutes. 'This was not correct,' his alibi stated.

> On Friday 25th of January 2013, I went to a yard situated at 155 Concession Road at around 8 o'clock or shortly thereafter. I went to this yard with the sole intention of loading large volumes of diesel waste cubes onto the back of a lorry already on site with the use of a forklift. Prior to my arrival at 155 Concession Road I received instructions from [a known diesel launderer] and [Mr C] via telephone regarding the loading of diesel waste cubes onto a curtain side lorry situated on site at 155 Concession Road. I was instructed by them to load as many diesel waste cubes [as I could] onto the lorry.

In his notice of alibi he stated that he hopped the gate to gain entry to the site, which was in complete darkness.

> I proceeded to walk towards the forklift situated at the rear of the lorry. The forklift failed to start, I made further attempts to start the forklift without success. I reached for a can of Easy Start underneath the seat of the forklift and sprayed the contents of the can into the air filter. After some time it managed to start and from there I commenced loading. Whilst I was loading from the back, staggering locations so as not to place too much in one

place, I was able to load two cubes at a time. I would lift two cubes onto the floor of the lorry.

He claimed that this process took between one and a half hours and two hours, due to the rough terrain and poor lighting as well as the forklift cutting out occasionally. 'Once I had completed as much of the process as I could I moved the forklift back to position and left the yard to return to 10a Lough Road.' Explaining the phone calls to Mr C and another associate the following day, he said this was to inform them that the job had been completed. It was the story Aaron Brady was now sticking to in an attempt to prove his innocence.

15

THE DPP VERSUS AARON BRADY

The capital murder trial began on 28 January 2020 in Court 6 of the Criminal Courts of Justice on Parkgate Street in Dublin. Because the case was expected to last five months, an extended pool of 15 jurors was selected in case any person serving on the panel took ill or had to drop out during that lengthy period. While there were reports of a Coronavirus strain spreading from Wuhan in China, the virus had not seen any mass outbreaks in Europe. It took almost two hours to select the panel, with more than 40 prospective jurors excused by the judge, while ten were challenged by the prosecution and defence. Shortly after midday, the jury of six men and nine women were sworn in, with the trial commencing that afternoon before Justice Michael White. The legal teams on both sides were made up of some of the most experienced and respected members of the criminal bar in the country.

Leading the prosecution case was Brendan Grehan, a lawyer with over 30 years' experience who had been appointed in the inner bar as a senior counsel in 2003. He had previously prosecuted two teenage boys accused of the murder of 14-year-old schoolgirl Ana Kriegel. The youths, known as

Boy A and Boy B, were 13 years old at the time of the killing and became the youngest people convicted of murder in Irish criminal history. He had also prosecuted serial killer Mark Nash, who was convicted of the murders of 55-year-old Sylvia Sheils and 67-year-old Mary Callinan in Grangegorman in March 1997.

Due to the amount of evidence in the Brady case and the length of the trial, a second senior counsel had been appointed to both the defence and prosecution. Lorcan Staines, accepted to the inner bar in 2018, was also on the prosecution team. He had previously served on the defence team for Tipperary farmer Patrick Quirke, accused of the murder of Bobby Ryan in the high-profile 'Mr Moonlight' murder trial. He had also worked on the defence team with Mr Grehan in the Anglo trial, defending the bank's former director of lending, Pat Whelan, in relation to the provision of illegal loans prior to its collapse. The junior counsel for the prosecution were Jane Murphy and Dean Kelly, who has since been appointed as senior counsel.

The legal team defending Aaron Brady was led by Michael O'Higgins, a former journalist who became a barrister in 1987 then a senior counsel in 2000. Renowned mainly for his work as a defence counsel, he had recently defended Patrick Hutch, accused of being a cross-dressing gunman who was part of the hit team that carried out the murder of Kinahan gang member David Byrne at the Regency Hotel in 2016. The charge against Hutch was later withdrawn, following a dramatic trial at the Special Criminal Court. Mr O'Higgins's fellow senior counsel was Fiona Murphy, an equally respected prosecutor and defence barrister, while Justin McQuade BL was the junior counsel assisting the defence.

That morning, after the jury were sworn in, Aaron Brady was formally arraigned on two counts. The registrar stood up and read out the charges to him, stating that on 25 January 2013 at Lordship Credit Union in Bellurgan, Dundalk, County Louth, he did murder Detective Garda Adrian Donohoe, then a member of An Garda Síochána acting in the course of his duty. Brady, wearing a blue suit and white shirt, replied: 'Not guilty.' The second charge was then read out, stating that he robbed Pat Bellew of approximately €7,000 in cash and assorted cheques at the same location on the same date. Again the accused replied: 'Not guilty.'

Brendan Grehan opened the prosecution's case against the defendant, saying matters concerned events seven years earlier, on a cold wet night in Dundalk, where gardaí were tasked with escorting those carrying the weekly takings from different credit unions on the Cooley Peninsula. He outlined the movements of the cash escort and how it was taken up by Detective Gardaí Donohoe and Ryan. He described how the convoy had arrived at Lordship Credit Union and was making its way towards the car-park exit. 'If you can picture the scene, ladies and gentlemen, as I have described it, within 60 seconds everything you are going to be concerned with is over.' Mr Grehan said that a car on the road moved into position to block the exit and that four young, athletic men wearing balaclavas hopped over the wall at the back of the car park. Two gunmen, he said, 'both went directly with deliberation and without hesitation for the garda car'. Mr Grehan described how they had ignored the other vehicles and that Detective Garda Donohoe, who had stepped out to see what was blocking the exit, 'was blasted in the face with the shotgun'. He outlined how the rest of the robbery unfolded before the gang fled to the Volkswagen Passat driven by a fifth raider.

All that happened in 58 seconds, and we can be that precise about it because there is CCTV footage. Even though it is dark you will be able to make it out. It's quite graphic and chilling in terms of the sheer organisation of those that were involved. It will be apparent, ladies and gentlemen, that this was a very slick operation, highly organised, with quite a number of people working together as a team. It was carried out, the prosecution says, for a base criminal motive. This was done for money, nothing else. There is no suggestion in the investigation of any connection whatsoever to any kind of cause. This was a robbery done for money, picking on something perceived to be an easy target and for an entirely selfish motive.

The prosecutor said: 'The slickness of the operation obviously took a lot of planning.' It involved knowing the schedule and timetable of the route of the escort, communications with walkie-talkies, the procuring of weapons and the getaway car, as well as choosing the escape route. 'They had to have a top-class driver to get them out of there at maximum throttle, and knowledge of the whole area. There would have to be a second vehicle available to get them back from where the burn site was. It has all the hallmarks of a well-planned and executed crime, only achieved with intimate knowledge of the local country.' The jury were told that very few clues were left at the scene, no evidence was retrievable from the burn site, and the firearms used and stolen cash were never recovered.

Mr Grehan told them that Aaron Brady was 21 years old at the time and spent the entirety of the day in question with two friends, James Flynn and Benny Treanor, whom the media referred to as Suspects A and B during the trial. He outlined the evidence they would hear, including statements given by Aaron Brady, telecommunications contact, and CCTV evidence. 'On this occasion the phones of persons involved are active during the day, but a curious thing happens. Aaron Brady's phone goes off the radar, so to speak, immediately before and after the robbery occurs. Curiously the same thing happens with James Flynn's phone. Curiously still with Benny Treanor's phone the same thing,' he said, describing it as a 'telecommunications blackout'. He said a factor in this case would be that Aaron Brady was under money pressure coming into the weekend, that he lied about his whereabouts when stopped by gardaí after the robbery, and that he called others to provide him with a false alibi. 'Then just before the trial the accused, through solicitors, put forward a new alibi that he was at a yard at 155 Concession Road in Armagh at the time of the robbery.' He said on the day of the robbery Brady had been sending texts to a person he knew, setting out how he was going to be busy the night of the Lordship robbery, specifically between 8 p.m. and 10 p.m. 'The prosecution say indeed he was busy,' Mr Grehan said, adding that the person who they say pulled the trigger was Aaron Brady.

Outlining the law relating to the capital murder charge, he explained that the accused must have known or been reckless to whether the victim was a garda acting in the course of their duty, as there are additional protections for gardaí.

While others run from danger, they'll run towards it. When we call them, we expect them to answer. When violent persons threaten us or our communities, they respond. And in short gardaí can find themselves in harm's way so that we are all kept safe. They serve and protect us so that we are kept out of harm's way and can feel safe, and because of that they sometimes have to put themselves on the line to protect us from violence, thuggery, anarchy, and ultimately the chaos that would ensue in a lawless society if you do not have the police. And sometimes they have to give their lives for that value, as they patrol that thin blue line that keeps us all safe.

'It is in recognition of that value and that service,' he said of the extra protections for gardaí under the legislation. He told the jury that Brady left Ireland shortly after the robbery and murder 'as the investigation ramped up, and he went to the United States and settled in New York, 3,000 miles away, believing he was beyond the reach of the long arm of the law'. The jury were told they would hear various conversations Aaron Brady had had with people while living on the other side of the Atlantic. 'When you hear all of the evidence, you can be satisfied to find him guilty of the capital murder of Detective Garda Donohoe,' the jurors were told.

The beginning of the evidence was delayed and the jury was asked to wait as Michael O'Higgins expressed his concern at the opening remarks, saying it had been stated that the accused was allegedly motivated by money and that this was juxtaposed with the blue line Detective Garda Donohoe was protecting. Mr O'Higgins said it was 'wholly unacceptable' in this case that the jury should get an opening in that form, adding that his complaint was at the prosecution's attempt to engender sympathy for the deceased personnel. 'When I say the word sympathy, you would want to have a heart of stone not to have sympathy for the deceased person, that's taken as a given,' he said, adding that 'sympathy is the handmaiden of prejudice'. He continued: 'In telling the jury this is the line he is protecting; his wife, brothers, that he has children: that's not evidence. It's not said for no reason – it's said to engender sympathy.' Justice White said he would address the jury specifically in their role in terms of being independent and not to have sympathy. The defence also requested that retired Detective Inspector Pat Marry be asked to leave the court while witnesses were giving their evidence, as he himself would be called at a later stage.

The jury were brought back and the first gardaí were sworn in to describe the layout of the border region and various sites including the crime scene using maps and images. CCTV footage was also played to the court, including the moment the armed gang struck and Detective Garda Donohoe was shot dead. Aaron Brady, sitting in the dock, looked up at the video footage playing on the monitors in the courtroom that captured the moment he allegedly shot the detective dead. One by one, witnesses who were working in the various branches on the Cooley Peninsula were called to give their recollection of events that night.

The next tranche of witnesses to give evidence were those in the car park at the time of the robbery. Detective Garda Ryan recalled hearing 'banging noises' behind him, and when he looked to his side, he saw two men approach the vehicle from the right. The first raider, he told the court, was holding a long single-barrelled shotgun in his hand. Detective Garda Ryan said he heard a loud bang and saw a flash from the front of the shotgun. He said at this stage he could not see his colleague, who had exited the vehicle, and believed it was a warning shot. He told the court that the person armed with the shotgun then threatened him and said: 'I'm going to fucking kill you, I'm going to shoot you. Give us the money.' He described this man as being around 6 foot 1 and speaking with a border accent. The witness told prosecuting counsel Brendan Grehan SC that there was a second individual armed with a handgun, which he believed was a SIG or Glock firearm, and described him as being around 5 foot 7 inches and speaking with a border accent. The witness also said he was thinking during the incident that he would prefer to be shot with the 9mm handgun than the shotgun because there would have been a 'better chance of survival' with the smaller weapon. After the gang fled, he said he drew his handgun and pointed it at the getaway car but assessed that there was no further threat to anyone's life and decided not to shoot. He checked on Mary Hanlon in the Nissan Qashqai before returning to the garda car where he noticed his colleague lying on the ground. 'He had a serious wound to his face, and I went over to him. He was lying facing the front of the car on his back. I could see he was lying in a pool of blood. I could see brain matter on the tarmac,' he told the court. 'I knew at that stage he was dead, but I went for a pulse anyway. He was dead – there was nothing there could be done for him.'

Bernadette McShane broke down as she recalled the events of the robbery, describing how she heard two loud noises – most likely the gunshot and Mr Bellew's car window being smashed – and then saw Detective Garda Donohoe falling to the ground and not moving. After this, she told the court, an individual ran towards her. Ms McShane wiped away tears before saying that she thought he was coming 'to kill me because I'd seen too much'. This individual smashed her driver's side window and told her to give him 'the fucking money' before fleeing with her handbag. Footage was also played to the court from a dash camera in Pat Bellew's car that captured some of the incident, in which screaming and shouting could be heard, outlining the sheer terror of what had unfolded. Mary Hanlon, whose Nissan Qashqai was blocked in by the stolen Volkswagen, said her gut instinct was that the driver of this car, whom she saw from a side profile, was a female with blonde hair, wearing a beanie hat, aged in her 20s or 30s, but that it equally 'could have been a fella wearing a blonde wig'. After hearing the shot, she told the court: 'My initial reaction was that guards had fired at these guys and they cleared off.' She described the gang as 'very fit and very fast' and that after they left she realised what had actually happened. Further testimony would be given by gardaí who were immediately on the scene after the shooting.

The court sittings were long, normally lasting from 10 a.m. until after 4 p.m. For Brady, this created an issue with getting exercise while being held on remand in Mountjoy Prison, and his legal team asked the judge to recommend that he get the chance to exercise on returning to prison in the evenings.

On 12 February, Dr Edward Connolly of Forensic Science Ireland gave evidence of examining samples from the scene, including the garda car, a cigarette butt, chewing gum, and a mobile phone. After giving evidence-in-chief under questioning by the prosecution, he was asked by Fiona Murphy in her cross-examination to confirm that there was no DNA match to Aaron Brady from any samples tested at the scenes. 'No,' Dr Connolly replied.

Gardaí who encountered Brady in the hours and days after the robbery also gave evidence, including John Moroney, now an inspector, who had stopped Brady with Flynn in the BMW at Ballymascanlon roundabout the following afternoon. Inspector Moroney explained that the conflicting accounts

given by both men, along with Brady's claim that he had only
heard about the murder when he woke up even though he was
staying inside the cordon, 'felt strange', leading to him writing
up a report on the encounter.

*

The following week saw the first clash between the senior counsels in the absence of the jury as Mark Phillips, who had been
promoted to detective inspector, was being cross-examined
during legal argument about Aaron Brady's statement and off-
the-record account given in February 2013, not long after
Detective Garda Donohoe's murder. Mr Grehan raised an issue
about the defence, mentioning that documents would be given
to the witness that the prosecution intended to introduce
anyway and that he was 'slightly concerned' about the way this
was being done. His opposing counsel said he did not see any
potential difficulties with this, adding that 'every opportunity
we get to make our case the prosecution are intervening, trying
to put impediments', describing the objection as 'ridiculous' and
an attempt to thwart the defence in putting their case to the
witness. A clearly unimpressed Michael O'Higgins also said
that he had 'never seen a prosecution conducted in this way'
and alleged the objection was without merit and only to make
'more difficulty for the defence to make its case'. The prosecution counsel retorted: 'I will strip the anger out of your
response,' saying that he had a responsibility to contribute to
the proper running of the case and that he was not trying to
stop his counterpart doing anything.

The defence then continued cross-examining Detective
Inspector Phillips, in front of the jury now, at length over the

course of several hours about why the yard at 155 Concession Road was not searched after Aaron Brady claimed he was there on the night of the robbery. The witness said that the PSNI were asked to conduct a trawl of Concession Road for CCTV but couldn't say why the PSNI weren't asked to carry out a search of the yard as he was not the SIO at the time. Detective Inspector Phillips said that any information given in Brady's account to gardaí was not deemed to be true at all. In re-examination he told Mr Grehan that he had been sent to Dundalk to investigate the murder of Detective Garda Donohoe and the robbery at Lordship Credit Union, and that he had no brief to investigate diesel laundering. Asked why they had not investigated Brady's alleged presence at Concession Road, Detective Inspector Phillips said: 'Because it took place sometime between 8 p.m. and 9 p.m. and further statements, at the time, placed him at Lough Road later that night.' Asked when he first became aware that Aaron Brady had suggested he was at the diesel-laundering yard during the murder, the witness said December 2019.

One of the next witnesses called was Jade Fitzpatrick, who had been in Jessica King's home on the night of the robbery. Questioned over why she had initially told the PSNI that Brady arrived at the house earlier than 9 p.m., she said: 'Jessica asked me to, more or less peer pressure in regard to his curfew at the time.' The curfew was related to the bail conditions he was under over the Dundalk ramming charges. She agreed that she then thought better and went back the following day to amend her statement. Cross-examined by the defence, she agreed that Brady was a 'cheeky fella in an out-going way' and did not appear preoccupied or worried when she saw him that night.

During the trial, Aaron Brady's father attended every day, while his mother was also present most days. His sister Laurene was also present on occasion and was there to support him on 26 February. The following day a juror brought it to the attention of the court that he recognised her from his local shop in south Dublin where she worked. Justice White said the juror was uncomfortable with continuing because of this association and discharged him.

That day Aaron Brady's former girlfriend was called to testify. She had by this stage long moved on from Brady and recently had a child with her new partner. As Jessica King walked past him towards the witness box, her ex-boyfriend kept his head down. Outlining their relationship, she said they began dating in September 2012 and it ended some time the following year. 'I probably went to America – we did see each other a couple of times over there, but shortly after we stopped seeing each other. I can't remember the exact month,' she told Lorcan Staines. When she was questioned about messages she deleted from her phone, in particular one in which Brady said he was planning on loading a lorry on the night of the robbery, Jessica King said: 'I was just worried about getting him in trouble about the diesel so I deleted the message.' She was then asked about their phone conversation immediately after he was stopped by Inspector Moroney.

> He called and told me he was stopped at the Ballymascanlon roundabout by the guards. He said it was at a checkpoint, people were stopped. It could have had something to do with the road closed off, something to do with what happened [the previous night] at the credit union. He just said him and Jimmy were questioned about it and said:

'If anything is mentioned to you just say I was there a bit earlier and left a bit earlier,' just in case he got in trouble for his curfew.

Ms King added that when she was brought down to the PSNI station she realised 'things were a bit more serious', saying she panicked and deleted some messages. She also admitted lying when she initially told the police that he was in her house from 7.30 p.m. until 9.30 p.m., saying: 'I was afraid of getting him into trouble over the curfew and I didn't realise what it was about so I just lied for him.' The witness also told the court that she later spoke to Brady, who told her to 'go in and change that and tell the truth about the actual time I arrived at'. Under cross-examination she was asked about a text in which Brady had said he had work between 8 p.m. and 10 p.m. on the night of the murder. Jessica King said of this: 'I don't know what he meant ... I never asked him, it must have been away with the lads.' She said he was normally 'good craic, talking away', 'a messer', as well as smiling and joking. Ms King said his demeanour was the same when she saw him on the night of the murder, and when asked if there appeared to be any bother on him, she replied: 'No.' With that her evidence concluded and she was shepherded out of court.

*

Much of the evidence that the prosecution intended to call was robustly challenged by the defence. The images of Brady and Flynn posing with a gun and wearing balaclavas, which were identified by Detective Garda Joe Ryan as being similar to the ones worn by the raiders, was ruled inadmissible by the judge.

The state also wanted the jury to hear that Brendan Treanor was a suspect in the first Lordship robbery, saying it was relevant because of his alleged involvement in the 2013 raid and his ties to Aaron Brady. Justice White said he had no difficulty in the jury concluding that the gang could have acquired local knowledge about the previous robbery to help with their planning and execution on 25 January 2013. However, he ruled that there might be an improper inference for the jury to draw and did not allow them to hear evidence that Treanor was arrested for the previous Lordship robbery. The phone calls made by Brady while in prison in which he spoke about US witnesses were likewise ruled out.

The prosecution were also having trouble getting key witnesses to come before the court. Colin Hoey, who had given Brady an alibi but then retracted it, had failed to turn up despite a witness order being served on him. The judge said that Hoey was 'quite deliberately in the face of the court refusing to attend' and issued a warrant for his arrest to come before him 'at the earliest opportunity'. Hoey would later be jailed for 21 days and fined €2,000 for contempt of court, claiming he received implicit threats by criminal or paramilitary elements not to attend. Justice White also issued a bench warrant for the arrest of Tommy McGeary, who had failed to attend court after being served with a witness order.

Further complications for the trial were to come. By 13 March, the World Health Organisation was declaring Europe the epicentre of the Covid-19 pandemic. That week, Taoiseach Leo Varadkar announced the closure of schools, bars, and public houses and advised against house parties in an attempt to curb the spiralling number of Covid cases. On 20 March, the jury were informed that they would not be required for four weeks as lawyers dealt with legal arguments, while special arrangements were put in place within the court to ensure the safety of those involved in the case. Two rooms would be made available so jurors could socially distance on their return, while the panel would have to utilise seats in the body of the court normally used by the public. The trial had also moved to the larger Court 19 on the sixth floor, with the building like a ghost town as the capital murder trial remained the only live case for several months. People not directly involved in the trial, including journalists, members of the public, and some gardaí, were moved to an overflow room in Court 22 where they could watch proceedings via video-link. The number of people permitted in the court was limited to 30, and those who remained there were the legal teams, the jury, the main members of the investigation team, Brady's immediate family, Detective Garda Donohoe's family, and court staff.

By 27 March, the situation had deteriorated, with 2,100 confirmed cases and 22 deaths; the Taoiseach addressed the nation outlining a stay-at-home order while banning non-essential travel and contact with others. The situation in New York, where many of the key witnesses lived, had also escalated, and Justice White granted a prosecution application to allow them give evidence via video-link.

*

On 20 April, Michael O'Higgins brought an application to discharge the jury, saying that the gravity of the charge together with the length of time since the panel last heard evidence and the current health pandemic were grounds for a discharge. He argued that the 14-person panel had been in recess for several weeks and that this would total eight or nine weeks by the time the trial was scheduled to resume. The period for which they hadn't sat, he said, was presumptively putting the trial in hazard. 'They're being asked to deliberate on my client's liberty for 40 years, or not, in circumstances where this is a global pandemic and are not, and cannot, in my respectful submission, be free from the type of worry, anxiety, and distraction to pronounce a verdict in which a fellow citizen is facing a 40-year jail sentence,' he told the court. Mr Grehan said that the severity of the sentence upon conviction was 'irrelevant' and 'without merit', as there is no 'sliding scale of fair procedure'.

The defence also said that they would make a submission on representations made by the court in an email to the jury and the consequences of this, saying the judge was not in a position to give any medical reassurances to jurors. A visibly angered Justice White said he totally rejected that he was 'in any way trying to encourage jurors to do one thing in breach of their health. That is simply untrue and an outrageous allegation to make.' The application was opposed by the prosecution, and the following day the court gave its ruling on what it described as a 'very sensitive issue'. Becoming irate over the claims made against him, Justice White's voice grew increasingly louder as he stated:

With honour, with honour, I would never try to influence a jury – never would I try influence a jury to do anything they don't want to do and I take that allegation very, very seriously and I am very upset by that. Under no circumstances was that email to the jury to do something they didn't want to do. The prosecution and defence have my solemn word on that. Let it be said, I'm not in a situation, I respect everybody that comes into this court. If my integrity is called into question, I'm not going to have it, basically. That's my bottom line. I'm not allowing my integrity to be called into question.

Refusing the application, he said the president of the High Court had declared that jury trials should continue to their conclusion and that he wasn't discharging the jury at this point. By the following day, matters had cooled, with the judge saying he lost his temper and apologising. Mr O'Higgins responded by saying there was no requirement for him to do so and himself apologised if he had caused any unnecessary upset. There would be more disputes to come between the legal teams and judge.

*

That week, Aaron Brady also sacked his solicitor, with Richard Corrigan of Phoenix Law coming on the record to represent him. The next application brought by the defence was to have Brady's return from the United States deemed inadmissible, with Fiona Murphy describing it as a 'de facto extradition' of her client. While not reported on at the time because it was in the absence of the jury, Brady was called to give evidence as part of this application. He outlined the circumstances of his arrest in New York, saying he had applied for a green card prior to his detention. Under cross-examination from Brendan Grehan, he said: 'I did explain to the agent at no stage did I want to go to the Republic of Ireland, that I fled to America on an English passport.'

The senior counsel wasn't having any of it, saying Brady never contested his removal at the time and told him: 'Come on, Mr Brady, you knew the plane was going to Ireland, to Dublin.' The defendant said he expressed 'several preferences' that he wanted to go to the UK, adding: 'I was telling them all this time I didn't want to go to Ireland.' The judge ruled that there was no subterfuge by gardaí assisting in his removal, as there were live charges against him over the Dundalk matter, and that his arrest and charge over the capital murder was not in any way affected by his deportation.

At the beginning of May another juror was discharged because of their concerns over the Covid pandemic, reducing the panel to 13. With the case expected to progress to the evidence from US witnesses, forces were at play in the background trying to ensure this would not happen.

16

A CAMPAIGN OF INTIMIDATION

The first indication that there was potential interference in the case came when Brendan Grehan was responding to a defence argument about records of witnesses being released, saying the proffering of that information could lead to trouble being made for somebody living in the United States. 'It's a matter of great concern for me given the tenor of communications we have had,' he said, adding that there had been communications to people associated with witnesses from people connected to Aaron Brady, 'all to the effect of seeking to make life difficult for them'. The defendant, he said, also 'has boots on the ground in New York telling him exactly what's happening with Homeland Security'. The campaign of intimidation escalated weeks later.

On the morning of 8 May, the senior counsel stood up and asked that ordinary members of the public be excluded from the hearing, in particular Eugene Flynn Snr, who was present in the gallery. He said that the previous night Detective Inspector Phillips had been notified of a WhatsApp message circulating in the border community. It included a text message and four excerpts from the video statement given by

Ronan Flynn, which were recorded from a laptop by a mobile phone. The message read:

> Aboy Ronan Flynn giving the guards a statement about that guard getting shot. That's over in New York he was supposed to get extradited back over here for beating a boy with a hammer and had drugs charges in New York. Got all his charges dropped and got the green card. Touting on his own cousins and then they flew him over to America and gave him a job.

Detective Inspector Phillips agreed that the association of the word 'tout' with the videos sent was an attempt to intimidate both Ronan Flynn and other witnesses. Mr Grehan said that Aaron Brady had been provided with a laptop to view electronic exhibits, including the video statement, and that the matter was being investigated by a separate unit within the NBCI. The barrister said that it was a 'very pointed attempt to intimidate a witness or witnesses' and that the reference to 'tout' has a 'very, very strong connotation' in South Armagh. He also said the timing was interesting, given that they had just applied for video-link facilities for the evidence of New York witnesses. Michael O'Higgins described it as 'wholly reprehensible and beyond comprehension', with the judge agreeing that it was intended to have an adverse effect on witnesses. A representative from WhatsApp was requested to attend a special court sitting that evening to determine what could be done. In truth, there was very little, given the platform the video was being circulated on. Justice White summed up his frustration at the situation, saying: 'Today is a very sobering day for the administration of criminal justice in Ireland. It is the most outrageous contempt I've ever come across in my time as a judge. It seems the court is powerless to prevent its dissemination at this point in time.'

As part of the criminal investigation into the matter, detectives took possession of the laptop provided to Aaron Brady and, in the preliminary stages of the inquiry, believed that the contents uploaded and shared on WhatsApp were recorded from Brady's laptop. The prosecution were also objecting to Brady's being provided with a replacement laptop and, because of a lack of trust in him following the leaking of Ronan Flynn's statement, suggested that sensitive documents should be read to him by his lawyers rather than a physical copy being in his possession. Brady's senior counsel said the dissemination of the footage and the text accompanying it was not something associated with the defence team and was 'unhelpful', as Ronan Flynn was 'a most important witness from the defence's point of view'.

A report was also compiled by Detective Inspector Phillips on communications from Brady's associates. One such instance occurred in April, when a former girlfriend of Christopher Morton was contacted on Facebook by Sonya Brady, in which she wrote: 'I'm not sure if you're aware my brother Aaron is in court for the murder of a policeman in Ireland. I can tell you for sure he had no part in it. The Irish police have given people in New York money, arranged visa green cards, left people off with crimes and criminal records.' She also claimed Mr Morton was 'forced to tell lies' about her brother, adding: 'I promise you all the Brady family want is the truth and we won't stop until we get the truth. We're asking people who have any or some knowledge about this behaviour no matter how small to help. We have information about Chris but we will continue to dig for more.' The message, which wasn't responded to, was followed up by another communication, asking for his ex-girlfriend to have a 'casual chat' with Brady's solicitor.

Molly Staunton also received a Facebook message from Danielle Healy which read: 'Dear Molly. I'm sorry to bother you, I've been asked by Aaron's solicitor to write to you to ask would it be possible to speak to you by phone. [It would] take up a very short time. Thanks a million for your time and help. I can send you his number, or if you send me your number I can pass it to him. Kind regards.'

The previous year, Daniel Cahill had been approached by a friend of Aaron Brady in New York, asking if he had made a statement to gardaí. On 11 August 2019, he was contacted by Sonya Brady via Facebook asking if they could speak to him about the case – before the fact that he had given a statement had even been disclosed to the defence.

There was another incident inside the court on 10 June, when Detective Garda Jim McGovern alleged that as he was leaving the witness box Tony Brady muttered something at him. He told the court: 'Judge, Mr Brady there as I walked down looked me in the eye and muttered words – I don't know what he said, I took that to be addressed to me, so that's all I can say. Yesterday a similar thing happened as I walked by the first time in the box but I said nothing. That's why I raised that there.' Tony Brady said there was 'no interference' on his part and was warned not to make any comments to witnesses.

*

The evidence continued before the jury when they were brought through the phone data and CCTV footage over several days, including the material connecting Aaron Brady to the theft of the Volkswagen Passat. Garda analyst Ed McGoey told the court it was 'unusual' that on the night of the credit union robbery the suspects' phones went inactive, stayed inactive, and were reactivated over a very similar time period. The only previous period that month during which all phones were silent was on 7 January, although Brady's, Flynn's, and Treanor's phones all went inactive hours apart. A car identification expert, Andy Wooller of Acuity Forensics, also gave evidence that James Flynn's car matched the BMW captured on CCTV at key times linked to the crime, including near the scene where the Volkswagen was stolen, driving in convoy with the stolen car after the burglary, and again travelling towards the burn site after the credit union murder.

On 11 June, the first US witness was called to give evidence, and Molly Staunton was connected to the court via video-link from her sitting room in New York. She began by outlining to the court her own background and how in January 2016 she was working at the Press Box pub in the city and later met Tommy McGeary. She recalled how that summer she was sitting on the couch in the apartment with her boyfriend and Ronan Flynn when Aaron Brady came in. Asked what she heard him say, Ms Staunton told the jury: 'That they had murdered someone in Ireland and that he had to carry around that guilt of having murdered a cop in Ireland.' She said Brady was in distress, crying, while he was also concerned about being a bad father to his own son.

Molly Staunton recalled Brady saying 'they were the biggest gangsters in Ireland' and were 'going on about how he had actually murdered somebody, that he took someone's life, they were big shots in Ireland, that they were the biggest gangsters'.

Questioned by Mr Grehan if Brady said who he had murdered, she replied: 'No, he didn't say who.' She continued: 'What I heard Aaron Brady say was that he was upset about having a child and not being there for his child. And he was upset that he wouldn't be a good father and that he didn't want to do construction. And that was all that he had said.' Under further examination, she went on to say that Brady was 'intoxicated and was going kind of crazy', adding: 'He said that he was in fear of the cops coming to the apartment because he had shot a cop in Ireland.'

The witness was then cross-examined by Fiona Murphy for the defence. As the senior counsel was getting into her questioning, Ms Staunton told her that someone was coming into her apartment. Following a brief break the examination continued, with the barrister asking if she was telling the court what she remembered or what she'd read from her statement. She told the court: 'Once I read the transcript it all came back to me. I had not read the transcript previously.' Ms Staunton again stated Aaron Brady said he had murdered someone in Ireland and that he spoke about the guilt of having taken someone's life. 'I didn't just pull this out of thin air – I remember him saying a cop was involved.'

However, her stance deviated under further questioning. Ms Murphy put it to the witness that the height of what her client said that night was that he was worried about police looking for him but that he didn't make any admission. 'No, he did not,' Ms Staunton told the jury. It was further put to her that the words that came from Aaron Brady's mouth were that he was upset about being sought by the guards for the shooting of the policeman, to which she replied: 'Yeah, that's correct.' The proposition that he never made an admission was put to her again, with Molly Staunton saying: 'That is correct.' It was a significant departure from the statement she had given to gardaí almost three years earlier and the testimony given moments before. The prosecution asked for the jury to be removed and said that the witness had not come up to proof in terms of her evidence, despite her previous statements, and they were considering treating her as a hostile witness.

Fiona Murphy responded by saying she was concerned about what had happened during the cross-examination with somebody whispering to Ms Staunton, indicating there was another person in the room, noting she looked 'very upset' before the jury left. The defence counsel raised concerns that there was no regulation on the other end of the camera. When she returned on screen, Molly Staunton told the judge that the room was now secure and that she'd got annoyed when a person came in unannounced.

The trial was adjourned until the following day but there were more issues overnight. That evening Ms Staunton's ex-boyfriend appeared to be about to contact her via the Snapchat app – she saw that Tommy McGeary had begun typing a message, but no communication was sent. She contacted Special Agent Matt Katzke, who said that if she had any immediate concerns she should contact 911.

The following afternoon the jury continued hearing evidence from Ms Staunton, but the testimony was interrupted once again. A radio was playing in the background, and the young woman was heard speaking to a person offscreen, identified as Seamus.

Molly: 'Seamus, they're hearing it – you have to turn it off. You got to turn it off – they just heard it.'

Seamus: 'Get back in your fucking room.'

Molly: 'I'm begging you, this is a murder case. Will you just leave? I can't focus.'

Seamus: 'I don't give a fuck. You need to be fucking [inaudible].'

Molly: 'You just want to terrorise me.'

Seamus: 'You terrorise everyone else.'

Molly: 'You have to leave. The judge, he wants people … No, you can't do this, Seamus. This is a murder trial – this is my life. I'm asking you to leave, I'm asking you politely. I'm politely asking. I'll make it up to you.'

Seamus: 'It's too late now. Swear on it.'

Molly: 'I swear.'

Seamus: [Inaudible.]

Molly: 'Fine, you want to listen to it then.'

Seamus: 'Just fucking do it.'

Molly: 'The judge just asked to get you to leave.'

Seamus: 'Tell them what you're supposed to tell them.'

Molly: 'I'm not telling them.'

Seamus: 'Tell them what you're supposed to tell them.'

Asked to clarify who the person was, she said it was her friend and that he had left, and she declined a request to have a police officer sent to her home. The defence again raised concerns around the environment in which the witness was giving evidence and the lack of regulation. In re-examination, Ms Staunton once again failed to commit to evidence she had given, saying that Aaron Brady only said he was concerned about gardaí looking for him. In the absence of the jury, Brendan Grehan applied for her to be treated as a hostile witness, after she initially gave evidence in accordance with her witness statement before it changed. Despite defence protestations, Justice White agreed that Ms Staunton had given 'completely contradictory evidence' and allowed the application.

In the absence of the jury, the video of her statement was played to Molly Staunton. She accepted that it was what she said at the time, that it must have been clearer in her head then, and that she would give this evidence in front of the jury. Ms Staunton said she would testify in front of the jury that Aaron Brady 'definitely said he shot someone' and that she knew from what he had told her that a 'cop was involved'. The jurors were brought back in and the case continued. However, just as she was about to testify to what Aaron Brady had admitted, the abusive friend once again returned to the room.

Molly: 'One second – can you leave?'

Seamus: 'Will you fuck off … put a stop to this, put a stop to this.'

Molly: 'No, I have to.'

Seamus: 'There's no more testimony. You can stop right now, there's no more testimony.'

The final comments were spoken into the laptop, as if he was speaking directly to the court, and with that the device was shut and the live feed cut off. The court was stunned into silence as the judge, lawyers, jury, and gardaí attempted to understand what had just happened. A frantic effort was made to contact Molly Staunton in the US to check on her safety, while the jury were ushered back to their rooms. Around 15 minutes later they reconnected with Ms Staunton in New York, who assured them that she was safe and that her friend didn't know she was still on a video call.

Before the jury were brought back in, Fiona Murphy argued that the value of Molly Staunton's evidence was hugely compromised and, at worst, could be held against her client if certain conclusions were reached about the interruption. With the jury back in the room, Molly Staunton was again asked what she had heard Aaron Brady say and was again non-committal, saying: 'As far as him admitting to killing a cop, I can't say he admitted to it.' The footage from her garda statement was then played to her in front of the jury, to which she said: 'Now that I have re-seen the video, I stand by my statement of what I said. He did say he killed a cop.'

There would be further sinister attempts to intimidate the young woman after she finished giving her evidence. That evening she received a video on Snapchat from McGeary in which her ex-boyfriend made a gun gesture with his left hand and told her: 'Bang bang you're dead.' A short time later she got a second message, which read: 'You silly silly girl' followed by ten emojis depicting a crying laughing face. Ms Staunton rang Detective Inspector Phillips saying she was extremely concerned about the threats and had looked up information on the IRA, South Armagh, and informants getting kneecapped. The young woman was considering moving out of New York because of the threat but was fearful of leaving her apartment.

The senior investigator calmed her, telling her that they had no immediate concerns for her welfare, which reassured her.

As a result of the interruption, the defence made another application for the jury to be discharged. Ms Murphy stated that a portion of the evidence, although not before the jury, was not recorded and was in breach of the Criminal Evidence Act. The second and more pressing reason for the jury to be discharged was the inadvertent prejudice stemming from the interruption of the testimony, with Ms Murphy saying it would be highly prejudicial against the accused and that there was no remedy for it. Brendan Grehan disagreed, saying there was nothing to suggest a connection between 'Seamus' and Aaron Brady and that no complaint was made about the evidence actually given. Mr Justice White said in his ruling that he could not see how any prejudice would fall on the accused. He refused the application to discharge the jury and said that he would direct the jury that the difficulties during Molly Staunton's testimony had nothing to do with Aaron Brady.

The following week the second US witness was called to give evidence via video-link. Given what had happened with the previous witness, Homeland Security had agreed to the exceptional measure during the pandemic of supplying facilities at JFK Airport for Daniel Cahill to give his testimony and be supervised by a person unconnected to the investigation. There would be further robust confrontations between the barristers prior to the witness being produced, and they would see Justice White pushed to anger once again.

During one argument, he had previously revealed that he had a document in front of him that he read every day that included advice such as be patient, keep calm, do not get distressed, do not be provoked, and be courteous at all times. The document also reminded him not to make spontaneous judgments but to go away and think before responding to arguments made by barristers. He told the senior counsels about the document to explain to them the pressure he was under and said that on several occasions he had walked out of court 'very, very angry' but hadn't shown it on the bench. On another occasion he said it was the most difficult trial he had sat in since the so-called Annabel's trial, a high-profile case in 2004 regarding the death of 18-year-old Brian Murphy, who was beaten to death outside a nightclub attached to Dublin's Burlington Hotel.

Days before Daniel Cahill was due to be called, Michael O'Higgins became embroiled in an argument with his opposing counsel over whether the witness's evidence should be delayed until they had completed legal arguments on a separate issue. The defence refused to tell the court what the separate issue was, with Brendan Grehan saying it was outrageous that Mr Cahill's testimony should be delayed over an issue that the prosecution knew nothing about. An angered Justice White said the continued accusations between two of the most senior advocates in the Irish bar during a capital murder trial was 'disgraceful', adding: 'Allegations of professional misconduct are being thrown around here like snuff at a wake.' Calling for improved relations between the barristers, he said the allegations 'must stop for the dignity of the Court and of the Bar'.

*

In the middle of the trial, another detective would lose his life in a fatal shooting. Forty-three-year-old Detective Garda Colm Horkan was on duty on 17 June when, shortly before midnight, he responded to reports of a motorbike driving erratically on

Main Street in Castlerea, County Roscommon. At the scene Stephen Silver, a man with a history of mental illness, approached the detective and a struggle ensued. He took Detective Garda Horkan's weapon and struck him with the butt of the gun before shooting him several times. Colm Horkan, from Charlestown in County Mayo, was struck 11 times and was pronounced dead at the scene despite the best efforts of colleagues to revive him. Detective Garda Horkan, who was nicknamed 'Bear' and described as the 'quintessential local guard', became the 89th member of An Garda Síochána to die in the course of their duty. Stephen Silver was later found guilty of capital murder and is currently serving the minimum mandatory sentence of 40 years' imprisonment.

*

On 22 June, Daniel Cahill was sworn in to give evidence via video-link. He outlined how he had worked in the Coachman's Inn bar for several years, during which he would have encountered Aaron Brady almost every weekend. He recalled the first time the defendant confessed to him, while Brady was bloodied and his ego bruised after being beaten up in a bar fight. Mr Cahill said he followed the trail of blood into the toilets where he saw a 'shook' Brady staring into the mirror. 'He just kept repeating that he was going to kill Shane Farrell, that he didn't know the things he was capable of, of what he's done and who he is,' the jury were told. 'He said Shane Farrell should know better because he had shot a member of An Garda Síochána in Ireland and it was a stupid thing to retaliate or mess with him.'

Cahill told the jury about another occasion where Aaron Brady was drinking heavily in the bar until the early hours. 'He

asked me had I ever killed anyone. I said: "No, no I haven't."
He told me how he felt at the time, how he'd done it. He told
me the consequences of what would happen, how he would
feel after he'd done it, the impact it had on his life. He said he
had nightmares.' Daniel Cahill also said: 'He mentioned how
a robbery had gone wrong and led to him shooting somebody.'
Asked if Aaron Brady had said whom he shot, the witness
replied: 'A garda síochána. He never mentioned the person by
name or said where.'

Mr Cahill recalled being at a house party the following
year after work with Aaron Brady and others. 'These people
were trying to outdo each other in almost a pissing competi-
tion would be my best words. Who was the man, who was the
person you would not want to be getting on the wrong side of.
Aaron decided he was the person there with the most experience because he said that he was the only person there who had
killed someone.'

As the afternoon wore on the jury continued listening intently
as Mr Cahill recalled a fourth time that Brady had admitted
his involvement in the shooting. By this stage the witness had
begun working in a different pub and was driving home when
he encountered the defendant. 'He was talking about how the
papers back in Ireland all the time, how they'd written articles
about him. He took his phone out and showed me one of the
articles … I remember the headline "Man who shot a cop in
New York". He told me that was him in the picture.'

Finally in his evidence-in-chief, Daniel Cahill recalled his
last encounter with Brady some months later. 'He mentioned
the fact that gardaí were trying to speak to a lot of people.
They'd been down to Micky Leneghan, and he believed they
were looking for him in New York. I don't think Aaron was

under the impression that people were going to speak to the police because they were intimidated by him, but he was very worried he was going to get caught because he felt like the net was closing on him.'

After several hours the prosecution had finished its questioning, and it was the defence's turn to cross-examine Mr Cahill. Over the following two days he was subjected to a robust interrogation by Justin McQuade that at times drew the ire of Justice White. Mr Cahill was first asked if he had any convictions in the United States, replying that he had tickets for disorderly conduct. McQuade then asked the witness why he was hiding in his attic when the HSI agents came to his house the previous year. 'I didn't know it was law enforcement – you're painting a picture as if I ran from Homeland Security. If I'd have known Homeland Security were at my door asking about Aaron Brady, we'd have had a longer, better conversation.' The barrister shot back: 'Do you always hide in your attic every time there is a knock on the door?' The questioning then turned to his interaction with off-duty gardaí in Connolly's Bar in Manhattan on St Patrick's Day in 2017. The witness said that he had told the gardaí at that time about what Brady had told him, but also told the gardaí he didn't believe Brady then. 'What would you expect members of An Garda Síochána to do with that information as soon as they received it?' he was asked, responding that he didn't know as they were off duty.

McQuade: 'Mr Cahill, you're a smart fella.'

Cahill: 'You're not speaking to me like I'm a smart fella. You're asking me what gardaí do – I don't know what gardaí do.'

McQuade: 'I consider it a matter of common sense.'

Cahill: 'You just said I'm smart, now you're saying I've no common sense.'

McQuade: 'A child would know the answer to this. You think they would discuss it?'

Cahill: 'I don't know what a bunch of drunk people do when they're in New York with their jobs back in Ireland. It depends on a person.'

McQuade: 'Do you think they would tell somebody?'

Cahill: 'I don't know.'

McQuade: 'Mr Cahill, a child of ten would know the answer to that.'

Justice White interjected and told the barrister that he could not comment on the response. Mr McQuade then put it to the witness that if he had dropped 'this bombshell' to gardaí in 2017 the investigation team would have been on the next plane over, but that this didn't occur because it was a lie. 'No, sir,' Daniel Cahill calmly replied. The barrister continued by saying that Mr Cahill had come up with a 'self-serving story' to 'save your skin in the United States'. Again the witness replied: 'No, sir, that's not true. That's false.' The barrister was corrected by the judge for not allowing the witness to answer a question before continuing: 'It beggars belief, Mr Cahill, that this is what you're asking a jury to accept. It beggars belief that you told off-duty members of An Garda Síochána that Aaron Brady made these admissions to you and they did nothing about it, an alternative you're asking the jury to accept.' Mr Cahill, who had remained composed throughout, responded that he had told the gardaí in 2017 that Brady had said things to him but that he didn't believe them at the time.

The cross-examination then turned to Daniel Cahill's life in Dublin and his friendship with the Ryans.

McQuade: 'Alan Ryan was murdered in September 2012. Vincent Ryan was murdered in 2016.'

Cahill: 'Yes.'

McQuade: 'Did you attend the funeral of Alan Ryan?'

Cahill: 'No, I did not. I went to work in Malahide on that day – I couldn't get time off.'

McQuade: 'Were you part of the Ryan Crew?'

Cahill: 'No, I'm not, I was not. I didn't go to the man's funeral; I went to work instead. You're asking me am I a member of an illegal organisation, I wasn't. I didn't go to the man's funeral; I had a job as a hairstylist. I'm answering the question you're asking me. You're trying to tell me I am friends with these people in 2013. They were childhood friends, these people, like many people from the neighbourhood.'

McQuade: 'You said you grew up with these people.'

Cahill: 'No, I grew up with Vincent.'

McQuade: 'I put it to you that you were a member of the Ryan Crew.'

Cahill: 'No, I was a hairstylist – I told you that. If you want to look where I was on Alan Ryan's funeral, I was in work. These are the facts.'

McQuade: 'I'm putting to you that you were part of the Ryan Crew – what I mean is the Dublin Real IRA.'

Cahill: 'That is completely false. That is a ridiculous statement to say. I never committed a crime or anything like this in Ireland – to accuse me of being a member of something, that's a ridiculous statement to make.'

McQuade: 'I'm putting to you that you were a member of the Ryan Crew.'

Cahill: 'And I've answered multiple times it's false. I didn't even go to the man's funeral, never mind being a member of his crew.'

McQuade: 'What I mean is an associate of [Alan] Ryan and engaged in dissident IRA activities.'

Cahill: 'No, that's completely false.'

At this point, Brendan Grehan rose to his feet and described it as an 'outrageous line of cross-examination', asking the court for a ruling on the matter and for the jury to be removed from court. He said what had been put to the witness in a public forum was 'unfair and outrageous' and wanted to know the basis for the questioning. 'I demand to know where the instruction came from. In my submission, it's in breach of the barrister's code of conduct: it's improper and unprofessional conduct for a barrister to ask questions which are scandalous or intended only for the purpose of vilifying, annoying, and insulting a witness.' Justice White agreed that it was an 'outrageous' and 'over the top' question, saying it was a collateral issue and that the defence can't throw mud at the witness.

When the jury returned, McQuade told the witness: 'I apologise for asking the last question, which overstepped the mark.' Mr Cahill was then asked about a picture of him with a group of men holding a banner for the 32 County Sovereignty Movement, a political group often linked to the Real IRA. The witness said he was asked to hold the banner for a picture following a sponsored walk but that he knew nothing about the organisation.

The following day the cross-examination continued with allegations put to Daniel Cahill that in 2015 he was involved in an assault on the defendant, during which a knife was held to Aaron Brady's toes in the alleged aggravated burglary at his apartment. The court was told the alleged incident occurred after claims that Brady had slept with another man's partner. The prosecution objected to the line of questioning, with the defence barrister saying they were the instructions from his client. The matter was broached several times with Daniel Cahill, who at one point replied: 'This has nothing to do with me. I've never assaulted Aaron Brady. I've never touched a hair on Aaron Brady in my whole life. I've never put hands on the man. The common denominator between all this is him, not me. He's the one who slept with someone's girlfriend; he is the one who caused these problems, not me.' He also said that he was working that night, which could be proven if checked. The judge would say in a later ruling that 'a lot of muck was thrown for the most tenuous of reasons' and that this was down to Aaron Brady and the way he instructed his counsel.

The examination then returned to the HSI agents arriving at Mr Cahill's house in July 2019, with him telling the barrister: 'If your client hadn't shot a guard then that wouldn't have happened.' He also said that Special Agent Mary Ann Wade had told him that he did not have to speak to the gardaí but that he volunteered to do so. At the end of the examination Daniel Cahill said: 'You've picked apart my past. I've answered every question and I will continue to do so. I wouldn't have put myself here if this was for me – this is for the family of Adrian Donohoe and this is for the justice system in Ireland.'

After two days of intense questioning, Brendan Grehan stood up for his re-examination and asked the key witness just one question. 'Mr Cahill, have you lied to the jury about what you said Aaron Brady told you about shooting a garda in Ireland?' The barman responded: 'Not once, sir, I have not lied at all in this. My recollection has got me on some aspects but I have not lied.'

17

A SKILLED AND PRACTISED LIAR

The prosecution had intended to call five more witnesses who had given statements about Aaron Brady confessing to his involvement in the shooting, but they never testified for various reasons. The evidence of Christopher Morton was ruled inadmissible after Justice White found that the process of identifying Brady had not been conducted properly. The testimony of Ronan Flynn, he said, was 'not available because of clear intimidation'. Both he and his family living in Ireland were subjected to an 'ongoing campaign of intimidation', Mr Grehan said, adding that there had been further incidents even since the WhatsApp messages had circulated. Anthony Maguire, who was assaulted by Brady and warned to keep his mouth shut, had engaged the services of a solicitor and was refusing to come to Ireland to testify. A decision was made not to call the Cork man whom Detective Inspector Marry had spoken to in 2018, with Mr Grehan saying this man was 'petrified' since coming into possession of information about the murder. Justice White said the situation of Tommy McGeary could only be described as 'bizarre', as he had made it clear that he wanted to go home from the United States when he gave a voluntary statement

implicating Brady, but had since refused to attend court and a
bench warrant had to be issued for his arrest. Further to this,
he had also engaged in the intimidation of Molly Staunton after
she gave her evidence.

The prosecution case was nearing its end, with a number
of witnesses left to call. One of those was Detective Inspector
Marry, whom the defence wanted to examine on the manner
in which the investigation had been conducted, Aaron Brady's
involvement in diesel washing, and the accused's relationship
with other fuel launderers. Recalling his cross-examination,
Detective Inspecter Marry says:

> The SIO is always a target for the defence barrister to
> create doubt in the jury's mind – that the investigation
> was not solid and mistakes could have occurred. I had
> encountered Michael O'Higgins before, and I knew I was
> up against one of the best, if not the best, defence barris-
> ters in the country. He was revered by gardaí and highly
> respected by me. I knew I was up against a formidable
> opponent with intellect and experience, while his ability
> to think on his feet was excellent. I knew he would at all
> times be doing his utmost for Aaron Brady and repre-
> senting him to the best of his ability.
>
> It was 2 July 2020, and it was my time to give evidence.
> Michael O'Higgins rose to his feet, and the cat-and-mouse
> chase began. I felt okay, and I could see he was exam-
> ining all the aspects of the investigation, when suddenly
> he asked me about a book I wrote in 2019. He raised an
> issue about giving long answers to defence barristers to get
> extra details into evidence, and was accusing me of doing
> the same now. He returned to the book later on in front of

the jury. I asked him: 'Have you read it? Give me it and I'll sign it for you.' The jury started to laugh, as did people in the gallery. Even Justice White smiled at the response, but the defence barrister wasn't impressed.

The cross-examination shifted towards Brady's claim that he was moving diesel waste cubes at the time of the offence, with Mr O'Higgins asking the witness why the yard on Concession Road hadn't been searched. Detective Inspector Marry said that CCTV of the area had been canvassed that showed different vehicles near the yard that evening, but none were identified as James Flynn's BMW. He also described Brady's account as 'bunkum and lies', saying the investigation team believed Aaron Brady was in the car park at Lordship Credit Union at the time of the murder. He added that in Brady's original account the defendant claimed he was only in the yard for 15 minutes, well over an hour before the robbery.

The defence was also putting forward the argument that Aaron Brady was in contact with four people that night who were connected to diesel laundering. One of these was Mr C, himself a suspect in the robbery, while another was a fuel launderer who remains a person of interest in the inquiry. Detective Inspector Marry said he believed these men's phones were not switched on that night and that, from his experience, people involved in diesel laundering would have their phones operating so they could be informed by scouts if police or revenue were nearby. When counsel put it to the witness that the investigation had gotten tunnel vision, he replied: 'I totally disagree with that – that's an unfair comment. I was investigating a capital murder. I wasn't investigating what is a revenue offence of diesel laundering.'

Special Agent Mary Ann Wade was called to give evidence and, in an often-spiky encounter with Mr O'Higgins, repeatedly refused to answer questions about the immigration situation of Daniel Cahill, citing a letter of scope from her employer limiting her testimony on matters including a person's visa status. She also repeatedly stated that the key witness wasn't offered any inducements to give a statement or testify.

A brief number of witnesses were tendered before the prosecution closed its case, as the defence then went into evidence. There was surprise among journalists in the courtroom when Michael O'Higgins turned to his client and said Aaron Brady's name, indicating that the man on trial for capital murder would be giving evidence in his own defence. It is rare, but not unprecedented, for a defendant on trial for murder to give evidence in their trial, with this opening them up to intense scrutiny under cross-examination in front of the jury.

Aaron Brady, having spent months listening to the evidence against him and taking detailed notes, made his way from the dock towards the witness box and sat down. His senior counsel began with three direct questions: 'Did you kill Detective Garda Adrian Donohoe? Did you take part in the armed robbery with a firearm? Have you ever admitted to killing Detective Garda Adrian Donohoe?' Brady responded with an empathic 'No' after each question. He was then taken through his life growing up, before moving on to the day of the crime. He told the jury that he was loading a trailer full of diesel waste cubes at the time of the robbery, and while he accepted he had told lies to gardaí, this was to avoid alerting them to the fact that he was involved in diesel laundering. Asked why he told lies to Inspector Moroney the day after the murder he said: 'Not for one second did I think gardaí would be serious about me being involved in this, the murder of Adrian Donohoe.' He moaned about the pressure he was put under after being linked to the robbery by gardaí and the media, saying: 'I was devasted as well. I was in a state of depression. I wouldn't leave the house.'

He said that after fleeing to America he worked with James Flynn but explained their falling out after he went missing in New York. He repeated the allegation made against Daniel Cahill that Cahill assaulted him, describing the key witness as a 'lying psychopath' and saying that he was 'terrified of the man'. Aaron Brady said that Molly Staunton wouldn't interact with them and let out a laugh when it was put to him that he confessed to her about the murder. Asked about the interaction he said: 'I was saying that I'm afraid of losing Danielle because the guards had called and she might leave me. Under no circumstances did I say I shot anybody, or a cop or a detective. "Cop" wouldn't be in my vocabulary – "guard" I would have said.' Michael O'Higgins concluded the examination by asking Brady his height, with the defendant responding that he was between 5 feet 6 inches and 5 feet 7 inches.

It was then Brendan Grehan's turn to cross-examine the man he was prosecuting for firing the fatal shot that killed Detective Garda Donohoe. His first question was a sign of things to come for Aaron Brady over the next five days. 'So let me get this right, you're the victim in all of this?' he asked, with the defendant saying he believed he was. The senior counsel put it to Brady that he was an admitted liar. 'You lie easily and repeatedly. You tell big lies and small lies. You lie for personal gain or when it suits you.' Brady agreed with the assertion but claimed that he had only lied to hide his involvement in diesel laundering.

He went on to tell the prosecution that he couldn't recall where he was on the night of the creeper burglary in Clogherhead but added that he 'certainly didn't steal that car'. Brady denied 'any casing' was taking place when Flynn's BMW drove by the credit union on the afternoon of the robbery and, while he accepted that he had no alibi for the time of the crime, said that 'people know I was in the yard'. He was asked when he started going out with Jessica King but initially claimed he didn't know the precise date. When pressed further, he said it was 12 September 2012, because he had the date tattooed on his back. 'Another lie,' Grehan remarked, with Brady complaining that it was embarrassing because his wife was in court. Asked what date he started going out with Danielle Healy, he said he couldn't remember, before turning to her in court and saying: 'Sorry, Danielle.' Over several days, Brady blamed the media and gardaí for forcing him to leave Ireland and claimed that Inspector Moroney acted 'out of malice' when taking details of his account the day after the robbery. He also falsely claimed that the inspector was rebuked by a judge in a previous case when he gave evidence that Brady used cocaine.

The defendant said that he took his solicitor's advice when lying to gardaí that he was only at the diesel-laundering yard on Concession Road for 15 minutes, and alleged he never asked Colin Hoey to give him an alibi. Questioned about James Flynn and his brother's involvement in the gang, he said: '[They] wouldn't be stealing cars. They were making six figures in America – what would they be doing stealing cars, doing armed robberies?' Questioned about the Ford Transit van pictured at the diesel yard being spotted near the burn site six months before the robbery, he denied having dumped diesel waste at Cumsons Road and said he had never been there.

At one point, going through his texts to Jessica King about meeting someone at Ballymascanlon on the afternoon of the murder, Aaron Brady said he couldn't remember who he was meeting. 'This is one of the most important days of your life, Mr Brady. What are you saying – you can't remember?' Mr Grehan asserted. The defendant was then taken through his phone contacts on the night of the robbery, saying he believed his phone call with Mr C, made over an hour before the raid, was to do with the diesel-laundering yard. Asked about Brendan Treanor's eight failed attempts to ring him an hour before the murder, he said: 'How am I supposed to know what that's about? I didn't receive the calls.' When asked if he believed two cars passing by Cortamlet Primary School towards the burn site were the getaway car and support vehicle, he confidently responded: 'That's for the people who done it – that's not for me to comment on.' The defendant also said he had issues with how the garda investigation was carried out and that the yard at Concession Road should have been searched for tyre marks.

Throughout the five days of cross-examination, he boldly continued to insist that he was loading diesel waste cubes for around two hours before going to Jessica King's home to fix their relationship after their fight the previous night. He described Molly Staunton as 'vulnerable' and 'mistaken' and said that what had happened to her while giving evidence 'was disgraceful'. At one stage Brady laughed when it was put to him that he claimed to be the most feared man in Ireland, and towards the end of his questioning, he again described Daniel Cahill as a 'lying psychopath'. Mr Grehan put to him that a psychopath is 'somebody with no morality, no moral compass, that blames others and manipulates others. That lies to get out of any situation by playing the victim.' Aaron Brady interrupted him to say that this was what Cahill was. 'I'm suggesting when you look closer to home it describes somebody as well,' the barrister told him.

After five days of unrelenting cross-examination and being pummelled by one of the most experienced barristers in the country, Aaron Brady was allowed to stand down and returned to his seat in the dock. Another witness called by the defence was immigration lawyer Kerrie Bretz, who told the trial it would be 'very unusual' for Homeland Security not to take any further action against Mr Cahill over his immigration status.

On 27 July, Lorcan Staines gave the prosecution's closing address to the jury, saying the state's case was one of overwhelming circumstantial evidence tied together with Brady's admissions and wrapped in a litany of his lies. He told them that the accused was under money pressure at the time of the robbery and knew he was facing jail time the following month over the Dundalk dangerous-driving incident. The evidence, he said, indicated that Aaron Brady intended to kill Detective Garda Donohoe when he fired the fatal shot. The defence had put an emphasis on the height of the killer being described as 6 foot 1 inch by Detective Garda Ryan. Mr Staines said this had to be taken in the context that the garda didn't give this description until his third or fourth account, that he was in a sitting position when the shot was fired, and that he was highly stressed.

Mr Staines said the communications blackout of the suspects' phones coincided with the theft of the getaway car and the robbery itself. 'It's not just the phones are off: it's the fact that a multitude of phones are inactive that were in contact beforehand and afterwards. If that were innocent, it would be an extraordinary, unusual, and unlucky coincidence.' He described as 'palaver' the names of other fuel launderers and phone contacts with them being 'bandied around the place' and said this was a 'try-on in open court' in front of the jury.

'I'm going to be candid. Aaron Brady has taken advantage of the enormous disclosure that he received from the prosecution. And he had a long period of time to slowly and carefully assess the disclosure … and used it as building blocks to construct a detailed false alibi,' Mr Staines told them, describing the defendant as a 'skilled and practised liar'. He said that Aaron Brady 'was very convincing' when he claimed that Inspector Moroney was rebuked by a judge and had lied out of some sort of personal animus against him. After this was disproven, he said, there was a mealy-mouthed apology from Brady, with the defendant claiming he was mistaken. 'Mistaken!' Mr Staines exclaimed. 'He looked you dead in the eye and lied to you about Inspector Moroney and he told you he had been rebuked by the judge. This is the measure of the man you are dealing with.' The prosecutor said this lie was told by the defendant to distance himself from the fact that he was the person who shot Detective Garda Donohoe.

He said Brady fled to New York and settled in Woodlawn believing it was a safe haven, working in construction, socialising, and playing football. He came to believe he was beyond the long arm of the law. 'As time went by his confidence grew, and he wore the shooting of Adrian Donohoe like a badge of honour. He used it to intimidate; he used it to curry influence among others. He wouldn't be the first person to think at the time he got away with it. He was confident when police came over that nobody would talk. He was wrong about that,' Mr Staines said. The jury had heard evidence of the defendant lamenting his involvement while drinking and bragging with his chest pushed out. He said the accused never denied the incident with Molly Staunton took place, simply saying she was a 'nice girl' but 'mistaken'. He also described what Aaron Brady had instructed his lawyers to do to Daniel Cahill as 'disgraceful' and that it was simply mud-throwing and baseless claims.

'Aaron Brady told you he considers himself the victim in this case. The victim of a garda campaign, the victim of the media, the victim of circumstances, and it would be easy for me to ridicule that suggestion but I'm not going to. Let's examine it.' He asked the jury if this could all be an enormous mistake, a lie, and bad luck. There would have been a lot of strange circumstances that had to happen if so, the prosecutor said. It would have been an unfortunate circumstance that Brady, the Flynns, and Treanor weren't involved in stealing the Passat, that Flynn was fuelling up late that night to go somewhere else other than Clogherhead, and that the car on CCTV near the scene was a different BMW 5 Series with a modified roof. That the passenger-side window of the BMW 5 Series was down as it drove by the credit union on the afternoon of the robbery, not because it was scoping the premises but for some other reason. That the specific time Aaron Brady claimed he was on his own in the diesel yard just happened to coincide with the time a separate, distinct local gang of young, athletic men were partaking in robbing the cash-in-transit convoy in Lordship. That the phones of the suspects all went off for more than two hours during the robbery for innocent reasons and that this timing was a coincidence. That a different BMW 5 Series, and not James Flynn's, was spotted driving past Chalybeate Road towards the remote burn site. That Aaron Brady didn't first hear of the murder the morning he woke up, but that Inspector Moroney was mistaken in this. That the first call the defendant made after being stopped by gardaí was to Brendan Treanor, just to see what he was up to for the day. That Aaron Brady lied repeatedly in his voluntary statements to gardaí, not because it had anything to do with the murder but to conceal his involvement in diesel laundering. That he fled to America, not because he was guilty of murder but because he was wrongly being blamed on social media. That the other suspects fled Ireland within weeks of the murder all for reasons other than their involvement in the crime. That two totally unconnected people gave evidence of Brady confessing to shooting a cop, one doing so because he had a personal animus towards the defendant, or was forced to over his immigration status, and the other being a US citizen with no baggage who was simply mistaken in what she'd heard Brady say. 'Is that reasonably possible, ladies and gentlemen?' Mr Staines asked the jury. 'That would be some string of unfortunate events. The prosecution leaves that determination in your hands.'

Closing the defence's case, Michael O'Higgins described the circumstantial evidence the prosecution relied on as 'smoke and mirrors', adding: 'But where is the fire?' He said Daniel Cahill claimed to be motivated by seeking justice for Detective Garda Donohoe's family but didn't come forward after the first, second, third, or fourth alleged confession made by Aaron Brady. 'Ladies and gentlemen, does this sound to you like someone with a burning desire for justice?' Mr O'Higgins described the witness as someone with a lot to gain from giving evidence and said that he was not a person whose credibility was undamaged. Molly Staunton's testimony was described as 'literally swinging left to right' like a pendulum, with counsel saying that her evidence could not be relied upon. He noted that the phone communications with the Flynn brothers,

Treanor, and Mr C were a key part of the prosecution case, but added that they had never even been arrested as part of the investigation and described the reliance on the phones' silent periods as evidence against his client as 'very dangerous and flawed'. He also said that Aaron Brady had told lies to cover his involvement in diesel laundering and that these lies had to be taken in the context of speaking to law enforcement in the border region. Mr O'Higgins criticised the garda investigation and said it was 'beyond comprehension' that aspects of his client's account, in relation to him being at the diesel yard, were never checked. He also described Special Agent Wade as an 'extremely difficult' and 'evasive' witness. Concluding his address, Brady's senior counsel asked the jury if the prosecution had proven its case beyond reasonable doubt. 'In my respectful submission, it has not,' Michael O'Higgins told them.

The trial had sat for 112 days, with 66 days of the evidence in front of the jury, who heard from 139 witnesses. In his charge to the jury, which lasted eight days, Justice White went through the evidence and told them that solely relying on the testimony of Molly Staunton could be dangerous. While the panel remained at 13 up to this point and would be reduced to 12 through the drawing of numbers for the deliberations, one juror voluntarily agreed to remove himself from the process. The jury of 12 were then sent off to consider their verdicts.

On the afternoon of Monday 10 August, the jurors had been deliberating for 12 hours and 35 minutes when they were called into the courtroom by Justice White, who informed them that he would now accept a majority verdict on the charges. Before the jury were sent back to continue their deliberations, they were asked if they had reached a verdict on any of the counts. Much to the surprise of the courtroom, the forewoman told the judge that they had. The issue paper was handed to the judge before the registrar announced: 'You say the accused is guilty on count two. Is that correct?' The forewoman responded 'Yes', confirming that they had unanimously found Aaron Brady guilty of robbery at Lordship Credit Union. Aaron Brady showed little emotion as the verdict was read out, knowing that he was now facing a lengthy sentence for his role in the robbery, at the very least. The jury were then sent out again to consider whether they believed he was the masked raider who shot dead Detective Garda Donohoe, with the judge informing them that he would accept a verdict if 10 people agreed. The deliberations continued over the next two days with little sign of a breakthrough.

On the morning of Wednesday 11 August, the jurors had been in talks for over 20 hours when word came in that they had reached a verdict. The court registrar walked out of the courtroom to inform the legal teams of the development, and barristers, gardaí, family members, and journalists hurriedly returned to the courtroom. Just after midday, the jury filed back from their rooms for the last time as the packed courtroom sat in tense silence. The forewoman confirmed that they had reached a majority verdict: 11 jurors were in agreement that Aaron Brady was guilty of the capital murder of Detective Garda Adrian Donohoe at Lordship Credit Union on 25 January 2013. Brady hung his head and stared into the distance, closing his eyes momentarily but making no other reaction. As the judge thanked the jury for their service, Brady's face turned pale as the reality of what he had just heard began to sink in. He would be spending the next four decades in prison.

The court briefly adjourned as the garda investigation team gathered outside and congratulated one another. After a gruelling seven-and-a-half-year investigation, they had secured their first conviction before the courts. Aaron Brady's supporters, including Eugene Flynn Snr, who had attended most of the trial, approached journalists covering the case after the verdict, expressing their annoyance and querying how Brady had been found guilty.

Recalling the verdict after the lengthy trial, Detective Inspector Marry said:

> It's a strange thing because you look at a jury during a trial and you just don't know what they're thinking. It can be especially difficult when a case is based on circumstantial evidence. Defence teams can put up very convincing arguments, so you never know if a jury have accepted the evidence or not. We had no golden nugget where some witness saw Brady at the scene, but his admission from his own mouth puts him fairly and squarely at Lordship Credit Union car park at the time of Adrian Donohoe's murder, and his comments established him as the shooter. Why would Aaron Brady boast about shooting a guard if he had not done so? The fact is, he did shoot Adrian Donohoe in cold blood, and the evidence proved that beyond reasonable doubt. After an eight-month trial, we were all tired, emotionally drained, and, in a way, looking forward to the end. I genuinely felt that not just me but the entire team did not let the side down and we were true to our colleague, An Garda Síochána, and the decent people of Ireland.

A large press pack of journalists and photographers had gathered at the front entrance of the courts complex where members of the investigation team and the Donohoe family were due to give a briefing. Before walking out, Chief Superintendent Christy Mangan gathered his team at the top floor of the court building and, with dozens of gardaí circled around him, had a private word with the investigation team before they walked out in unison. The Donohoe family, supporting each other and with the solid support of investigators, also took time to compose themselves and allow the news to sink in after the mammoth trial. Caroline Donohoe thanked the jury for sticking with the trial for so long and thanked her garda colleagues and the prosecution team on behalf of herself and their children.

Standing on the steps of the court, Adrian's brother Colm stood square in front of the nation's media, flanked by his brother Martin and his sister Mary. He thanked the prosecution team, the gardaí, the judge, the staff in the DPP's office, and the jury of 15 ordinary people who had been sworn in at the end of January.

We would like to express immense gratitude to Adrian's colleagues in Dundalk who investigated this while trying to grieve for the loss of a colleague. This has been one of the most comprehensive investigations in the history of the state. The professionalism and the quality of this investigation has been borne out by the fact that it has been able to withstand the most robust and forensic examination by the defence in this case. It is a huge credit to each and every person involved in the investigation that we stand here today.

He acknowledged the 'extraordinary help given to the investigation by law-enforcement agencies around the world'.

At this point in his statement, Colm Donohoe paused, steeled himself, and with a strong voice said: 'Aaron Brady was not alone in Lordship on the 25th of January 2013. The quest for justice for Adrian will continue and we appeal to anyone, near or far, who has any information and who may assist in this investigation, to come forward and do the right thing to bring those involved to justice.' He added: 'While justice has been done today, nothing will bring back Adrian to his wife, his two kids, his parents, his family, his colleagues, and his friends. As has been said at this trial, Adrian was a good man and the very least he deserves is that justice be served.'

*

On 14 October, Aaron Brady's sentencing hearing took place at the Central Criminal Court. It was a formality in regards to the term he would receive for capital murder. However, he also had to be jailed for his role in the robbery, while the court heard the victim impact statements from the Donohoe family, his wife Caroline, and the other people present in Lordship Credit Union car park that night. Detective Inspector Martin Beggy summarised the facts of the case to Justice White and outlined Aaron Brady's history of prior offending.

In a statement read on behalf of Adrian's parents, Hugh and Peggy, they described their first-born son as a model student growing up, who even after moving away from home would always return to help out on the family farm.

Adrian loved the guards; we remember how proud he was the day he graduated from Templemore. Our lives are divided in two – our lives before 25th January 2013, and our life since that awful night. It's hard to accept that such a good man would come across such evil on that cold wet night. We'll never forget that awful night – sitting in the kitchen, saying prayers – when the guards came to the door. It's news that no parents should have to deal with; it was such a waste of a good man by that evil, pointless act.

His parents spoke about how it was impossible to enjoy life, that they were existing now only for their children and grandchildren, while saying how fortunate they were to have such a caring family around them.

Adrian is such a loss to us – when we gather as a family there is such a big presence missing; he lived for family gatherings and happy occasions. He is such a big loss to us and the milestones he misses in his children's lives, it breaks our hearts. We visit his grave every week, which gives us some comfort, but it's no place for him – he should be here with us living life. Life was so unfair to him – such a good man deserved to live a full life to old age and not to be shot down in such a brutal way. He loved the guards but looked forward to his retirement – but he never got the chance to retire and live to an old age.

Adrian's wife, Caroline, said in her victim impact statement:

There are absolutely no words that can adequately express the impact the events of the 25th of January 2013 had on my life and the lives of my children and our extended family, colleagues and friends, and all who love Adrian. I will never recover fully from what I had to see at Lordship

Credit Union. My heart breaks every time I pass there and sometimes I can't get the images out of my mind for hours. Nothing or no one will ever replace Adrian in our home. Our children, Amy and Niall, have missed having their daddy at their communions, confirmations, and all the firsts in their young lives. We had a loving, happy family, everything was just perfect, but in just 58 senseless seconds everything changed forever.

Anne Donohoe, in a statement on behalf of Adrian's siblings, said he was an inspiration to them and that two of her brothers had followed him into the guards. 'Adrian was a huge child at heart, he loved children and gravitated towards them. We are angry and bereft that he has missed out on knowing so many nieces and nephews that were born after he died. They will never know their big uncle Adrian, nor the joy and laughter that he would have brought.' She said that the family had been distraught for the seven and a half years since his murder, adding that this sense of loss had not diminished. 'Possibly having this justice will help us heal, but all we are left with are photos and memories, and I don't think Aaron Brady will ever comprehend what he has done to our family,' Anne Donohoe stated.

Detective Garda Joe Ryan said that he suffered from PTSD (post-traumatic stress disorder) symptoms, including flashbacks, after the night his colleague was murdered and that he later left the guards and moved to Spain. 'I fear I will always experience flashbacks and always feel guilty that it should have been me and not Adrian. I think regularly about Adrian's wife, Caroline, and the children, that they have to live with the pain of not having a life with him, and will always feel guilty that it was him and not me.'

The judge praised the meticulous garda investigation and described as 'exemplary' the behaviour of Detective Garda Ryan who, despite having undergone 'a minute of terror' at the scene, immediately went to check on the welfare of others present. Justice White said Adrian Donohoe was a dedicated officer who was rooted in his community and held in the highest regard. 'I'm sure he was the type of officer who guided many young wayward men onto a different path,' he said. Turning to Brady, Justice White said his young age at the time of the crime was 'shocking' and that this was the only partly mitigating factor in the case. He also said it was difficult to comprehend the mundane everyday activities Aaron Brady carried out in the lead up to and after the shooting, including having lunch at a McCaughey's filling station, dinner at James Flynn's house, and a 'nonchalant' visit to his girlfriend's home. Justice White handed down the mandatory sentence for capital murder and a concurrent 14-year prison term on the robbery charge, backdated to February 2018 when Aaron Brady first went into custody. The judge remarked that there was no mitigation in the case, apart from Brady's age at the time of the crime, adding that anyone who had seen the CCTV footage of the raid at Lordship Credit Union would be 'shocked to the core'.

It was the first conviction as part of the long-running and demanding investigation, but gardaí were determined to bring the other raiders involved to justice. The man who fired the fatal shot would now spend at least the next 40 years of his life as Prisoner 74326, having become the first person to be convicted of capital murder since fellow Crossmaglen killer Michael McHugh, 35 years earlier. While Brady's hand was on the gun, there were many fingers on the trigger, including those present with him in the car park that night, those who helped with logistics and planning, and the people who supported the raiders after the fact. For the garda investigation team, the matter was far from concluded.

18

A PICTORIAL ADMISSION OF GUILT

Shortly after being sentenced Aaron Brady was moved to Portlaoise Prison, the country's only maximum-security jail where dissident republican criminals and senior organised crime figures are held. As Brady began his 40-year jail term, separate garda investigations turned to the other suspects involved in the Lordship robbery and the attempts made to intimidate witnesses during the capital murder trial. Members attached to the NBCI had even attended the final stages of the court sitting to arrest Brady on suspicion of attempting to pervert the course of justice should he have been acquitted and walked free.

In the background, before the trial had even concluded, the unit had carried out a number of operations into the intimidation of witnesses. On 23 June, a search was carried out of a cell in Mountjoy Prison in which a violent Dublin criminal was being held. Detectives seized a mobile phone and, when later examined, gardaí recovered a number of audio voice recordings allegedly showing an effort to threaten and put fear into Daniel Cahill during the trial. A month later, on 15 July, a major garda operation involving the NBCI and ERU led to a number of halting sites across north Dublin being searched as part of the inquiry, with several items of potential interest seized. That same day the prison cell of the Dublin criminal was once again searched, and while no phone was uncovered, gardaí found a piece of paper with several phone numbers on it. Gardaí suspected this was again linked to the attempts to intimidate Mr Cahill.

On 7 August, a prison officer entered the cell of 40-year-old Glen Holland, a Dublin man from the north-inner city with links to the Kinahan organised crime gang, who at the time was serving a lengthy jail term for firearms offences. The prison officer saw a Samsung Galaxy phone on the floor of the cell and confiscated it, with Holland moved to another cell. This was subsequently searched by gardaí on 27 August under warrant. During this operation, gardaí found a Huawei phone hidden in a sock in a bowl, stashed in insulation behind a sink unit. Holland's DNA was found on both devices, and when later analysed, investigators recovered messages from Holland to his partner asking her to have his WhatsApp call history remotely wiped. On 8 October, the investigation team arrested four people, including Holland and the other Dublin criminal, on suspicion of attempting to pervert the course of justice, and all were later released without charge. Two other Dublin criminals with links to organised crime were arrested weeks later as part of the same inquiry.

On 7 November, Aaron Brady's father, Tony, met detectives by appointment at Carrickmacross Garda Station as part of the witness intimidation investigation. He was questioned for several hours by Detective Sergeant Peter Woods before being released without charge. The following day, his son was taken from his jail cell in Portlaoise and brought to the local garda station.

Aaron Brady was also questioned on suspicion of attempting to interfere with prosecution witnesses in his trial and about the leaking of Ronan Flynn's recorded witness statement. He was the eighth person arrested by members of the NBCI team, before being released and returned to prison while gardaí finalised the substantial file for the Director of Public Prosecutions.

The following year, gardaí received directions from the state's prosecution service to charge several people as part of the inquiry. On 4 April, Aaron Brady was brought before a sitting of Dublin District Court where he was charged with perverting the course of justice and conspiring to persuade Daniel Cahill not to testify in his trial. Another man, 29-year-old Dean Byrne from Cabra Park in Dublin, was also brought before the court as part of the inquiry. They were both accused of conspiring with each other to persuade Mr Cahill not to give evidence, therefore attempting to pervert the course of public justice, between 8 April and 22 June 2020. Brady was also charged with a second count, alleging that on a date unknown between 20 February and 7 May 2020 he recorded the playing of a video-recorded witness interview between Ronan Flynn and members of An Garda Síochána, thus embarking upon an effort to pervert the course of justice. Both charges are contrary to common law and can result in unlimited fines and jail sentences on conviction.

Giving an outline of the evidence, Detective Garda Kevin Lawless said it would be alleged that an outgoing message from Dean Byrne's phone referred to Daniel Cahill as a 'fucking rat cunt', a 'smelly bastard cunt', 'and a 'rat bastard' who said: 'Brady told him he killed a copper.' The message added that 'Brady never even said that to him', Detective Garda Lawless said.

Both men were remanded in custody, and the DPP later applied for a certificate to have the case trialled before three judges at the Special Criminal Court, as the ordinary jury courts would be inadequate to secure the effective administration of justice. Both men are due to stand trial before the non-jury court in April 2024. Co-defendant Glen Holland was charged with unlawfully possessing a mobile phone in Mountjoy Prison between 7 and 28 August 2020, and his case was dealt with at district court level. He initially contested the charges, but later pleaded guilty and was sentenced to a total of one year's imprisonment.

*

The investigation into the murder and robbery at Lordship Credit Union was also ongoing and focusing on Brady's accomplices who were involved in the robbery. Detective Inspector Marry had been long retired by this stage but knew the inquiry would be in safe hands.

> The investigation, I knew, would continue, but who was to take over from me? I knew when I retired I was letting go of the reins, detaching myself from garda life and moving on. I recognised the abilities of my team, and there was only one man with the mental capacity to deal with such an investigation, and that was Mark Phillips. He is a superb investigator, and his knowledge of the case from day one was unquestionable. Upon my retirement, he was not yet the rank of detective inspector or a qualified SIO, and Detective Inspector Martin Beggy took over from me, a very capable person. I remember him ringing me once

for a chat and him saying: 'How in God's name did you cope?' I knew exactly what he meant.

Martin did a fine job of keeping the investigation going, but he also retired. It was with relief that I was told that Mark Phillips, who had since been promoted and was a qualified SIO, would be taking over the running of the investigation. I knew Mark's qualities, and in safer hands the investigation could not be. Aaron Brady was only one of five that took part in the robbery, but who were the others? And would they be brought to justice?

Gardaí had taken a fresh statement from Charlene O'Callaghan, Treanor's girlfriend at the time of the raid, in an effort to break his alibi for that night. Having originally said that Treanor was at home around the time of the robbery, Ms O'Callaghan clarified that she did not see him when she arrived home and spoke to him only as she was leaving to get food for them closer to 10 p.m. On the morning of 21 April 2021, detectives arrested Brendan Treanor in Dundalk under Section 50 of the Criminal Justice Act, 2007, in relation to murder involving a firearm. He was brought to the local garda station and over seven days was questioned over his alleged involvement in the Lordship Credit Union robbery. On the evening of Sunday 25 April, Brendan Treanor was released without charge and walked out of Dundalk Garda Station. Within weeks, gardaí submitted a file to the DPP recommending that both Treanor and James Flynn be charged with robbery at Lordship Credit Union. By this stage Flynn had sold his share in the Boston companies and returned to the UK, where he'd set up a car sales business in Newry. He had also become a father but, despite this, was living away from his pregnant wife and child for most of that year in England.

It didn't take long for the DPP to direct charges, and on the morning of 14 July investigators moved on the two suspects. Brendan Treanor was arrested in Dundalk and brought before the local district court, where he was charged with the Lordship Credit Union robbery and conspiring to commit burglary with James Flynn and others between September 2012 and January 2013. He was remanded in custody and later brought an unsuccessful bail application before the district court.

James Flynn was detained in Watford on foot of an international arrest warrant by members of the National Crime Agency and brought before a local magistrates' court, with a judge remanding him in custody as the extradition process commenced. While being held on remand he applied for bail three times, with the Crown Prosecution Service strenuously objecting on each occasion. In one hearing, Crown barrister Amanda Bostock said that James Flynn was the 'best friend' of Aaron Brady at the time of the robbery and that he provided him with a false alibi. She also argued that Flynn failed to cooperate with gardaí and knew he was a suspect early on in the investigation, after homes linked to him were searched on three separate occasions. The barrister said he was somebody 'who cannot be trusted on bail' and who had 'very, very limited ties to this jurisdiction'. In response, his barrister, Graeme Hall, said James Flynn 'absolutely refutes any involvement' in the offences and that the burglary charge relied on cell site evidence. He added that his client was a person of good character, with no previous convictions, and that there was no evidence James Flynn deliberately provided incorrect information to gardaí. The bail surety offered in the case also showed the significant finances Flynn and his family had access to. Some £195,000 in cash was being put forward as a security, along with £965,000 in the form of a surety, which included properties owned by his cousin and mother.

While he awaited his hearing in London, James Flynn's wife was sentenced at Monaghan Circuit Court over the fatal road crash in 2012. Now known as Colleen Flynn, she had pleaded guilty to careless driving causing the death of Ciaran McKenna. In his sentencing remarks, Judge John Aylmer said he could not say whether her moving to the United States was an aggravating factor, but that no credit could be given to the defendant for approaching the matter in a 'cowardly fashion'. Accepting her circumstances, he sentenced Colleen Flynn to 12 months' imprisonment, which was fully suspended.

Her husband's extradition hearing took place at Westminster Magistrates' Court on 8 April 2022. At the outset James Flynn attempted to delay the proceedings, arguing that because his solicitor had changed he didn't have time to consult with his new legal representative. Asking the judge to adjourn the case, he said he was suffering from PTSD and anxiety. 'I haven't slept in three days, your honour, because I was so worried about this case because I didn't know who was representing me,' he told the judge from the dock. He later added: 'As I said earlier on, I'm taking a panic attack right now, my heart is beating out of my chest, my hand is changing colour, I haven't slept in three days. How am I expected to stand here and bear witness to this?' The judge responded by telling him he appeared well composed and was making an impressive job of putting across his argument, and declined to adjourn the hearing.

Flynn's barrister argued that the extradition of his client would be unjust due to the passage of time and because the allegations against him had not been particularised. Mr Hall said there was medical evidence that his client's memory was 'significantly and adversely affected' and that he couldn't recall what took place in 2012 and 2013. James Flynn gave evidence denying he had evaded authorities, saying he didn't know he was a person of interest in the inquiry and that he was one of thousands of people spoken to by gardaí as part of the investigation. However, he later added that he believed there were efforts to put pressure on witnesses to implicate him in the crime. 'At no time did I ever think I would be prosecuted for something I didn't do. I knew the police were trying to build a case of lies against me,' he said. Ms Bostock responded by saying that the delay was due to the complexity of the case, which included over 6,000 lines of inquiry and thousands of statements. She also argued there was nothing to suggest Mr Flynn's PTSD was worse than at the time of the robbery and that he gave statements to police on three occasions in 2013 when his account was 'fresh in his mind'. The judge was told that the Irish state's case was that Flynn, his brother Eugene Jnr, Aaron Brady, and Brendan Treanor were acting as a criminal gang and predominately engaged in creeper burglaries to steal high-powered vehicles.

James Flynn's barrister then brought an abuse of process application, whereby a case can be prevented from proceeding if there are concerns about a defendant's fair trial rights or the integrity of the justice system is called into question. Tony Brady was present for the hearing in London and was called to give evidence as part of this application. He told the judge that he had 'serious concerns' about the garda investigation, saying there were 'glaring issues' in the case and that relevant CCTV footage was missing. He also made the bizarre and unfounded claim that the DPP and gardaí 'tampered with and used specialists to tamper with CCTV' footage. Amanda Bostock submitted that the Irish courts considered the trial safe and that the High Court judge would have been aware of these alleged issues when signing the extradition warrant. The presiding judge said he could find no conduct 'capable of amounting to an abuse of process in respect of the extradition courts process'.

On 28 April, after considering the arguments in the case, the judge ordered James Flynn's removal from the UK. Flynn lodged an appeal, which was unsuccessful, and was flown back to Ireland, appearing before the Dublin District Court on the morning of 30 July. Detective Garda Gareth Kenna gave evidence that when Flynn was charged with the credit union robbery, he responded: 'I strongly deny the charge. I was not present in the car park on January 25th; I'm a businessman who was running a successful business in the USA since 2011.' He responded to the second count of conspiracy to commit burglary: 'I strongly deny that charge.' James Flynn was remanded in custody and both he and Treanor were later sent forward for trial. Due to the intimidation that had featured in Aaron Brady's case, the DPP successfully applied for their case to be tried before the Special Criminal Court, with a trial date set for January 2023.

Prior to the case commencing, Brendan Treanor made another application for bail before the non-jury court, arguing that he had barely seen his newborn son as a result of being held in custody. Gardaí strenuously objected to him being granted bail, with Chief Superintendent Alan McGovern of the Louth garda division giving evidence of his knowledge of Brendan Treanor's involvement in criminality. The opinion evidence of a garda of that rank or higher is admissible before a court when objecting to an accused person receiving bail. He said the accused 'is a person of violent disposition' and 'one of the leaders of a violent and dangerous organised crime group involved in creeper burglaries and ATM thefts', of which a 'number of his close criminal associates have been convicted'. He said Treanor's crime progression became more audacious, culminating in the theft of ATMs in Dundalk in April 2020, using vehicles to block the exit from Dundalk Garda Station and setting the cars on fire. The senior garda said that gardaí 'were trapped inside their own compound and that these vehicles were stolen in creeper burglaries'. Chief Superintendent McGovern added that he believed Brendan Treanor 'is a director of an organised crime gang' involved in creeper burglaries and 'will continue to commit serious offences including perverting the course of justice' if released. Brendan Treanor was once again refused bail and remanded in custody ahead of his trial with Flynn the following year.

Detective Inspector Marry said of the upcoming case:

> I was delighted to hear that Jimmy Flynn and Benny Treanor were to face the courts concerning the robbery and their alleged involvement in creeper burglaries. A lot of the evidence that was to hand for their trial was developed and secured during my tenure, but Detective Inspector Phillips and the team developed more evidence that had convinced the DPP to charge them. The intimidation that unfolded during Aaron Brady's case was a big factor in their trial being before the non-jury court.

*

The case opened at the Special Criminal Court on 1 February before presiding judge Justice Tony Hunt, sitting with Her

Honour Sarah Berkeley and Judge Alan Mitchell. Senior prosecuting counsel Lorcan Staines outlined how the state's case relied on circumstantial evidence, including the accused men's association with Aaron Brady, mobile phone contacts before and after the robbery with one another and other suspects, the silent period at the time of the raid, Flynn's involvement in conducting reconnaissance of the credit union on the night before and afternoon of the raid, and his connection to the theft of the Volkswagen Passat used in the robbery.

The prosecution contended there was evidence of a scoping exercise taking place near the credit union the night before the raid. CCTV footage tracked James Flynn's car driving to a closed petrol station near the premises at 8.58 that night, which Mr Staines said gave them 'a good viewpoint to Lordship Credit Union'. He added that in doing so they were able to 'obtain as much information as they can regarding the locking up taking place'. The prosecution also alleged that Flynn's BMW driving past Lordship Credit Union on the afternoon of the robbery was another scoping exercise of their target that night. Flynn, Treanor, and Brady were all in the car when it passed by with its passenger window momentarily rolled down on the rainy afternoon, the judges were told.

Treanor's ex-girlfriend gave evidence that on the night of the robbery she returned home at around 9.15 p.m. after having hair extensions put in. Ms O'Callaghan told senior prosecuting counsel Brendan Grehan that she went upstairs to watch television and took a shower before leaving to get food, having spoken to Treanor as she left the house. The court was told that their house was around 10 minutes away from the Superbites fast-food outlet in Crossmaglen, and CCTV footage showed her arriving there at 10.06 p.m. This, the prosecution contended, meant there was enough time for Treanor to have been dropped home immediately after the robbery before the getaway car was driven to Cumsons Road and burnt out.

Another exhibit that the prosecution relied upon to link Brendan Treanor to the crime was a large tattoo covering his upper back. The tattoo was drawn in 2018, five years after the raid, and depicted artwork relating to items connected to the crime at Lordship Credit Union. There were four gangsters, a woman wearing a balaclava holding a gun, and knuckledusters. There was also an image of a long-barrelled shotgun, the weapon used to murder Adrian Donohoe, a handgun, rolls of money, and a BMW with the registration plate 'Boss BFT'. This tattoo, the prosecution said, was a pictorial admission by Brendan Treanor, an act of hubris on his part, and an attempt by him to glorify his role in the events at Lordship Credit Union. Referencing the masked woman in the picture, Mr Staines noted that, at the time of the robbery, gardaí were initially investigating if a female had acted as the getaway driver.

Another witness called was Colin Hoey, who, having failed to turn up at the previous trial, had decided to testify this time around. He had to be treated as a hostile witness and, when asked if his account of not seeing Brady at all on the day of the murder and robbery was correct, said it was his position now. In summary, Colin Hoey agreed that in his second statement he'd said that he had not seen Brady and James Flynn 'at all' on 25 January 2013, and it must have been the previous night when they'd called to the house at Lough Road. CCTV footage showing the BMW travelling towards the burn site after the raid and statements from a farmer who saw a BMW 5-Series driving away from Cumsons Road were also used to link Flynn to the robbery.

In relation to the burglary conspiracy, the prosecution asked the court to draw inferences from phone contacts between Flynn, Treanor, and Brady at the times of the break-ins, including the locations of the cell sites their phones pinged off around the times of the offences. There was evidence of a satnav stolen from one car during a creeper burglary being found on Eugene Flynn Snr and partially burnt documents taken from a home in Cavan being discovered on the grounds of the house where Aaron Brady had lived until March 2013. Lorcan Staines said there was a 'fluidity' in relation to the people involved, which changed from time to time. James Flynn was in America in September and October 2012 and therefore was not involved in three of the alleged burglaries, but the prosecutor said Flynn returned to Ireland that November and 'became an integral part of the conspiracy that was continuing right up to' the murder of Detective Garda Adrian Donohoe. Taking all the burglaries together, he said, the pattern 'becomes clear in terms of the individuals involved in these highly similar crimes'.

The conspiracy-to-commit-burglary charges related to crimes across five counties in the four months leading up to the Lordship robbery. On 12 September 2012, a Volkswagen Passat was stolen from Thorndale Park in Kingscourt, County Cavan. The prosecution said evidence from call-data analysis showed Brendan Treanor utilised a cell site in the area to call Aaron Brady on the morning of the burglary. A month later, on 11 October, an Alfa Romeo was taken from a house in Virginia, County Cavan. Partially burnt documents relating to the car owner were found when Brady's house at Lough Road was searched in April 2013.

The prosecution also relied on telephone communications to prove the conspiracy. A message recovered from Eugene

Flynn Jnr's phone showed a text sent after midnight on 15 December 2012 to his brother asking if Brady was 'working later'. In response, James Flynn wrote: 'Dunno think he is cause he is stuck for money so prob wanna try get someone else tonight.' In a text conversation five days later, Brady asked Eugene Flynn Jnr: 'Let me know where we are going tonight.' CCTV footage showed a number of cars leaving Dunroamin House that evening and returning in the early hours of the morning. In the middle of the night of 8 January 2013, three creeper burglaries were carried out in the Montcourt estate in Monaghan. In one crime a handbag with £300 was reported missing but the vehicle wasn't stolen. On 11 January, two creeper burglaries took place in Mullingar, County Westmeath, during which two Toyota Avensis cars were stolen, with the criminal enterprise involving at least five people. On 15 January, a creeper burglary was carried out at a house in Virginia during which a grey BMW was stolen. The car was later returned to the owner, having been abandoned after coming to the attention of the PSNI on Concession Road in Armagh, close to where the suspects lived. The prosecution said that James Flynn's phone pinged off a cell site at the Parkgate Hotel in the town on the night the car was taken. The state relied on much of the same evidence presented in Aaron Brady's trial to link James Flynn to the theft of the Volkswagen Passat from Clogherhead on 23 January, through CCTV footage tracking the movements of what the prosecution alleged was his BMW near the scene of the theft.

After hearing evidence over four months, including lengthy legal arguments on phone traffic, cell site analysis, and CCTV footage, the prosecution closed its case on 16 May. Lorcan Staines pointed to the multiple coincidences in the case and that, in terms of the totality of the evidence, there were one, or two, or 20 coincidences too far, and that the court in considering the case 'would be in a position where they could no longer stomach the coincidences disclosed by the evidence'.

There had also been a break in the prosecution's closing speeches when the state applied for Tony Brady, who had attended most days of the trial, to be removed from the court. This related to material from the proceedings that was posted online and accused one garda witness of committing perjury. The court was shown the video, and as his face appeared on the screens, Mr Brady walked into the body of the court, apologising to the judge for being late. 'You are neither late nor early. You are not obliged to be here,' Justice Hunt fired back. Mr Brady said he believed he was entitled to give his opinion, with the judge responding that he was not entitled to accuse somebody of perjury or contempt of court. Tony Brady pointed to journalists sitting in the gallery who had reported on proceedings from the previous day, with Justice Hunt responding: 'I'm sure they did – that's their job. I'm sure they didn't come to the material conclusion that somebody is a liar or in contempt of court.' The judge said that Mr Brady was attempting to defend his position by pointing to bona fide press members but added that he couldn't claim any equivalence with that. He said the three judges agreed that Mr Brady had abused his presence in court by publishing offensive opinions and acceded to the prosecution application to remove him from the court. After the ruling was made, Tony Brady asked the judge if he could make one point of clarification, with Justice Hunt simply responding: 'No.'

The defence barristers then gave their closing speeches. Sean Guerin SC, for Treanor, said his client was friends with

Aaron Brady and that they'd spent time together on the day
of the incident, doing 'what friends do'. The court was told
there was an abundance of telephone evidence but the fact of
a friendship and the association that comes with this is not in
itself probative of guilt. Mr Guerin said that the prosecution
couldn't point to anything that had happened relating to the
commission of the robbery, except for an 'incredible claim' that
a three-second drive-by of the credit union earlier that day was
a reconnaissance operation. He also said that the evidence of
the silent period was 'of no real value'.

The non-jury court was told that there was an 'enormous
empty hole' in the middle of the prosecution case leading up
to the robbery. Mr Guerin said there was 'no evidence' that
Brendan Treanor left his home that night after being dropped
home by James Flynn at 7.45 p.m. He submitted that, even if
Treanor had left his home, the prosecution case would mean
that he was sitting soaking wet in a muddy field for 45 minutes
before the robbery. The accused would have also gotten into
a car with the person who had discharged a shotgun, running
the 'grave risk' of having firearms residue on his clothing. But
Mr Guerin said there was no evidence of this when Treanor's
girlfriend saw him at home around 15 minutes after the
robbery. He said Ms O'Callaghan gave testimony that he
wasn't in muddy attire or trying to get rid of clothes, but rather
he appeared to have been watching TV or going about the
house in a normal way. He also said that there was a 'much
more convincing case' to be made against two men not currently before the court – Mr C and the other fuel launderer who
was also in contact with Brady. Mr Guerin submitted that the
closer you examine the prosecution case, 'the further from Mr
Treanor you get', and asked the court to acquit his client of the

robbery charge. He added that the burglary-conspiracy charge was 'fundamentally unfair'.

Bernard Condon SC, representing Flynn, said there was not 'one iota of evidence' to prove that his client was involved in the robbery. Flynn's association with Brady, counsel said, 'cannot be asserted as a fact of guilt or guilt by association', adding that evidence linking his client to the theft of the getaway car was 'deeply problematic'. He pointed to the timings given of vehicle movements around Clogherhead, which he described as 'unreliable' and 'dangerous' to place any weight on. John Larkin KC (King's Counsel), for Flynn, addressed the court on the conspiracy-to-commit-burglary charge. He said it was a matter of 'common sense' that if there was not enough evidence of one substantive charge of burglary, there could not be enough evidence of an overarching conspiracy to commit burglary. Mr Larkin also pointed out that the prosecution had accepted his client was in America for two months of the alleged conspiracy when three burglaries took place. The barrister questioned if it was therefore 'at all plausible' that Flynn 'retrospectively embraced' an agreement that had already been put in place. After hearing the closing arguments, the three judges retired to consider their verdict, saying this would take several months to complete.

The case returned before the Special Criminal Court on 11 September 2023 for the court's judgment to be delivered. Unlike in jury cases where the reasons for deciding on a verdict remain secret, the three judges in this case had to set out detailed reasons for arriving at their decision, and it took the court several hours to read out its ruling. Justice Hunt said that the cell site data used by the prosecution 'would be compelling evidence' but was not proven in a proper way and therefore could not be relied upon to prove that both men were involved in the burglary conspiracy. The judge said that, while Eugene Flynn Snr was found with the stolen satnav device, there was nothing to link Flynn Snr to the burglary and he had not been charged with handling stolen property. In relation to the theft of the Volkswagen in Clogherhead, the judge said they were satisfied beyond reasonable doubt that it was James Flynn's BMW 5 Series recorded driving close to the scene on the night of the crime. The court found that the CCTV footage of vehicle movements and communications between Brady and the Flynn brothers demonstrated that they were involved in nightwork 'of a criminal variety on this occasion'. The judges amended the charge, finding James Flynn guilty of conspiring with others to commit burglary that night by stealing the keys of the Volkswagen Passat. Justice Hunt said there was no basis to infer that Brendan Treanor was a passenger in the BMW that night and couldn't find that he was a participant in the conspiracy beyond reasonable doubt, clearing him of the charge.

Moving to the robbery charges, the judge said it was 'theoretically possible' for Brendan Treanor to be in his house having a conversation with his girlfriend immediately after the murder and robbery at Lordship Credit Union. However, he noted that, if so, he would have been in a wet field, carried out a violent robbery, and been packed into a car with a person who had recently discharged a firearm. The court said it was difficult to see how he would have had time to clean up and dispose of his clothes, while if he had not cleaned himself up there would have been 'noticeable signs of recent excursions'. Justice Hunt said the calls between Treanor and Aaron Brady 'reek of suspicion', while his eight failed calls to Brady an hour before the robbery are 'consistent with some involvement by Brendan Treanor in this matter'. However, the court said this did not place him at the scene and was more consistent with anxious inquiries being made by him on how matters were progressing in his absence.

Justice Hunt said the accounts given by Treanor were not truthful or honest, with the court regarding them as self-serving and unreliable. He said the tattoo was 'the most striking and colourful' part of the evidence against Treanor and that a component of the artwork was the crime committed at Lordship. This, he said, signified his approval of the crimes and was a 'despicable declaration' by Brendan Treanor. He added that it did not uniquely imply that he was one of the four gangsters in the tattoo or in the car park of Lordship Credit Union. While it found that he was a member of the criminal gang involved in the raid, the court said there was insufficient evidence to place him in the car park during the robbery and found him not guilty.

Moving on to James Flynn, the court said it had been established beyond reasonable doubt that he was an active member of the gang that had carried out the robbery and that he was intimately involved with his brother and Brady in the theft of the getaway car. The judge also said that Flynn drove his BMW to the site where the getaway car was burnt out and removed the culprits from the burn site, therefore making him an accessory before and after the fact. 'There is no doubt at all as to the general complicity of Aaron Brady and James Flynn in this matter, but ultimately we are not satisfied beyond reasonable doubt that Flynn was one of the direct participants in the robbery,' Justice Hunt said.

While the non-jury court accepted that Treanor and Flynn were part of the gang involved in the robbery, it said there wasn't enough evidence to place them at the scene carrying out the physical robbery. The court also acquitted him of robbery as his family members gasped in relief, embracing each other. There was no reaction from the garda investigation team, while Adrian Donohoe's siblings, who had been present for the hearing, quietly left the court after the judgments were read out. Flynn was remanded in custody ahead of his sentencing hearing for the conspiracy-to-commit-burglary conviction in November. His co-accused, Brendan Treanor, despite being acquitted of all charges, was also taken back into custody, as he had other charges pending.

19

HOLDING OUT HOPE

The verdict was a hammer-blow to the investigation team, who believed that there was more than enough evidence presented against James Flynn to convict him of robbery. However, it didn't mean that he would walk free. In a sentencing hearing on December 21, Justice Tony Hunt said that Flynn was involved in stealing the Volkswagen Passat 'with the specific purpose in mind' of the car being used in the credit union robbery. The judge said there was 'no doubt' that this wasn't a random burglary, but instead one designed to steal a fast car suitable as a getaway vehicle in a pre-planned and organised robbery by a criminal gang. Justice Hunt added that any doubt over Flynn not knowing the purpose of the burglary was 'put to bed' with his conduct alongside Aaron Brady in the period between the burglary and robbery, including two visits to Lordship to carry out surveillance. Taking into account the overall wrongdoing, the group aspect involved and the 'serious organised crime' element, the non-jury court sentenced him to eight years imprisonment, backdated to when he went into custody in the UK in 2021. Speaking about the verdict, Detective Inspector Marry said:

I was numbed when Judge Tony Hunt concluded James Flynn was not guilty of the robbery. There is no doubt in my mind the circumstantial evidence in this case would more than convince a jury of someone's involvement in the robbery at Lordship. The evidence, even though circumstantial, strongly supported one particular inference – that being their involvement in the robbery – and alternative explanations were in effect ruled out. Circumstantial evidence allows a trier of fact to infer that a fact exists but, despite finding Flynn was involved before and after the fact, they didn't think there was enough evidence beyond a reasonable doubt to put him in the car park at Lordship during the murder and robbery. To put James Flynn in the car park in the 58 seconds of the robbery, he would have to have admitted he was there, or someone else who was involved and was there at the time would have to have named him as being there too. This was never going to happen, as border criminals don't cooperate with police.

The circumstantial evidence, in my mind, put James Flynn as being a participant in the robbery. To conclude Jimmy Flynn conducted surveillance, collected the culprits in his car after the robbery and lied about his whereabouts at the time of the robbery, had his mobile phone turned off at the relevant time the robbery occurred, and was rubbing shoulders with the convicted murderer all evening and after the robbery, all to find that he wasn't one of the four, defies logic. However, the sentence handed down for conspiracy to commit burglary, and the judge's comments, reflected Flynn's overall involvement in the criminal enterprise. I accept that the evidence against Treanor, in relation to the robbery charge, was not as strong. With border criminals, their mindset is different: they don't conform to any sort of authority and are born and bred to despise law and order. Thinking someone was going to cooperate was futile and not in the make-up of the border criminal.

Despite giving crucial evidence that led to the conviction of Aaron Brady, neither Molly Staunton nor Daniel Cahill ever sought the substantial reward for information. The €105,000 remains unclaimed, waiting for someone to come forward and give information about the other gang members. Brady has appealed his conviction, while he is also due to go on trial in April 2024, charged with perverting the course of justice relating to his murder trial. The verdicts in relation to his two alleged accomplices are, however, not the conclusion of what, to this point, has been the largest criminal investigation in the history of the Irish state.

While murder probes on average generate hundreds of lines of inquiry, there were in excess of 6,000 in the Lordship murder and robbery investigation. Over the course of the decade, gardaí took 4,950 witness statements and seized 45 phones, while over 65 call-data records were requested to be analysed. Over 40,000 hours of CCTV footage was seized and in excess of 1,200 potential exhibits recovered, while over 2,000 questionnaires were completed, and each meticulously evaluated, with Detective Inspector Marry saying:

Adrian's case was a mammoth task and the biggest murder investigation the state ever undertook, leading to the longest murder trial in Irish legal history. Did I read all the statements? I did not, but the ones of interest I did, including the statements taken from Aaron Brady over a two-day period by Mark Phillips and Jim McGovern, two top-class detectives. When you take the definition of a criminal investigation, each word of Brady's statement was analysed, and as a result decisions were made to verify or disprove his version of events on the night of 25 January 2013. It transpired at his trial that Aaron Brady constantly lied in his statement and throughout the trial itself, even though he claimed he was the victim in this investigation.

John Moroney took charge of the divisional search team and it was good fortune that, the day after the robbery, he decided to stop Aaron Brady and Jimmy Flynn while tasked with the search strategy. That stop by Inspector Moroney was so important in the context of the overall investigation. Both men concocted lies to him and were eventually found out.

A new phenomenon which I used, and most investigations use now, is the service of garda analysts, which is invaluable to investigators. Their analysis of phone records and chart completions assists in painting the picture as the investigation progresses. They help track timelines of statements made, movements of persons, mapping of phone movements, and so on. I worked closely with Ed McGoey, the analyst who gave me invaluable assistance and, no doubt in my mind, helped me immeasurably in solving serious crimes, including the Adrian Donohoe murder.

A senior investigating officer will amount to nothing if he does not value his team and inspire them to meet the challenge – in this case, solving Adrian's case. By inspiring your team, you have to give honest feedback and praise for a job well done. With 6,000 lines of inquiry, I was constantly managing performances, and all of my team were enthusiastic and had Adrian in their hearts and minds. I knew their strengths and weaknesses, but I have to say I was blessed with the calibre of gardaí I worked with in the Louth division. They were excellent people with an abundance of qualities far greater than I possessed. It's all about team play to reach professional standards. I always told the team that we were public servants and accountable to our superiors, the courts, and the public, and to never lose sight of that. Each and every one of them had values and ethical standards. Homeland Security and its agents were also on the ball and understood what we required. Not once did Matt Katzke ever question the garda investigation, its integrity and focus.

The cold-blooded murder of Adrian Donohoe shocked, numbed, and indeed left an indelible memory in every decent person's life, no more so than his work colleagues'. Adrian was a decent human being with an appetite for all things good, family, community, and the job of being a detective. I missed him and I still do – he should never have been taken the way he was.

*

The list of 207 persons of interest at the height of the inquiry was whittled down to just 26 at the time of Aaron Brady's trial and included those who had information about his involvement in the murder, people who provided the gang with logistical support or false alibis, and the suspected gang members themselves. Following his conviction, the list was further reduced, and now around a dozen people remain live persons of interest. This includes Mr C, the fuel launderer who gardaí suspect was one of the men in the credit union car park that night. He has since married and continues to be linked to criminality in South Armagh. Others on the list are those who gave him an alibi for the night of the murder. The alleged getaway driver, a close friend of Aaron Brady at the time, also remains a person of interest and has come to the adverse attention of authorities several times over the past decade, although not for violent crimes.

An SIO is still in charge of the inquiry, although most of the original investigation team have moved on upon promotions, transfers, and retirements. While the possibility of more prosecutions appears unlikely, investigators are still continuing their efforts to litigate the men who provided logistical support to the gang, following the findings by the Special Criminal Court in the Flynn trial. Gardaí also still hold out hope that if someone develops a conscience and speaks out, the other gang members who were with Aaron Brady in Lordship Credit Union car park on the night Detective Garda Adrian Donohoe was shot dead can be brought to justice.

ACKNOWLEDGEMENTS

Pat:

This case could not have been solved if it were not for a dedicated team who gave their all to see Adrian get justice. I have to acknowledge the following for their dedication and hard work. My incident room coordinator, Detective Garda James Doherty, who was the nucleus of the incident room and whom I can't speak highly enough of. My incident room manager, Inspector Ciaran Clancy, who always had his eye on the ball and was invaluable to the investigation. Sergeant Karen Coughlan, who was exhibits officer and took responsibility for thousands of exhibits for the duration of the case. A most trustworthy, honest and decent woman, thank you, Karen. Detective Garda John Kissane and Detective Garda James Comisky RIP, the two people I had put in charge of reading statements. It was Detective Garda John Kissane's eye for detail that led to the first break, establishing the identity of a car which followed the getaway car on the night of the murder. Sergeant Eugene Collins, who was tasked with all the house-to-house inquiries and completing questionnaires. Sergeant Vincent Jackson and Detective Garda Gareth Kenna, who managed to collect and log all the CCTV gathered and accessed during the investigation, two very valued members. Detective Garda Kenna excelled in giving evidence of CCTV relied on during the trial; a true professional. Detective Garda Ronan Duffley assisted in the CCTV analysing and coordination, a highly qualified person and a member I could trust to the end.

Detective Garda Brendan Duffy was the man who would not let me forget and constantly brought things to my attention on several investigations. A pure gentleman, an outstanding detective and a trojan horse for work. Thank you, Brendan.

An incident room requires personnel who have a knack for administrative work, filing, logging, cross referencing. Detective Garda Yvonne Snell was one such person who kept the records straight and helped in preparing the file for the DPP, an excellent worker. Superintendent Gerard Curley dealt with the press and had the responsibility of running a very busy district of Dundalk. Chief Superintendent Christy Mangan, who took over the Louth division and was a pleasure to work under. I have to acknowledge the members on the ground who ploughed through the mundane inquiries that had to be done. A huge thank you to Inspector Darren Kirwan, Detective Sergeants Kieran Reidy, Shane Farrell and Paul Gill, Sergeants Padraig O'Reilly, Andy Barron, James Corden and Dave O'Leary, Detective Gardaí Sean Finnegan, Noel Mohan, Paul Flynn and Sean Fitzpatrick, Superintendent Pat Connell, Gardaí Nuala McQuade and Aiden Hanlon, and Superintendent John Moroney, who made a very important car stop which was of immense help in progressing the case.

I have to acknowledge help and assistance from the Special Detective Unit: Detective Inspector Bill Hanrahan, Inspector Padraig Boyce and Detective Sergeant Kieran Regan, and members from the National Bureau of Criminal Investigation, Detective Sergeants Ian McLaughlin, Dave Gilmore, Paddy Cleary, Mike Smith, Adrian Murray and Peter Woods, and Detective Inspector Brian Hanley. I have to mention Detective Garda Bobby Ogle, who was only on the investigation for a short time before he retired but played a vital role in breaking the suspect's alibi. A man with a natural ability as a detective, a most honourable person, it was a credit to have worked with him. There were two members from the National Bureau of Criminal Investigation who made a distinct difference when it came to dealing with suspects and developing circumstantial evidence: Detective Inspector Mark Phillips and Detective Garda Jim McGovern, what professionals they are. I can't thank them enough for their dedication, professionalism and trust in me as Senior Investigating Officer. Mr Ed McGoey, a garda analyst I engaged in most of my murder investigations who became aware of how his skill set could benefit an investigation. I depended on Ed to decipher large amounts of data and convert it into logical formats to allow it to be understood. Ed was very important to an investigation of this size. We all appreciated your work, Ed, and thank you. Superintendent Brian Mohan and Detective Inspector Martin Beggy took over the driving seat on the investigation at times when I was not available. Well done for keeping the case alive. I have to say at this stage that a lot of members contributed who stepped in and out of the investigation over the years and for any member I have not mentioned, I am sorry. The PSNI dedicated one of their Murder Investigation Teams to the case and they covered a lot of ground for us in the north. I thank them dearly. Chief Inspector Gareth Talbot did an excellent job.

There is no doubt the case would not have been solved without the professional approach of Homeland Security Investigations. Their help and understanding of knowing what it was like to lose a colleague was outstanding. I have to name Special Agent Matthew Katzke, a pure professional, a gentleman and a guy I can not talk highly enough of. A genuine, deep-felt thank you, as you were the man I relied on in the USA for guidance. You will never be forgotten by all those on the investigation team. Special Agent Scott Crabb was another hugely helpful agent who assisted us in bringing the case to a conclusion. Special Agent Mary Ann Wade shepherded us on several occasions while making inquiries in New York. We will not forget you and your colleagues for your honesty and care, thank you. The prosecution team, in particular Brendan Grehan SC and Lorcan Staines SC, worked tirelessly on the case. I wish to acknowledge my co-writer Robin Schiller who was a pleasure to work with. I must acknowledge Detective Garda Joe Ryan (retired) whose clear recollection of the events of the night put me and the investigation on the right track. You did Adrian proud and a genuine thank you from us all. My wife, Niamh, who put up with me disappearing for long periods of time to work on this book, thank you for your patience. My daughters who are bored to the end of me talking about this book. Thank you Cheryl, Jade and Doireann, who always encouraged me.

Robin:

I would like to offer my sincere thanks to those who can't be named for sharing their knowledge and insights into the investigation of Adrian Donohoe's murder and the robbery at Lordship Credit Union. I am grateful to my colleagues within the media industry for their continued support, in particular *Irish Independent* crime correspondent Ken Foy, *Irish Sun* crime correspondent John Hand, *Irish Independent* political editor Philip Ryan and my former *Irish Independent* colleague Niall O'Connor. I would like to acknowledge journalists Paul Williams and Barry Cummins for their help in getting the book off the ground and for their guidance and support, particularly in the early stages. A thank you to court reporters Eoin Reynolds and Alison O'Riordan of Ireland International News Agency, for their assistance on all court matters. A thanks to my employer Mediahuis Ireland: Editor Cormac Bourke, Head of News Kevin Doyle, News Editor Gareth Morgan and the team for their support and giving me time to work on this book. A special acknowledgement to my wife, our baby boy and family for always supporting and encouraging me. I would like to thank my co-author Pat Marry, whose expertise on this case made the book possible and for being a pleasure to work with. We also want to thank Drummond Moir, the MD of Atlantic Books, and Atlantic's group associate publisher, Clare Drysdale, for putting their faith in us.